T0366368

THE CREATIVE LIVES OF ANIMALS

ANIMALS IN CONTEXT
General Editor: Colin Jerolmack

When Animals Speak: Toward an Interspecies Democracy
Eva Meijer

Just Like Family: How Companion Animals Joined the Household
Andrea Laurent-Simpson

The Creative Lives of Animals
Carol Gigliotti

The Creative Lives of Animals

Carol Gigliotti

NEW YORK UNIVERSITY PRESS
New York

NEW YORK UNIVERSITY PRESS
New York
www.nyupress.org

© 2022 by New York University
All rights reserved

Excerpt from *The Gift: Imagination and the Erotic Life of Property* by Lewis Hyde, copyright © 1979, 1980, 1983 by W. Lewis Hyde. Used by permission of Random House, an imprint and division of Penguin Random House LLC. All rights reserved.

Excerpt from *The Evolution of Beauty: How Darwin's Forgotten Theory of Mate Choice Shapes the Animal World—and Us* by Richard O. Prum, copyright © 2017 by Richard O. Prum. Used by permission of Doubleday, an imprint of the Knopf Doubleday Publishing Group, a division of Penguin Random House LLC. All rights reserved.

References to Internet websites (URLs) were accurate at the time of writing. Neither the author nor New York University Press is responsible for URLs that may have expired or changed since the manuscript was prepared.

Library of Congress Cataloging-in-Publication Data
Names: Gigliotti, Carol, author.
Title: The creative lives of animals / Carol Gigliotti.
Description: New York : New York University Press, [2022] | Series: Animals in context | Includes bibliographical references and index.
Identifiers: LCCN 2022002174 | ISBN 9781479815449 (hardback) | ISBN 9781479815463 (ebook) | ISBN 9781479815487 (ebook other)
Subjects: LCSH: Animal behavior—Juvenile literature.
Classification: LCC QL751.5 .G49 2022 | DDC 591.5—dc23/eng/20220203
LC record available at https://lccn.loc.gov/2022002174

New York University Press books are printed on acid-free paper, and their binding materials are chosen for strength and durability. We strive to use environmentally responsible suppliers and materials to the greatest extent possible in publishing our books.

Manufactured in the United States of America

10 9 8 7 6 5 4 3 2 1

Also available as an ebook

To Calder and Kendra for their love, strength, and compassion, to Copernicus, who was with me through everything, and to all the creative beings on this planet.

CONTENTS

Introduction. Animals as Creative Beings   1

1. Animal Intelligence: Pigeons and Higher Math   19

2. Communication Unlimited: Do Not Ask What That Prairie Dog Is Saying about You   49

3. Play as a Creative Source: Finding Your Inner Kea   76

4. Creating Built Environments: Nests, Lodges, Bowers, Avenues, Tunnels, and Hives   106

5. Sexual Exuberance: Ratchet-Pointing, Water Dancing, and Same-Sex Enjoyment   138

6. Emotional Agency: The Empathy of Chickens   164

7. Culture across Species: Tools, Songs, and Moral Codes of Conduct   194

Epilogue. Creativity Has Its Reasons   225

Acknowledgments   233

Notes   235

Bibliography   253

Index   275

About the Author   289

Introduction

Animals as Creative Beings

The gift is not merely the witness or guardian to new life, but the creator.

—Lewis Hyde, *The Gift*

Animals create.

Some use their intelligence, self-awareness, and flexibility, three essentials for creativity, to build homes. Beavers engineer their elaborate dams and canals by controlling and creating water flow to transport food and building materials. Understanding exactly what needs their unique habitats demand, they devise appropriate and creative strategies to meet them. Each caddisfly larva, using the same creative qualities as the beaver, constructs a unique protective case around themselves using sticky silk threads expelled from their head. Individuals carefully choose just the right material, such as plants, sand grains, wood fragments, pebbles, and small shells. With these, they construct the exquisitely intricate cases in which they live for up to two years until shedding them as adults.

Whether they are building, communicating their feelings of anger, empathy, or affection, showing their personalities, improvising a new song, charming and seducing a mate, inventing a new game to play, or adding to their collective cultures, their creative processes enhance their lives and often contribute to the diversity of this planet.

If I had said these things even five years ago, the amount of argument I would have received would have stopped this discussion in its tracks. Audiences who read books on nature, the environment, animals, and science and are now familiar with new thinking on animal intelligence, emotion, and self-awareness will find additional reasons to see animals as valuable and powerful beings. Those readers who still find this thinking surprising will find explanations of how the creative behavior of animals rests on these and other qualities once considered to belong only in our species.

Most of us view animals through a very narrow lens, one that sees only bits and pieces of beings who seem mostly peripheral to our lives. In actuality, animals are complete individuals with the potential for creative behavior in many aspects of *their* lives. Hearing the gorgeous and uniquely pure whistles of a sparrow refreshes our spirits. Recognizing those whistles as part of the creative languages of birds cracks open a wider view of animals' place in the world. What we might not know is that many songbirds are not born knowing how to sing. For these birds, their songs are not innate; they learn their songs. Not only that, but where the songs are learned, when they are learned, and from whom they are learned are unique to each species. The ability to learn in varied ways points to traits we evoke when discussing the foundations of cognition, consciousness, and creativity in humans and is just as useful in discussing those foundations in animals.

Male bowerbirds of New Guinea and Australia practice for many years carefully constructing lavishly decorated bowers of several types, all for love. To further charm and seduce their prospective mates, they also dance and sing. Some bowerbirds indirectly cultivate a berry plant they use not as food but as decoration in their bowers. Others collect specific colors of glass shards, plastic toys, straws, flowers, and, for one bower, a glass eyeball.

Like bowerbirds, humans have often designed, engineered, and built beautiful domiciles for love. Our creative urges are mixed with emotions of all kinds: curiosity, compassion, revenge, sorrow, and empathy, among many others. Birds, long accused of being stupid, possess perceptive and cognitive abilities that serve as the basis for their intricate social behaviors. Birds, scientists have now learned, have complex brains as inventive as any mammalian brain. Chickens—although I have noticed people often forget that they are birds—are social diplomats within stable groups, at least in healthy and open environments. Able to differentiate at least 100 individual chickens by recognizing the idiosyncrasies of their facial features, they are avid communicators and use at least 30 different vocalizations that researchers have interpreted via careful documentation. The human creativity research community considers social diplomacy a valuable creative trait, and those who spend time with chickens have long known how socially adept they are. While the idea that animals have the capacity for various forms of creativity is not new, only recently have scientists considered it a serious source of investigation. As with us, animals' creative choices affect their social, cultural, and environmental worlds. Their lives as emotional beings also affect their creativity. In a recent study conducted at the University of Bristol, researchers found that domestic hens exhibit a clear physiological and behavioral response to their chicks' distress. The researcher explained, "We found that adult female birds possess at least one of the essential underpinning attributes of 'empathy'; the ability to be affected by, and share, the emotional state of another."[1] Empathy helps prepare for a creative solution. Understanding another's distress is essential in alleviating that distress.

Animals as Creative Beings

Describing animals as creative beings brings up all kinds of questions that demand revaluing both animals and creativity. I made the decision to focus on the creativity of animals not in comparison or in contrast to human creativity but to see both as part of a "deep source" of encompassing creativity. Nevertheless, the following questions have emerged as I made my way through this journey of discovery. Does suggesting this mean that animals are creative in the same ways as humans? How do these findings affect how we think of our creativity? Might asking these questions change the way we define creativity? Will this redefinition of creativity affect the way we perceive and act towards animals? Might it contribute to changing the way we view our place in the world? My book takes on these questions by looking at specific behaviors of animals in the constantly changing circumstances of their lives and what that might mean for our current definition of creativity, which does not include them.

I am defining creativity as a dynamic process in which novel and meaningful behaviors are generated by individuals with the possibility of affecting others at cultural, species, and evolutionary levels. My definition does not confine itself to one species, the human species, for instance. It includes individual animals as creative in their individual, cultural, and species-specific ways and incorporates the evolutionary effect their accumulated creativity has on biodiversity. It includes animals who practice their creativity as part of a larger community of beings, such as ants or bees. These individuals contribute to a larger goal, what is often called the "hive mind."

I emphasize the process of creativity, instead of the products, for several reasons. If we are to learn anything about the creativity of animals, we must be able to appreciate the sometimes complex and iterative processes by which an animal solves whatever problem they are confronted with, or goal they want to achieve. Even in human terms, although there is no template for the creative process, overall creative processes are domain general.[2] In other words, for humans, whether the goal is scientific or artistic, similar processes are at work. While some scientists in this book see these processes in animals as driven by the needs of adapting to their current surroundings, others see individual animals choosing how to guide that process. One example of the latter is the spread of grass earrings originally worn by Julie, a chimpanzee studied by researchers for over a year in the Chimfunshi Wildlife Orphanage Trust in Zambia. Julie initially stuck a stiff piece of long grass in her ear, adjusted it, and then wore it through daily activities. Eight out of the 12 members of this chimpanzee group engaged in the same behavior for the year, documenting a spontaneous and rather creative fashion tradition in this chimpanzee community.[3]

I suspect Julie uniquely solved the problem of living in an enclosed environment, even one with native habitat. Her goal might have been a bit of creative control over her behavior in otherwise limited circumstances. Neophilia—being excited by new experiences—encourages new behavior among individual animals. This openness may lead to a combination of exploration, working memory, and cognitive power enabling a truly new product, such as a tool, that is useful to the creator and others of their species. The range found in animal creativity, just as seen in human creativity, is very broad and deserves our open minds, a willingness to experience behaviors in a new way, and comfort with complexity. These qualities, the same qualities associated with creative behavior, will assist us in appreciating animals for who they are, and understanding how creativity is often an integral part of their everyday lives.

You will note that my definition does not limit what is or is not creative. As research on creativity in neuroscience progresses, we are learning why limiting what kinds of thought or behavior contribute to creativity is unhelpful. How creative processes work is being studied across varying activities and cultures. The creative process is often a zigzagging activity, returning many times to aspects of the ongoing process. Neuroscientist Rex Jung explains, "Only very recently have neuroscientists discovered brain mechanisms that appear to underlie such 'task unrelated thoughts.'"[4] Thinking about the past, the future, or the thoughts and feelings of others, for instance, while not related to the task itself, may play a crucial role in the creative work at hand, in both its inception and its production. If you have created anything, whether that something is a favorite recipe, a garden plan, or a new app, you know that thoughts about the past, the future, and the feelings of others often arise in the creative process you used to make that dish, plan that garden, or design that new app, and may influence it.

There is a difference between creativity and innovation. Biologists Patrick Bateson and Paul Martin divide the terms into the idea and the product. Creativity, as they see it, is "having" an idea while innovation is applying that idea. This seems like an uncomplicated definition of both words. I cannot help but feel that the ease with which those two words are divided also may be what limits the boundaries of how we currently think about creativity both for humans and for animals. I am interested in the *creative process* of individuals and groups of animals. Sometimes that process produces innovation in behavior or an item, such as a song, a tool, a nest. Sometimes, however, the creative process itself is integral to what is being constructed. The production itself is a creative act. At other times, nothing new seems to come out of the creative process, but the behaviors involved in the process may be new for the individual and useful in other areas of their activity now or in the future. Since animals are not employees of corporations, they do not have to be innovative to be creative. Innovation may result in a goal being met or a product being produced, but the creative process does not require a product, and sometimes that process produces a failure. The process may not be visible to an outsider, existing only as a thought process or a thought experiment. But a fragment or remnant of that process might produce something considered creative years hence.

Definitions of creativity abound. In history, they span from the Greek notions of creativity as a craft or practice to medieval Christianity's insistence on only divine creation to contemporary definitions from multiple disciplines, including those in the social sciences, the arts and humanities, economics, education, neuroscience, and computer sciences, to name just a few. As expected, definitions often assume the different perspectives of those disciplines on what is categorized as creative. A working definition that continued to crop up in my reading on animal creativity and innovation relies on both "novelty" and "appropriateness." Most creativity researchers agree on these two concepts, although the term "original" may replace the word "novel," and "useful" or "valuable" may replace the term "appropriate."

Still, as behavioral and evolutionary biologist Gordon Burghardt contends, the conflation of the two words "creativity" and "innovation," in popular thought and among biologists, limits the understanding of how those processes might work in animals. As Burghardt says, "The history of work on creativity cannot be summarized that easily."[5] Burghardt gives a helpful overview of theories of creativity, at least from the field of psychology, from 1951 on. He explains that animal creativity has helped pin down the essentials of ideas around human creativity. Psychology has worked on defining and separating a continuum of creativity. At one end of the continuum is "little-c," personal creativity, which may be innovative for the individual involved. At the other end is "Big-C," the creativity that affects a culture, with an emphasis on icons of human creative endeavor as creators, what are called "geniuses." Think Picasso, Einstein, Ada Lovelace, Marie Curie. Lewis Hyde, however, tells us that the Romans, and their ancestors the Etruscans, referred to each person's guardian spirit as their genius. The Etruscans believed that each animal also had their genius. Hyde describes the belief that one must cultivate one's genius that has come to one at birth. "It [our genius] carries with it the fullness of our undeveloped powers. These it offers to us as we grow, and we choose whether or not to accept, which means we choose whether or not to labor in its service."[6] For the Romans and the Greeks, rather than genius residing in a few lucky people, each being had the opportunity to sacrifice and labor in grateful reciprocation to the genius responsible for their gifts.

Those interested in how creativity works have recognized the importance of cultural influence on the creativity of an individual or group. An interest in how the creative impulse works across many domains, not only the arts, has fostered a reluctance to limit creative license to only a few special individuals. Together with digital media and its use by all kinds of people, the idea that creativity may be a common quality throughout human activity has emerged just as ideas about animal creativity are gaining traction in the biological sciences.

The late marine biologist Stanley Kuczaj, in his essay on "Animal Creativity and Innovation," combines these qualities to highlight the little-c notion. For him, "Novel behaviors will be considered creative if they are purposeful and meaningful to the individual."[7] He argues that the most foundational element of creative behavior is curiosity, with personality (bold versus timid, for instance) also playing a role. He suggests that play is "an important context for animals to explore possibilities and develop flexible problem-solving skills."[8]

Jung argues that the broadly accepted definition of creativity referring to the production of something novel and useful is plausible since it applies not only to humans and animals "but also to species and across evolutionary time."[9] He also identifies two obstacles to understanding the processes of creativity. The first is the singular focus on the iconic genius, and the second is an "undue focus on an encompassing definition around which largely unedifying academic arguments ensue."[10] In comparison, he notes that the concepts of "gene" or "intelligence" have no commonly accepted definition although mountains of research continue to accumulate in these areas.

My experiences teaching not only traditional visual art students but students involved in computer animation programming, graphic narratives, design, interactive media, and video allowed me firsthand knowledge, primary research if you will, on how the creative process works. We can compare creativity to one of the four fundamental states of matter, liquid. Like a liquid, it may have a definite volume but no fixed shape. As these students often moved across disciplines, flexibly diving into new areas with an acute curiosity and a willingness to fail, they often brought knowledge and methods from one discipline to another. Just as often, they were open to learning new rules of engagement that they would then break or convert to their needs.

Creativity has played an enormous role in my life, inspired by both humans *and* animals. As a child, I took solace in both being with other animals and practicing the arts I was exposed to: music, visual art, and opera. My teenage and college years revolved around literature, and learning the art of acting and performance. After years of embodying others' words, I wanted to engage with my own thoughts, and in the visual arts of drawing, painting, and printmaking, I found opportunities to do so. While I was working towards an MFA in printmaking, my concerns about and commitment to animals became a driving force of my creative life. While teaching art in a large urban high school, I was introduced to an Apple IIGS. Immediately I saw its possibilities for combining my passions for art, words, sound, and animals, and I decided to investigate animation. With a PhD from the Advanced Computing Center for the Arts and Design at Ohio State University, I began my university teaching career.

I was lucky to have witnessed thousands of examples of how the creative process works through the students I taught over many years. Their ability to form the most minute experience or selected object into a layered process of discovery often led to novel perspectives. One of my all-time favorite teaching experiences is the intervention assignment I gave to students in my introductory course on interactive digital production. The parameters of the assignment were to choose an assumption they thought needed changing and then reflect that change by engaging visually with the campus and surrounding island that the university sat on. Given this kind of freedom, students threw themselves into a heightened state of exploration, thought, preparation, and production. Hearing from people who came across these projects in midconstruction or when they were finished was a powerful experience. Whether the feedback was good or bad, whether the viewer agreed or disagreed with the point of the work, students felt they had learned a great deal about what it meant to take complete ownership of an idea and of a creative project designed to communicate that idea.

The animals I have lived with surprised me with their ingeniousness in the same way that my students did. Like many of us, I have often searched for those moments when the clarity of the world was sufficient and my thinking about it became unnecessary. I have found those moments most often in my engagement with the creative process and my involvement with animals.

There is a space, sometimes several, in a process of creating when the individual who creates becomes one with what they are creating. There are no boundaries between the maker and the made, no barriers between the idea and its manifestation, no difference between the present moment and infinity. This flow, as it has been aptly described, is an experience sought by humans.[11] It seems to me it is experienced by animals within the context of their lives.

Being with, thinking about, and attempting to understand animals by making my own art with images and words has encouraged me to question the assumptions about animals still circulating even in educational settings. I am still surprised when acquaintances respond to my concern about a group of animals with a shrug and the phrase, "They are just animals." It has been clear to me for much of my life that animals are intelligent, emotional, self-aware, and individual beings who matter. There were moments when each of those qualities in a particular situation with a particular animal drove the point home, and I recount some of them throughout the book. That animals are also creative was something that took longer to come to. The knowledge was always there in front of me, so obvious that I had to work at recognizing it.

One of the first instigators of a desire to rethink assumptions about creativity and animals was rereading physicist David Bohm's book *On Creativity*.[12] While Bohm explores human creativity, he does so by linking the processes of creativity to the processes of the universe at large. For me, reading this book was a life-changing experience in several ways. To offer a more concrete example, here is one quotation from the book that has resonated with me, even after many years.

> It cannot be too strongly emphasized that what is being suggested here is that intelligence does not thus arise primarily out of thought. Rather, as pointed out earlier, *the deep source of intelligence is the unknown and indefinable totality from which all perception originates.*[13] (emphasis mine)

If those sentences seem opaque to you, they remained so to me for many years until I was immersed in writing this book. I reread Bohm's book, and this time the meaning became clear. Could creativity be described in the same way Bohm talks about intelligence? *Is the deep source of creativity the unknown and indefinable totality from which all biodiversity originates?* And if so, are animals' creative processes contributing to the biodiversity of this planet? This thought has been my guide in researching and writing this book.

I had been collecting anything I could find on animal creativity for many years. Biologists Simon M. Reader and Kevin N. Laland edited and published a pioneering book on *Animal Innovation* in 2003.[14] They state categorically in their preface, "Until recently, animal innovation has been subject to almost complete neglect by behavioral biologists." In that book, Reader and Laland use the word "innovation" to describe the products of animal creativity, leaving open the question of whether insight and creativity underlie innovative behavior in animals. However, in his more recent book, *Darwin's Unfinished Symphony: How Culture Made the Human Mind*, Laland, says,

> Our investigations, and those of other animal innovation researchers, provide compelling evidence that humans do not have a monopoly on creativity. Many animals invent new behavior patterns, modify existing behavior to a novel context, or respond to social or ecological stresses in an appropriate and novel manner.[15]

His work in this field is important because it has placed research on animal innovation and creativity firmly in the sights of younger researchers. Some in the biological sciences had been unwilling to even consider the possibility of animal creativity.

But even Laland, in the closing chapter of his new book, emphasizes the more "evolved" state of human innovation based on humans' ability to share ideas through social learning. He sees human cultural production as both the driver and the result of these abilities. Laland admits that his entire career has been based upon his desire to understand "the majesty of human culture" and its uniqueness, but his description of how humans lack a monopoly on creativity is not a trivial matter. We will see that many of the traits that Laland and others have listed as necessary for innovative behavior, including cultural transmission, exist in many species, not just ours.

In 2004, I came across an article by the biologist Allison B. Kaufman and the psychologist James C. Kaufman entitled "Applying a Creative Framework to Animal Cognition."[16] This article made me realize that I was not the only person thinking along these lines. Although our approaches differ, their helpful model and respectful tone toward animals in using the word "creative" in their title encouraged me. From then on, it was a matter of collecting research as I found it. Allison and James Kaufman published an edited academic book entitled *Animal Creativity and Innovation* in 2015.[17] I was delighted. This was the first scientific book, at least in the last 60 years, that applied the word "creativity" to animal behavior. By incorporating essays from human creativity researchers, psychologists, biologists, and ecologists into the book, the Kaufmans emphasize creativity as a dynamic process and encourage a transdisciplinary approach to what is a global phenomenon. The present book also brings together information from researchers in human and animal creativity, psychologists, biologists, cognitive ethologists, behavioral ecologists, conservation biologists, neuroscientists, and evolutionary biologists. While much of my writing in animal studies has relied on philosophical, social, and political approaches, it became obvious that investigation supporting the presence of creativity in animals is predominantly found right now in the biological field sciences, much of it from scientists who have spent years in the world of a particular species. Similarly, I included experiences and opinions from sanctuary workers who have spent a great deal of time with specific groups of animals.

The amount of research on animal innovation and creative behavior emerging from these fields grows every day. As I wrote the bulk of the book, there were so many pertinent articles that I was having trouble deciding which examples of creativity in such a wide variety of animals I should include. What I have tried to do in this book is to offer a synthesis of both the established and the emerging questions about the creativity of animals gleaned from researchers who have spent not just hours but years with particular animals. I have relied on my knowledge and experience in the creative process in my own work or in teaching to ensure an open mind as I considered how creative methods might help us understand the creativity of animals. My own creative process in researching and writing this book with the goal of engaging readers of all kinds included lateral and metaphorical thinking, along with storytelling and affective narratives. While I stayed true to the research used throughout the book, the goal was to highlight disruptive ideas often buried within the academic jargon of science, allowing readers to speculate with me how these might open our eyes to the realities of the creative lives of animals.

We are faced with vast species extinction, catastrophic changes in climate, and pandemics caused by human interference with animals. We have triggered these breakdowns in planetary life not only through our ignorance but also, more recently, through deliberately denying our reliance on nature. It behooves us to rethink our estimation of human culture as "majestic." The history of unchecked creative endeavors is filled with examples of unexpected or ignored repercussions. Nuclear fusion was a creative discovery that led to the atomic bomb. The sequencing of the human genome is expected to create beneficial diagnostic and treatment options for those suffering from diseases. However, applying this knowledge to genetic technologies such as transgenics and genetic modification has opened doors to the possibility of changing life on earth to mirror only human needs. Considering the creativity of other species might help us grasp what our creative decision-making processes lack when we exclude ourselves from the limits imposed upon this planet by nature.

Can we only think of animals as merely useful contributors to our human needs? Or, as I will argue, are they creative beings whose contributions to the world are being wasted by our limited view of them? We desperately need to grasp the complexity of the rest of our fellow species on this planet and value both their individual and their communal contributions to what we think of as only *our* home. Unless we grasp how completely we depend on the nonhuman world, the many choices we make as we creatively innovate are open to unprecedented and possibly irreversible decisions.

Openness to new ideas is a crucial characteristic of the creative process, yet disregarding the possibility of animals being creative has blinded us to alternative and richer ideas about what creativity is and how creativity operates across species. Should we try to squeeze the creativity of animals into our human categories of creativity, or along with animals', is our creativity part of a larger picture of the creative urge we have yet to discover? Linking the concept of creativity to animals' behavior is, in its own way, a creative move—one I think perfectly suited to rethinking creativity in today's perplexing world.

While comparisons to human creativity and innovation have a place in understanding how creativity works in other species, this book concentrates on the creativity of animals in *their* lives, not ours. Constantly comparing the rest of the species on this planet to us leaves very little room for understanding gifts unique to their species and behaviors giving great value to their lives. We are, we need to remember, only *one* of an evolving and unique planet populated by the latest (disputed) estimate of roughly 8.7 million other species.[18]

Anthropomorphism as a Methodology

There is one more point I would like to make about how scientists study and understand other species. Several of the animal researchers referenced in this book have noted the need for a more open and cross-disciplinary approach in studying intractable subjects such as creativity in animals. This turn is linked to another change in how scientists study animals. Once, the fear of anthropomorphic thinking, ascribing human characteristics to nonhuman things, was a sin of the highest degree, right up there with suggesting that the world is flat. But, over the last five decades, beginning with Donald Griffin's 1976 book, *The Question of Animal Awareness: Evolutionary Continuity of Mental Experience*, things have changed.[19] While anthropomorphic thinking supported by reams of data is now part of mainstream science, when his book was published, Griffin took a professional beating for attending to the shared biology of human and animal consciousness. Today, many scientists are using this approach to understand and appreciate not only how different animals are from us but also how similar. The book incorporates research from some of these scientists, such as Marc Bekoff, Culum Brown, Gordon Burghardt, Frans de Waal, Donald Kroodsma, Jane Goodall, Kay Holekamp, Cynthia Moss, Joyce Poole, Richard O. Prum, Con Slobodchikoff, and Françoise Wemelsfelder, to name just a few. Not that there is complete agreement about this approach in all areas of research on animal behavior. One complaint is that this method limits our knowledge of animals less like us—insects, for instance, or amphibians. You will find in the following pages descriptions of the work of scientists who have used what Burghardt calls "critical anthropomorphism," in which "statements about animal joy and suffering, hunger and stress, images and friendships are based on a careful knowledge of the species and the individual, careful observation, behavioral and neuroscience research, our own empathy and intuition, and constantly refined publicly verifiable predictions."[20] Burghardt's research often involves reptiles, amphibians, and fish, leaving no doubt that he is considering animals other than mammals when using empathy and intuition to understand the complexity of animals' lives.

To understand the phenomenon of anthropomorphism, two University of Vienna behavioral biologists focused on the cognitive processes underlying anthropomorphism, or "mental state attribution." They found that we share a social toolbox across the animal kingdom and that this helps us and other animals make sense of other living creatures. We, as animals, are endowed with "processes evolved in the social domain, such as motor matching mechanisms and empathy, and by domain-general mechanisms such as inductive and causal reasoning." We and other animals use "empathy and intuition" to make sense of "other minds."[21] Far from being a rejection of a scientific approach, critical anthropomorphism is a useful and biologically based faculty for understanding many species. How else do we as human animals understand each other?

A Peek at What Is in the Book

Animals often rely on creative solutions to their unique circumstances. Each chapter offers detailed examples of situations in which an individual animal or a group of animals relies on their unique creative processes to solve problems and sometimes pass those results on to others. As I interviewed prominent biologists and ethologists whose ongoing research is in the study of animal behavior, cognition, and consciousness, I found that many of their findings supported my arguments for recognizing the creativity of animals and the importance of rethinking our notions of creativity.

Each chapter in the book holds anecdotes, research, and discussions that build on the others. My inclusion of many animals across the chapters, rather than focusing on one or two, is a response to the vast body of research available. In addition, the goal was to emphasize the existence of creativity across species, so as not to regress into older ideas about it only existing in animals considered to be more like us—mammals, for instance. You will find here many examples of creativity in many animal species.

The first two chapters address elements integral to any kind of creativity: cognition and communication. Chapter 1 reviews research on animal intelligence over the last 50 years and what that might mean for understanding animal creativity. It then reviews these findings in three animals often maligned in human culture and not always thought of as intelligent or creative: ants, pigs, and pigeons. The first third of chapter 2 engages with the work of animal behaviorist and conservation biologist Con Slobodchikoff on animal language, particularly prairie dogs as a model species and how they sometimes use their language skills creatively. The second section of the chapter offers research on and examples of animal languages in a variety of species, from cuttlefish to red-eyed tree frogs to elephants. Animals communicate with each other all the time, and while making that point, this chapter also includes examples of how they might do so creatively. The last section of the chapter looks at the work of ornithologist Donald Kroodsma and others on bird song, and what roles creativity might play in one of the most exquisite sounds of the natural world.

Chapter 3 argues that play is one of the most understudied and yet crucial elements of a creative state of mind. Leading animal-play researchers Gordon Burghardt, Marc Bekoff, and Patrick Bateson argue for animal play as an important and unique subject for investigation. My visit to Canada's Fauna Foundation Sanctuary, where chimpanzees who have come from medical research and zoos are living out the rest of their lives, delves into the impact of trauma on the ability to play. Taking away the ability to play from animals leads to a dampening of creative behavior, among other abuses more often described.

In chapter 4 we look at the architectural talents of animals as diverse as beavers, caddisflies, bees, and bowerbirds and many examples of tool creation and use in animals across species, including an interspecies artwork initiated by a crow and documented by the artist who was chosen as a partner in this creative endeavor.

Chapter 5 adds another level of investigation to our journey, one that looks at sexual selection not only as an indicator of individual choice but also as a contributor to biodiversity, the biologically creative system that manages the variety and abundance of all life on earth. Richard O. Prum's research and theories on how sexual selection has coevolved into attraction help explain how the aesthetic choices of animals are important contributions to biodiversity.

Chapter 6 draws on recent findings on animal emotions in a wide variety of species and addresses how and why emotion is an important driver of creativity in animals as it is in humans. The associated area of animal personality research offers important insights into the creative process in individual animals. Chapter 7 concentrates on the creative impulse in animals within the context of another emerging area of research in animal behavior, animal culture in the context of what might be "Big-C" creativity for animals. This elaborates on the last section of my definition: "*the possibility of affecting others at cultural, species, and evolutionary levels.*" Biologists Hal Whitehead and Luke Rendell's research on whale and dolphin culture has been an important model for studying the cultures of animals. It includes their questions of the place of morality in animal culture and how we might understand the moral impulse and its impact on the creative behaviors of some animals.

How to Understand Animal Creativity: Be Creative

I started this journey with a few essential thoughts. The first was a fuzzy but strong sense that not only are animals creative, but they are creative in ways that are both similar to human creativity and decidedly unique. Some general qualities of creative beings that I had either learned from teaching or had experienced in my own creative processes were the second things I brought to this investigation. The following are the words I, along with others, have used to describe the qualities most often appearing in any creative process: "flexibility," "intelligence," "curiosity," "inventiveness," "persistence," and "comfort with complexity." Please, keep these available in your pocket as a reminder to step outside your box and breathe in the difference.

The third idea I packed was one that I had glimpsed earlier in my own experience, but emerged as the overarching outcome of my research: *the creativity of animals exists on the individual, group, species, and ecosystem level, and the loss of an individual animal is the loss of that individual's unique contribution to those interacting levels.* I hope this book is a starting point for that idea. In the descriptions of individual animals, the reader will recognize that animals are important not only to themselves but to those with whom they share their lives and to the world in which they live.

One more thing: creativity, as I perceive it, works on many levels. More traditional human assumptions about creativity have placed its manifestation in only the most celebrated of human artists, scientists, or innovators. Current thinking about creativity, however, has expanded to accommodate the ordinary individual and cooperation among groups of people in creative ventures of all kinds. The larger and more universal creativity I refer to in this book is one that exists for humans only on loan or as a gift, a gift that we need to understand and value for itself, as a process that exists throughout the world with or without human input. That is what I have learned while writing this book. I hope you too will consider this an opportunity to reconsider what creativity might mean to you as an individual, a member of a community, and a member of your species, which is only one of the millions of species who inhabit this planet.

1

Animal Intelligence

Pigeons and Higher Math

Every species deals flexibly with the environment and de-
velops solutions to the problems it poses. Each one does it
differently.
—Frans de Waal, *Are We Smart Enough to Know How Smart
Animals Are?*

Ayumu, an 11-year-old chimpanzee, waits for the day's activities to begin.
On a large touch screen before him, the numbers one through nine flash
for milliseconds before they are concealed by white squares. Ayumu's
goal, or so it appears, is to get as many peanuts as he can by selecting
the squares in numerical order from memory. The researchers' goal is to
see just how smart Ayumu is by recording how many times he is correct
in using his "working memory capability for numerical recollection."[1]
They also compare his performance on this test with that of humans,
whom he consistently out-performs by as much as 40 percent.

Ayumu has been taking this test for the last eight years, during which
time the number of milliseconds allowed for the numerals to flash across
the screen has decreased from 630 to 420 to 210, faster than the blink of
an eye, literally.[2] In 2008, Ayumu pulverized the 2004, 2008, and 2009
British Memory champion, Ben Pridmore, at the same test; Ayumu
scored 90 percent while Pridmore scored a humiliating 30 percent.[3]

These memory tests, along with others meant to test chimpanzees'
intelligence, emotional capabilities, and cultural learning, take place in
the Primate Research Institute at Kyoto University in Japan. Ayumu has
remembered the placement of almost every number he has seen in those

eight years. One cannot help but wonder what Ayumu has concluded about the intelligence of the researchers in those eight years. Aside from considering them exceptionally slow learners, he might also wonder why they are so obsessed with numbers.

The fact that Ayumu was born in the lab to his mother, Ai, who is also a working memory expert, may prompt other questions about what kinds of intelligence animals might reveal when not captive, but in their natural environments. If chimpanzees, for instance, can ace our memory tests and often beat a human memory expert, can we not assume that they are just as intelligent in their home environments, the forests and jungles from which we have taken them? Do they remember the placement and amount of things? Do they remember relatives or enemies they have not seen in a while? Are they, as other research has made clear, possessed of self-awareness, a combination of consciousness and long-term memory? Assuredly, the answer to all these questions is yes.

So, what do the continuing memory tests of Ayumu and Ai help us understand? Along with proving that chimpanzees are intelligent because they have strong visual memory capabilities, these tests indicate other forms of intelligence in these captive chimpanzees. If one uses "the ability to learn or understand or to deal with new or trying situations" as a broad definition for intelligence,[4] it is a small step to see how captivity itself might be challenging and difficult for the animals involved. These tests, then, also speak to the ability of animals not only to cope with but also to make the most of "new or trying situations." What about other kinds of animal intelligence, those more valuable to animals in their natural setting? Could animals possess different kinds of intelligence from those that are considered part of the human intelligence toolbox? How do we gauge the intelligence of animals who are capable of perceiving light at wavelengths below 390 and above 750 nanometers, the limits to light seen by the typical human eye? How do we understand the intelligence of animals who communicate with each other through infrasonic rumbles or electrical charges? Is it possible that animals who have a natural ability—flying, for instance—show a particular kind of intelligence to navigate long-distance migrations?

Consider that desert iguanas emit scents that reflect ultraviolet light to mark their territories and other iguanas, seeing these ultraviolet-lit markings, stay clear of that territory.[5] Similarly, elephants use infra-sonic rumblings inaudible to humans to communicate with each other over long distances[6] while the South American knife fish uses bursts of electrical energy to connect with compatriots. These fish possess an internal mechanism, kind of like a dimmer switch, to save energy when they are not using it, something few of us have mastered without the help of external assistance.[7] Migrating birds evaluate how much assis-tance tailwinds can give them while climbing up through the air col-umn, among other variables they assess in their long flights across land and sea.[8]

Humans have long thought themselves to be more intelligent than any other species if we have considered other species to have any intelli-gence at all. Problem solving, planning for and predicting future events, and cooperating with others to accomplish a task were all believed to be the province of humans and, *perhaps*, the higher primates, but certainly not fish or reptiles. It was not until the latter part of the last century that animal behavioral scientists began to recognize that animals, other than humans and chimpanzees, could think abstractly and then act on those abstractions.[9] Generally, up until then, the ability of an animal to hold a piece of knowledge in memory—for instance, the particular location of a food source—and then to retrieve that knowledge not just to ac-complish a task but to create something new—a new way to find food, a more optimally located nest, a way to open a cage door—was considered nothing more than "instinct." It was not thought of as indicative of intel-ligent behavior or, in these examples, creative thinking. With important exceptions, the prevailing belief was that animals could *not* think, let alone think creatively. Over the last few decades, the idea that animals of all kinds do think has changed due to the hard work and pioneering at-titudes of scientists in a wide array of fields, such as ethology, behavioral ecology, animal behavior and learning, cognitive sciences, comparative psychology, and evolutionary biology.

Twenty years of teaching creativity in both the arts and the sciences have taught me many lessons, perhaps most importantly that the processes and sources of creativity should never be taken for granted. Often, students who are considered the most intelligent due to their consistent A grades—those who do all their homework, always do well on tests, and always do what the teacher or professor asks—have a much harder time thinking creatively than other students. While it can be frustrating to have to explain to these students why they need to stop asking me what *I* want them to do, working with them is often gratifying.

Watching someone reach deep inside to find a source of creativity that has been buried or silenced and produce a unique perspective on the world is an exhilarating experience. In contrast, sometimes it is those students who are considered less intelligent, due to their poor grades in other subjects, who give themselves over to particularly profound or ingenious creative projects. The notion that intelligence is a purely logical function simply is not accurate; the seemingly illogical language of creativity indicates intelligence as well.

Are Ayumu and Ai similar to the students who always do what the teacher asks them to do? In some ways, they are. They both have been successful in learning and repeating their assigned tasks. But, what if they had not been living in a lab? What would they be using this amazingly consistent memory for? If intelligence and creativity are helpmates, would Ayumu and Ai be considered the Ada Lovelace and Alan Turing of the chimpanzee world? Or would their creativity in the wild be uniquely theirs?

As with most interesting and, I would add, important ideas we have, it soon becomes clear that others are thinking along the same lines. Experienced scientists who have been investigating animal intelligence for many years have begun to talk openly about the creativity of animals. The more I have searched, the more I have found that the idea of animal creativity has been slipping into the conversations of scientists who study animals, if not always into their publications. A few of these scientists have approached their studies of animals with underlying questions about creativity, while others have been surprised when witnessing acts of creative behavior in the animals they are studying. But both have found evidence that points to the presence of the creative impulse in the animals they study.

My point above about not assuming that creativity emerges only out of a particular kind of intelligence still stands. Conflicting research results and theories about both intelligence and creativity in humans leave room for new ideas about both. One way to investigate creative behavior in animals, however, is through what we know about animal intelligence. This accumulated knowledge has allowed researchers from many fields to consider that some of what they have been observing in animals extends into what can be called creative territory. And while the mapping of that territory is still to be determined, we now know enough to be able to set out on an investigative journey concerning the creativity of animals, beginning with what we know about animal intelligence thus far.

A Short Overview of Animal Intelligence and What That Might Mean for Creativity

Intelligence turns out to be as confounding a concept as creativity. Those involved in intelligence research across many disciplines, from cognitive science to educational theory, are still in debate over what constitutes intelligence in humans. And since, until very recently, animal intelligence has been studied in comparison with human intelligence, much of what is known about animal intelligence mirrors the investigations of human intelligence research.

Over the last few decades, the sheer quantity of scientific data amassed on animal intelligence has challenged assumptions about the lack of intelligence in animals, in addition to many other traits we once believed made humans unique in the animal kingdom. Scientists have been documenting in animals what is thought of as higher orders of thought: learning and memory, the ability to understand grammar and symbols, categorization, understanding others' motives, imitating others, abstraction, and self-awareness. All of these are considered to be necessary skills in humans and animals for intelligent behavior. Revisiting the large quantity of research on creativity while collecting research on animal intelligence has clarified for me how these abilities are also important for understanding the underlying processes of creative behavior.

Learning and memory, as Ayumu and his cohorts have demonstrated, for example, play a major role in estimating the extent of a particular species' intelligence. For Jason Bruck, a biologist at Oklahoma State University, a captive dolphin remembering the signature whistle (more about this later) of a tank mate she had not seen for twenty years serves as evidence of long-term memory.[10] Stray dogs in Moscow, twenty dogs at last count, learning the routes of the subway system well enough to catch the correct trains that will carry them back and forth between the suburbs and the city, reveal a complex use of both learning and memory.[11] Dr. Andrei Poiarkov of the Moscow Ecology and Evolution Institute, who has studied these dogs in Moscow, explains that urban areas provide more opportunities for dogs to meet their needs, such as food from handouts, warmth on the train, and social reassurance from compassionate people. The dogs show an understanding of the subway system, something that would have had to be learned as it would not have come naturally, as well as a keen memory of when and where to board and disembark the trains.[12] One wonders, Was there a first dog to board a Moscow train and was he followed by others? Or was this behavior an example of a creative zeitgeist in the dogs that travel back and forth on these trains?

Scrub jays, and other birds of the corvid family, demonstrate an understanding of others' motives when caching food for later use. Not only do they remember weeks later where they have buried the food, but they are also particularly careful to hide the cache when other birds are not looking, something behavioral researchers call "tactical deception" and found in other species, including ants, pigs, cuttlefish, monkeys, and primates.[13] This kind of deception requires a complexity of thought that involves both evaluating the intentions of others and episodic memory— the ability to recall personal experiences and specific events. Individual creativity often makes use of personal experience and events to fathom and fashion something new.

Researchers now have begun to credit certain animals with an understanding of grammar and symbols. Baboons at the Cognitive Psychology Laboratory at the Aix-Marseille University are offering Jonathan Grainger[14] and other members in this lab insight into essential, more advanced elements of learning to read. The complex process of reading alphabetic script begins with identifying and understanding the visual elements of letters and their positions in particular words. "Orthographic processing"—recognizing and remembering the images that make up an alphabet—is considered to be the first "language-specific" stage of the reading process. The baboons in this study have displayed remarkable abilities to identify specific combinations of letters in words and recognize the difference between English words and gibberish. Even more striking is their ability to recognize differences in words they have not seen before, an ability eerily similar to that of humans.

The baboons involved in this study are tested through a computerized system controlled by microchips implanted in each baboon. These baboons remain within their social groups in captivity, and voluntarily self-test on computers in their large enclosure, day or night. This has encouraged their interest in the task. The high proficiency with which the baboons have learned to use the computer and also to process and differentiate words from meaningless combinations of letters prompted Grainger and his cohorts in this study to agree on this: "The primate brain might . . . be better prepared than previously thought to process printed words, hence facilitating the initial steps toward mastering one of the most complex of human skills: reading."[15]

And if reading is not enough to make us rethink our view of animal intelligence, marine scientists in both Scotland and Florida have discovered "the use of names" in both wild and captive dolphins.[16] Naming, another behavior we humans were once sure was exclusive to our species, is used by bottlenose dolphins to devise their signature whistle at a young age, a whistle that identifies them in particular. Other dolphins not only recognize these particular whistles but also use them to call to individual dolphins. Dolphins use this method to communicate with each other from over twelve miles away. I cannot help but wonder what they have been calling us behind those charming smiles that just happen to be the way their mouths curve?

Marine biologists working over decades on and in the ocean have discovered how complex the large groups in which dolphins live can be—a complexity that would have been impossible to decipher or attribute in captivity. These include long-term bonds, such as those between mothers and calves, those between adult males, and those between females. A society exhibiting these kinds of group social behaviors is sometimes called a "fission-fusion society," in which animals may merge into different groups, or split off to forage alone or into smaller groups.[17] Male dolphins develop what researchers consider to be higher-order alliances, which require a great deal of cognitive capacity in developing social strategies to deal with participation in two to three levels of shifting alliances in large groups, including cooperative networks.[18]

Not surprisingly, recent research on wild female dolphins interacting across species has demonstrated similar levels of higher-order alliances in addition to alliances with humans. These are dynamic societies in which social grouping changes over time in size and composition. Individuals embedded in these fluid social networks, where decisions at one level may have impacts at other levels, require the highly developed and nuanced intelligence of seasoned diplomats, exactly the qualities that adult dolphins possess.[19]

Memory is one of the essential aspects of intelligence. Early research on the cognition and behavior of bottlenose dolphins has documented that, like us, they have strong auditory, visual, and spatial memory. Captive dolphins have acted in rational and intelligent ways, indicating that they can remember and process complex information. These include examples of learning many types of abstract rules of human language, as well as spontaneously understanding and implementing these rules to meet requests from their trainers. Using random behaviors that often translate into tricks, such as flipper clapping and ball playing, researchers have developed carefully planned experiments in which the dolphins learned to decode and use the rules of a language not their own. Captive dolphins excel at understanding the demands of their trainers by learning *our* language.[20] Ask a human to use dolphin language and it doesn't go nearly as well. Dolphins and other animals who interact with humans have had to be very good at interpreting our auditory, visual, and behavioral languages to make up for our poor understanding of their languages.

An important factor of creativity is parsing ways of perceiving the world other than our own and acting on those perceptions. Dolphins and other animals are very good at doing just that. In the wild, dolphins swim alongside or above manta rays as they hunt for small fish among the waving grasses of the sea floor. The manta's undulating movements stir up the small crustaceans concealed in the grass as the dolphins swoop down and quickly scoop up a few as if they are browsing an appetizer buffet. In this situation, dolphins have watched and learned from another species, the manta, mainly a filter feeder. They have then manipulated that knowledge to their benefit by swimming above the manta and diving in to grab an easy meal.[21]

The dolphins imitate some of the mantas' behavior by swimming with them, but they also understand that the manta's goal is to find food, and they plan to get that food before the manta does. This kind of imitation, called "social learning," is a particular area of interest to researchers studying both animal and human intelligence. Imitation was once thought of as a poor cousin to what is now sometimes called "creative cognition," but more researchers are seeing it as a lynchpin to various forms of learning and cultural behavior. As in the example of the scrub jay's deception in hiding food when others are not looking and then being able to remember where the food is hidden, this kind of social learning is a prerequisite for more innovative behavior.

Baby birds babble, and that babbling helps them to practice sounds that will eventually help them learn the songs they need to communicate as adults. Human babies babble as well. When human children do this, it is seen as a sign of intelligence, but when animals do it, no one seems to notice—until recently. Studies with zebra finch babies showed that their babbling before learning songs was strikingly similar to that of human children, and in both species babbling was a form of practicing sounds that over time are used by the little ones to construct their respective languages.[22] In the past decade, acts of imitation in some animals and humans have been studied as the products of an entire system of cognitive, social, and neural mechanisms. What has changed?

In 1996, a neurophysiologist, Dr. Giacomo Rizzolatti, found evidence of what he called "mirror neurons" while researching the neural representation, or more simply a mental image, of motor movements experienced by macaque monkeys. The term "mirror neuron" alludes to the fact that, unlike other neurons, these neurons not only fired when the animal was engaged in planning a motor movement but also, more interestingly, fired when the monkey observed a motor movement in another monkey, or another species, such as a human. For example, when a monkey sees someone eat a banana, his mirror neurons fire, even though he is not eating a banana at that moment.

Over time, rather than assuming that thinking logically helps us to understand the feelings and actions of another, research on mirror neurons has offered a new view of perception. Seeing another act, eating a banana, for instance, in some way sparks particular neurons to fire and produce an internal simulation of that action. It is as if one were performing that action oneself. This is a revolutionary concept about how we understand others' motives, actions, even minds. What this finding has suggested is that feeling provides an understanding of others' intentions as well as their actions. In other words, we understand others not by thinking about how they might feel but by feeling that way ourselves.

Consequently, much discussion about mirror neurons has centered on the idea that these neurons, or the system in which they exist, is the basis of empathy, an essential ingredient of creative behavior. This discovery, originally not accepted for publication by a top scientific journal, was then published by another journal to a great deal of interest that continues today.[23]

Research on mirror neurons is important because it has supported the consideration of imitation as one of the most advanced cognitive faculties. For instance, let us say my son is watching me make lasagna. He is learning not only how I go about making lasagna but also how he might make it better. Imitation in animals is considered a valuable source of social learning that involves some degree of intentionality or goal directedness, such as the dolphins imitating the mantas' search for food. In the same way as my son learns to make lasagna from me as he plans ways of making it better, so the dolphin learns from watching the manta's behavior as he plans to catch the prey before the manta does. Human creativity is in part based on a similar sequence of processes. Artists, architects, musicians, scientists, and writers have always learned through imitation and future planning. Watching others' creativity has always been a conduit to understanding creative behavior.

A growing body of knowledge supports this elevated position of imitation in learning research. The convergence of findings in fields ranging from cognitive sciences and cognitive ethology to social psychology and neuroscience has helped to contribute to a solid framework on which learning by imitation has been linked to various forms of intelligence, including creative intelligence, in parrots, dogs, chimpanzees, dolphins, whales, rats, and birds.[24]

What about us? Do we have mirror neurons? Yes, it turns out that we do. For a time, after finding them in monkeys, many scientists doubted their existence in humans, but recent studies have shown us to have them as well.[25] What individual mirror neurons are responsible for and whether they are part of a larger neurological, psychological, and emotional system or not—my bet is that they are part of a larger system—are still up for debate.[26] But these findings in both animals and humans have encouraged an openness to perceiving animal behavior as coming from thoughtful minds with conscious awareness of their body parts, body image, behaviors, and knowledge. Self-awareness is a sign of what has been called "higher-order intelligence." But what does the ranking of various kinds of intelligence mean for understanding the intelligence of species not our own? How might labeling various intelligences "higher" than others blind us to discovering the intelligences of other species?

Cetaceans seem to be so human-like. We respond to their smiles, their playfulness, and their friendliness, and so we accept their intelligence and even the possibility of their creativity. We know that chimpanzees share 98.6 percent of our genes, as well as having, like us, large brains, stereoscopic vision, opposable thumbs, and flexible limbs. Their similar facial features and expressions, combined with their comparable nonverbal communication, allow us to entertain the idea that they too might share a "higher" order of intelligence. But what about other species we think of as less like us than, say, dolphins and chimpanzees? Are ants, pigs, and pigeons as intelligent as we are? And more to the point, is it possible that they too exhibit creative behavior?

Ants as Intelligent Beings

You are in the kitchen working on dinner for friends. Everything is set, so you decide to enjoy a glass of wine until the guests arrive. You reach into the pantry to find that bottle a previous guest has left and you see a trail of ants marching diligently across the shelf. Before you grab the newspaper or another sort of ant-killing aid, think about the words of entomologist Mark Moffett: "The astonishing truth is that the brains and central nervous systems of ants and human beings share closer evolutionary ties than was once believed."[27]

Moffett, an organismic and evolutionary biologist who studied with E. O. Wilson, has watched ants so closely and for so long in the field that he can distinguish the characteristics of individual ants by noticing their particular and repeated behaviors. Some ants are rather lackadaisical, while others dive into their work and devise solutions to problems. Behind those varying personalities, he believes, is intelligence: "We know a worker can evaluate the living space, ceiling height, entry dimensions, cleanliness, and illumination of a potential new home for her colony—a masterly feat, considering that she's a roving speck with no pen, paper or calculator."[28]

Ants display traits that are often considered examples of intelligence in primates and other species, including humans. One example we have discussed before is tactical deception, and this is practiced by the honeypot ants of the American Southwest in the form of ritualized behaviors intended to avoid lethal conflict. In a movement called "stilt walking," ants from different colonies will circle each other on tiptoe in an attempt to appear larger. They will even stand on pebbles to rise above their rivals.[29] Humans, most often males, display similar behaviors in the abidingly popular what-are-you-going-to-do-about-it ritual. While this particular similarity with humans may not lend much credence to the "acute intelligence" of ants, it is a useful use of tactical deception in individual animals.

Moffett also finds parallels between ant and human culture. Through ancient languages made up of chemical signals, ants respond to the bonds and needs of their nest-mates. Like us, they cooperate to meet those needs by altering nature, building fortresses, stockyards, highways, and nurseries. Moffett has shown that ants face similar problems to ours in organizing the myriad needs of their communities, such as obtaining and distributing resources and labor, preserving civil unity, and defending against intruders. And while Moffett sees ant intelligence leading to creative behavior, he specifies that another way to look at creativity is "at the level of the superorganism. Rather than seeking playfulness in individual ants, could it exist in the colony as a whole?"[30] While Moffett says he is fascinated by ants as individuals and has the patience to watch one for an entire day, he also offers several other ways of understanding ant colonies: as part of a society, as part of an organism, as part of a superorganism. And if individual ants are not known to play, perhaps, as Moffett suggests, their creativity lies within the superorganism to which they belong.

Another ant researcher, Antonie Wystrach, has been studying ant navigation using a bottom-up approach. Wystrach explains that this method allows researchers to look for the simplest explanations for complex behavior, all the while looking for higher levels of intelligence. Wystrach elaborates:

> Ants use a variety of cues to navigate, such as sun position, polarized light patterns, visual panoramas, gradient of odors, wind direction, slope, ground texture, step-counting . . . and more. Indeed, the list of cues ants can utilize for navigation is probably greater than for humans.[31]

But, he adds, they do not integrate these cues into a unified representation of space, at least not one that we would consider unified, but instead use distinct modules for different navigational tasks. Wystrach and his team were particularly interested in the abilities of the Australian desert ants they studied ten miles south of Alice Springs. This grassy area laced with trees provides rich visual cues for navigating ants. Wystrach and his team found that ants use backtracking behavior only if they have recently seen their nest's surroundings before getting lost. This demonstrated that the ants were able to take into account familiar visual terrain when attempting to find their way back and to combine that with other visual cues. The team points to this kind of navigational skill as evidence of these ants' intelligence. Wystrach thinks, "Even insect brains are far too complex to be fully understood in the near future." So, perhaps it is too early to assume that creativity is not one of the many kinds of intelligence used by ants.[32]

The Boredom of Intelligent Pigs

In our culture, pigs are primarily used for food. Animal researchers who work closely with pigs, however, know that they are extremely intelligent. They respond to verbal communication, identify objects they have not seen in some time, distinguish slight differences in similar objects, disregard irrelevant information, and accomplish all of these things with no instruction from the researcher, other than a direct statement, such as, "Figure out what you are supposed to do." They take on tasks with motivation and persistence and are capable of what is known as "one-trial learning." They are quick studies, comprehending how something works or what action is needed to achieve a goal on the first try.[33]

When rooting around for scientifically based research on pig intelligence, I was particularly frustrated. Much of what exists does so for two general reasons, neither turning out very well for pigs. One reason is to understand pig cognition—you may substitute the word "intelligence" here—so that pigs may be used as animal research models for human medical studies. That pigs share physiological and anatomical similarities with humans has led to their use in medical testing as far back as 250 BC when Erasistratus of Ceos, a physician in ancient Greece, used them to investigate the mechanics of breathing. When Erasistratus was granted permission to vivisect condemned criminals, their bodies were "slowly cut open, their bloody, trembling organs exposed, turned over, palpated, and inspected; all amid shrieks of pain and under the cool glance of the anatomists and their pupils and assistants."[34]

Pigs were subject (as they still are) to the same fate and the same misery, because of their similarity to humans in psychological, emotional, and cognitive functions. Today they are used in transgenics, as organ transplant models, in combat trauma training, and in the medical classroom. Given their similarity to humans, it is hard not to call the treatment of pigs in today's medical research and factory farms torture as well. Improving the appalling bit of life pigs are allowed before they are slaughtered for food is the second overarching reason for pig cognition studies.

It is clear to those spending time with pigs in research labs and sanctuaries that pigs possess capacities for learning and remembering in
large measure. Domestic pigs descended from the wild boar and, given
the chance to exercise their freedom, continue the behavior and social
organization of their wild ancestors. Wild pigs, then, live in matriarchal groups of two to five. During the breeding season, an outside male
might accompany a family; once grown, male offspring go off on their
own to become members of "bachelor" groups.

Animal behavior researchers Michael Mendl and Susan Held at the
University of Bristol have spent the last ten years developing tests demonstrating the kind of cognitive abilities that might be useful to pigs in
their wild state. Workers on farm sanctuaries (there are over 100 in the
United States alone) offer numerous anecdotes that support the findings
of Mendl, Held, and other researchers who focus on pig intelligence.
According to Mendl and Held, pigs can tell each other apart "even when
only provided with cues in one sensory modality (smell, appearance, or
sound)."[35] While Mendl and Held have not studied how long pigs remember their friends, Kim Sturla of the animal sanctuary Animal Place,
claims,

> Pigs develop close relationships, particularly if they have grown up to-
> gether. If they have the opportunity to mature together, the bond pretty
> much lasts a lifetime. They will make choices to be with one another—to
> sleep together, take mud baths together, and roam together. They become
> partners.[36]

In addition to being able to differentiate others, both human and animal, pigs are also able to remember particularly good hunting grounds
for a meal. Mendl and Held have studied deceptive behavior in pairs of
pigs. In one study, one pig knows where the food is while the other does
not. The informed pig, Harry, quickly learns that it was a mistake to
teach the other pig, Augustus, where the food is after Augustus bullies
him away from the food and scarfs it down himself. In response, Harry

begins to deceive his clueless but greedy pal by being much more secretive about where the food is located.[37]

Mendl and Held admit that this kind of deceptive, highly intelligent behavior is similar to that seen in chimpanzees and ravens, but they demur on how intelligent the behavior is. Most research I found on pig behavior followed the same pattern: despite a glut of evidence of the higher intelligence of pigs, some researchers still shy away from including teaching in pigs' intelligence portfolio. Describing the initial behavior of Harry, the informed pig, as *teaching* is something Mendl and Held did not do in the article describing this particular experiment. I described Harry as having *taught* Augustus to find the food because I wanted to point to an area of disagreement among researchers when it comes to describing particular animal behavior as intelligent.

Biologists and comparative psychologists have often deviated on their positions about whether animals teach since Nigel Franks, a behavioral ecologist at Bristol University in the United Kingdom, and his graduate student at the time, Tom Richardson, published a study in 2006 in the journal *Nature*. Their study was the first to show teaching in a non-human species, rock ants.[38] Then, scientists found strong evidence of teaching in three other nonhuman species: meerkats, southern pied-babblers, and superb fairywrens.

More recently, researchers who study social learning in animals have been documenting this behavior in other species, such as orcas, chickens, and elephants. According to Alex Thornton, senior lecturer and research fellow in biosciences at the University of Exeter, more biologists, zoologists, and cognitive ethologists are working in this area. They view "teaching" through an evolutionary lens rather than one seeking to find what kind of psychology underlies pedagogy, a concern in comparative psychology. For these scientists, Thornton says, teaching in animals is a type of cooperative behavior, like hunting or sharing food, something that Harry did until Augustus became a bully towards him.

Teaching requires intelligence and, for Thornton, is best studied by going "into the field to investigate the evolution and development of cognition and culture in the wild."[39] It is this new openness to disparate approaches to nonhuman cognition that is crucial to understanding how intelligence exists in animals, and it is vital to learning how intelligence contributes to their creative behavior.

As for pig intelligence, biologist and behavioral scientist Françoise Wemelsfelder does not balk at describing pigs as intelligent, but also as having consciousness, awareness of self and others, and conscious emotion. She offers one explanation for other researchers' reluctance to do so: scientists' resistance reveals how this might argue for a change in our relationships with animals. "To me," she recently wrote to me, "the creativity of learning and behavior is fundamental to understanding animals as sentient creatures and how they perceive their world."[40] If, when thinking about pigs, for instance, we recognized these signs of higher intelligence as part of a whole picture—one that regards them as beings with personalities and emotions—we might reconsider our tradition of eating them for food and using them in experiments. "Pigs," Wemelsfelder says, "that live in rich, spacious, natural, and social environments have more chance to develop and show creativity than pigs living in highly confined, barren, dark pens."[41] For a group of scientists, including Stephen Hawking and Irene Pepperberg, a scientist noted for her studies in animal cognition, particularly with parrots, this kind of realization led to a well-documented declaration from a prominent international group of neuroscientists in a well-publicized ceremony at the University of Cambridge in 2012. The Cambridge Declaration of Consciousness formally declared, "The weight of evidence indicates that humans are not unique in possessing the neurological substrates [emotions] that generate consciousness. Nonhuman animals, including all mammals and birds, and many other creatures, including octopuses, also possess these neurological substrates."[42]

Wemelsfelder agrees with this declaration on nonhuman consciousness. The last two decades of her research have explored the sentience of pigs. A senior research scientist at the Scottish Rural College in Edinburgh, Wemelsfelder has written several book chapters on animal boredom and the importance of "creativity and competence as goals for animals."[43] Seeing firsthand how healthy and well-fed pigs exhibit depression and helplessness when they are unable to live an active and sociable life in which their "creative flow of engagement"[44] flourishes, Wemelsfelder and her colleagues developed a new methodology.[45] The Qualitative Behavior Assessment (QBA) was conceived for judging the expressive quality of the whole animal and their engagement, such as body language, in their social environment. "Our research now encompasses other animals," she told me, "because the principles of creativity and sentience apply to all animal species, in my view."[46]

Sentience—the ability to feel, perceive, or experience sensations—is a term with an interesting history. The Latin word "*sentiens*," meaning "feeling," from the verb "to feel," was transformed into the mid-eighteenth-century meaning of "to be conscious *of* something." Earlier used to separate feelings from intelligence, the word shifted in its use and spelling to describe what was possible with the senses: if one felt something, then one must be conscious of that feeling. Looking at a graph of the history of sentience since 1800, one notices a deep decline from the early twentieth century into the late 1950s.[47] This dip corresponds with the rise of behaviorism, a version of psychology insisting that there is no need to resort to internal processes such as thoughts, ideas, or feelings to explain either human or nonhuman behavior. External processes, in other words, behaviors that could be tested empirically in the laboratory, were preferred.

John B. Watson, the cofounder with B. F. Skinner of radical behaviorism, insisted that all behavior can be explained as a result of learned associations between a stimulus—such as a cookie—and a response—such as grabbing the cookie. Behaviorism, in the early days, focused on how these associations can be reinforced or eliminated with rewards, such as getting to eat the cookie, or punishments, such as realizing one has put on an additional twenty pounds after always responding to this stimulus in the same way. The methods of behaviorism, originally meant to elevate psychology to the pantheon of objective sciences like chemistry and physics, seem barbaric today.

One of the more infamous examples involving humans was the 1920 emotional conditioning experiment at Johns Hopkins University called the "Little Albert" experiment, in which Watson and his assistant, Rosalie Rayner, exposed a nine-month-old human baby ("Little Albert") to a white rat and other furry animals and objects.[48] They allowed the baby first to experience the animals without any negative conditioning. The baby responded with curiosity and playfulness. Then the baby was submitted to what was called negative conditioning in the presence of the same animals and furry objects—in most cases a loud and strident noise made by a hammer against a metal pipe—and "Little Albert" was left sufficiently terrified of anything furry.

While these kinds of experiments were practiced on human subjects in the early days of behaviorism, they evolved to include animals. Current experiments on pigs,[49] for example, show that they become depressed after being injected with varying doses of the recreational drug Ecstasy—just like humans. The scientists guiding this test note that since pigs' brains are similar to humans' brains, the serotonin released by the drug into the brain puts both species at risk for depression. They add that it can even cause both pig and human physiological systems to lose control of body temperature, something we already know due to numerous deaths by dehydration of humans when willingly taking Ecstasy.

Rather than replicating experiments proving that pigs and people have many similarities, Wemelsfelder sees the multiple affinities between humans and pigs as a major reason for developing the QBA approach.[50] She is scientifically documenting how pigs suffer under intensive farming regimes. Wemelsfelder points out that engaging with one or several individual animals and developing a rapport with them goes a long way toward "showing us how animals express themselves with unexpected creativity in unexpected moments, giving us a sense of who they are as individual beings."[51]

While early behaviorists believed that there was no reason to even speculate that animals might have inner lives and points of view, Wemelsfelder insists that this mindset, while still surviving, is increasingly outdated. Her work involves finding ways to contribute to the "study of animal perspectives, *as perspectives* rather than objects."[52] Her work on animal boredom, one emotion barely examined by animal researchers, highlights

> the importance of recognizing the drive for creativity and competence as goals for animals. Animals may be well-fed, and healthy, and productive, but if they are not given the freedom to live an active and sociable life, then their creative flow of engagement dries up, and they can suffer from boredom, or eventually from depression and helplessness.[53]

Note how Wemelsfelder describes the creativity of pigs as "the creative flow of engagement." If we are to understand anything about how creativity works in animals, studying them in environments in which this creative flow is made to dry up due to their inability to engage with others, with everyday life, with any kind of movement, is hardly beneficial. There is a growing effort among scientists working with animals to include these anecdotes of individual expression in their scientific understandings of what she calls the "whole sentient animal." As the political scientist Raymond Wolfinger once said and renowned cognitive ethologist Marc Bekoff is fond of repeating, "The plural of anecdote is data."[54] Rather than exclude these more personal judgments of animal intelligence and behavior, Wemelsfelder has incorporated observations into her studies of pigs' quality of life in which engagement in the world is encouraged.

The crucial component of these studies focuses on how observers described pigs' behavior in a variety of farm conditions. Wemelsfelder and her group[55] first investigated humans' ability to assess animal intelligence and behavior by having the observers describe what they were seeing rather than using those descriptions typically provided in advance. This allowed the observers to base their descriptions on close observations of animals in a variety of situations, rather than on preexisting terms that might not fit the individual pig's behavior. Free Choice

Profiling (FCP), often used in food and consumer science but never before used in research on animal behavior, became a perfect fit for this investigation. I find this a sadly ironic turn of events given that the most commonly consumed meat worldwide is pork. The FCP protocol allows participants to describe in their own words animals usually seen as non-living products. A major reason Wemelsfelder decided on this method was that it allowed the study of people *as well as* pigs. The human participants were surprised at how easily they were able to evaluate nonverbal signs of an animal's state of mind, such as boredom, tension, playfulness, or calmness, with a high degree of nuance and sophistication. The method encouraged integration and judgment of animals' expressions rather than merely trying to fit what the observers saw and learned into a previously defined category.

"Pigs," Wemelsfelder tells me, "are such curious, lively, intelligent, affectionate, and playful beings—very like dogs. They are very expressive in ways easy to recognize for humans."[56] The idea that certain environments or situations encourage creativity is one that looms large in studies of human creativity. The link between our inability to see many animals as creative, conscious beings and the barren confines of the environments we keep many of them in, particularly domesticated animals used for food or research, indicates just how thick the filters through which we see them are. As with looking through a very dirty and rippled window, what we see is distorted, and we fill in the gaps of our understanding with our prejudices and assumptions.

Pigeons and Higher Math

The students spend many months learning the basics. Each day they are presented with 35 sets of three images on computer screens. Each image is filled with one, two, or three objects of different sizes, colors, and shapes. When they can differentiate the lower numbers of items from the higher ones and can choose them in order by touching the screen, they are rewarded. Finally, after much hard work, the big day arrives.

They are asked to perform the same task, but this time there are six to nine items. Everyone succeeds at this new, more difficult task without any prior instruction, and the reward is all the wheat they can eat. Wait . . . What? Oh, I forgot to mention that these students are pigeons.

My interest in pigeons started many years ago when I took in a homing pigeon that had flown from California to Washington, DC, where I lived at the time. Homing pigeons are bred to find their way home over long distances. Finding her in the park, I saw how weak she was and brought her home to care for her. I was able to identify her through the number on the band on one of her legs and called the owner in California, who said he did not want her back if she was ill. Shocked at his nonchalance, I took her to the vet, and following their advice, tried to nurse her back to health. She allowed me to hold her and gently cooperated with all my attempts to feed her and make her comfortable, but she died a week later. In the week I took care of her, I began to appreciate just how affectionate and individual pigeons are. I have had a special fondness for them ever since.

Even though many city dwellers despise pigeons, they were not always seen as pariahs. In ancient times, the dove represented the divine. As far back as the Iron Age, delicate representations of doves perched atop small clay shrines to Canaanite goddesses. The Greeks and Romans elaborated on this connection between doves and goddesses by revering the birds as sacred to Aphrodite and Venus and Fortuna. Both the Bible's Old Testament and the Babylonian Epic of Gilgamesh cite the dove as a messenger of the end of the flood and so the messenger of God. Christians' preferred symbol of the Holy Spirit was none other than the dove, a type of pigeon.

The pigeon that we see in today's city and the historically and religiously significant doves are one and the same. Pigeons all over the world descend from the blue rock pigeon, also called the rock dove. They were originally from Europe, northern Africa, and western Asia, and settlers of these areas introduced what are now city pigeons into the eastern United States as a domestic bird in the early 1600s. They expanded west, north to Canada and Alaska, and south to the southernmost tip of South America.[57] What does all this say about the intelligence of pigeons, you ask? As birds that seem to do nothing all day but peck, what possible kind of intelligence could pigeons possess? If anything offers an example of how much we have missed out on the intelligence of other species, the pigeon should be the poster child par excellence for animal intelligence.

Throughout history, we have used pigeons' navigational abilities in sending messages, in the military, in racing, and in aerial photography. Recently, their ability to recognize themselves in a mirror—a test developed almost half a century ago—placed them in an expanding group of animals we consider to be self-aware: primates, elephants, dolphins, and magpies, among others. Pigeons also have uncanny abstract reasoning skills. Once these kinds of skills were discovered by researchers, they began rethinking how they might test other animals for similar features. Scientists are developing newer methods of measuring animal intelligence, taking into consideration the widely differing sensory perceptions and motor activities of various species. One test for all animals (just like one test for all humans) is, simply stated, bad science.

Ed Wasserman, professor of experimental psychology at the University of Iowa, has used a touch-screen test based on the standard intelligence "string test" to more deeply explore pigeon intelligence.[58] His digital version presents the pigeons with a touch screen of icons connected by digital lines to either full- or empty-looking food dishes. Pecking the correct icon allows the virtual bowl to move down the screen and closer to the pigeon sitting at the bottom until the pigeon is eventually rewarded with real food. According to Wasserman, "The pigeons proved that they could indeed learn this task with a variety of different string configurations—even those that involved crossed strings, the most difficult of all configurations to learn."[59]

Wasserman and other scientists involved in this research also noted the pigeons' competence in connecting the virtual strings and the virtual dishes to the result of real treats. This faculty for abstract reasoning surprised another group of researchers who found that pigeons did just as well as primates in understanding abstract number rules.[60] Like Ayumu and his mother described at the opening of the chapter, pigeons were able to order image sets of objects holding low to high numbers of these objects. At first, they were only shown one to three objects in those sets, but though they were not taught to order a larger number of objects, much to the researchers' surprise, they were able to transfer the abstract rule of their initial trials to ordering screen images holding groups of four to nine objects. Even more, these larger groups presented a range of images, from familiar to novel or completely different in size, shape, and color. They made this cognitive leap without any help from the researchers.

While this may not seem like higher math to some, the studies in which these pigeons (in addition to primates) perform these tasks are not just about counting. They allowed the researchers to see that pigeons, and other birds as well, understand a fundamental concept of higher math, in this case, the abstract concept of what Wasserman calls "the relation of relations," or what is called analogical thinking.[61]

The fact that pigeons possess analogical thinking tells us that they can perceive not just what things are related to each other but *how* those things are related. Analogical thinking is fundamental to learning and discovery and is used to explain or understand new topics. Analogies help to transfer ideas across different concepts, situations, or domains, and analogy is a key mechanism in creativity. For many creative people, analogy lies at the core of their work.

Wasserman is more than happy to talk about how smart pigeons are, but in recent interviews, he also likes offering two other fast-growing ideas among scientists who study animal behavior. The first idea is cultural transmission: the social spread of particular ways of doing things shared by members of a community, seen in animal communities of all kinds.

Birds learn to chirp in dialects, whales learn songs that are repeated and changed over time and location, meerkats teach their young how to catch scorpions by bringing them dismembered ones in gradual stages, and a species of ant teaches others to find food with a poking and prod-ding technique researchers call "tandem running."[62] These kinds of cul-tural learning examples, in pigeons and other animals, speak to their ability to take learning further. Their ability to analogize or, as Wasser-man puts it, understand the "relation of relations," is an ability we have as well, but not until we are four to six years old. In an interview on animal cognition, Wasserman explained,

> The work with animals and their adaptability to changing environments tells us that all intelligence may reside in basic laws of behavior. Those basic laws of behavior may go a very long way to explain not only what animals do, but also what we do. To think that we are not part of nature, but are somehow above and beyond it is a kind of arrogance, a very dan-gerous arrogance.[63]

Wasserman proposes that foundational cognitive processes that are widespread among animals are the very same processes that underlie those human behaviors we consider being uniquely ours, such as cre-ating complex mathematical theories or poems. Many species have displayed high levels of success in passing or exceeding intelligence tests through their demonstrations of an understanding of cause and effect, sameness and difference, numerical abilities, categorization, imitation, complex communication, abstract thought, and the ability to learn and remember what they have learned.

So, what is the difference between animals and humans? Humans, after all, are a species just like chimpanzees and slugs, and many ani-mals can pass, and often exceed, the numerous intelligence tests we have designed for them. They demonstrate the cognitive processes that un-derlie creative human behavior. When we are faced with the idea that they might also be creative, the question often asked is, But, have they produced symphonies, great art, towering architecture, and complex and fascinating societies? The answer is, that is the wrong question. Our conceptions of what defines a symphony, a work of art, a style of architecture, or a civilized society match our adaptations to the world over time as *we* know it. Why do we think animal creativity must match ours? They are endowed with capabilities we do not have or have not developed. Perhaps it is time to ask ourselves, If we are so smart, why has it taken this long to see that multiple intelligences across species might exist just as multiple intelligences exist in ours? A much more helpful and interesting question is, What kinds of creativity do animals exhibit?

One of the most satisfying moments of my life in teaching was to come across the work of the Harvard psychologist Howard Gardner. Gardner's theory of multiple intelligences (MI)[64] emerged as a psychological theory, one that also drew on brain and genetic knowledge in the early 1980s, during the very time I was teaching art in a large urban high school in Arlington, Virginia. MI is a critique of the standard psychological view of intellect: that there is a single intelligence, adequately measured by IQ or other short-answer tests. These tests tend to assess linguistic, logical, and mathematical kinds of intelligences. Gardner's theory recognized intelligences, such as musical, bodily kinesthetic, spatial, and both interpersonal and intrapersonal intelligences, among others.

When I was teaching high school students, it was obvious to me that students learned in varying ways. As unique as they were as individuals, so they were unique in how they understood things. Some were able to listen to my explanations, others needed either written or visual amplification, and other students had to dive into the project to digest what it was that we were involved in. I, like other teachers who had experienced these kinds of differences in their students, leaped upon this theory to support our knowledge about the varied ways students learn, which up until then had been discounted.

Gardner is a psychologist and was surprised when the majority of interest in his work came from the educational community. But, he now has a home in the education department at Harvard, and over the years has consistently written about his theories and creativity and most recently been involved with the Good Project, a research collaboration on the place of ethics in schools. I imagine Gardner did not develop his theory of multiple intelligences to apply to animals' minds, but his work has influenced my teaching and thinking about creativity. The idea that multiple intelligences may be spread across species is an idea too interesting and revealing to pass up. Gardner refashioned the meaning of intelligence as "a biopsychological potential to process information that can be activated in a cultural setting to solve problems or create products that are of value in a culture."[65] If animals in their own cultures can solve problems or create products of value to them, it seems accurate to consider these acts as creative. It is obvious that we have lost a great deal by assuming for so long that animals are not intelligent. What will we have lost if we continue to assume that *homo sapiens* is the only creative species on this planet?

Thought and Language

Wasserman's description of our attitude toward animals as "a dangerous arrogance" applies to no human ability so much as language. In an article written with Leyre Castro, he offers this perspective on animals, intelligence, and language: "Although animals may not use words, their behavior may serve as a suitable substitute: its study may allow us to jettison the stale convention that thought without language is impossible."[66] Philosophers, linguists, and scientists have often submitted animals' lack of language as proof that we are superior to animals. Generally, they say, *if there is no language, there is no mind.* To see the obvious problems with that kind of generalization, one only has to think of attitudes towards indigenous languages that allowed colonizers to call the native tongues of the speakers "uncivilized." The predominantly verbal languages of humans are but one kind of communication. And deeming nonhuman languages as mindless closes the door to any understanding of the minds behind animals' multifarious methods of communicating, many of which we know very little about.

* * *

The garage attached to Emily Carr University where I taught for many years was home to a large group of pigeons. I enjoyed walking from my car to the garage exit every morning and recognizing individual birds by their various markings. The more you observe pigeons (and other animals), the easier it is to discern them as individuals. This was their home, and I was thankful to get to know them in a place out of the cold and rainy Vancouver weather.

Noticing differences in their color and feather patterns, watching their iridescence shift with the light, I was dazzled daily by how beautiful they were. I could not help but respond to their soft, cooing sounds, and attempted to emulate these in the hope that I might be able to link certain sounds with a particular behavior. One evening, a colleague of mine came upon me communing with the pigeons in the garage. She seemed genuinely startled and asked, "Are you talking to the pigeons?" I laughed out loud at the expression on her face, but I also was reminded that not everyone felt the same way about the pigeons making their home in the garage. About three weeks later, I was returning to my car after a day of teaching and meetings and found several workmen placing bird spikes along all the pipes and beams running along the ceilings of each floor of the garage.

Of course, I knew what they were doing, but I asked anyway. "Is there any way to let them have some of the garage?" I asked. The man I directed my question to turned from his work, gave me a sympathetic smile, and said, "It is the pigeon shit everywhere, that's what they want to get rid of." I continued asking questions, thinking I might be able to give the pigeons some reprieve at least, but as sympathetic as he was, at some point, he just ignored my presence and kept working. During this process, the pigeons had started lining up just ahead of where the workmen were attaching the spikes. They stood, five or six in a solid line, only inching further down the beam in unison as the worker implanted the next spike.

Activist that I am, I saw this behavior as courageously attempting to stop the addition of each spike. But perhaps they were just staying as close to each other and their former home as the spikes would allow. Having watched them behave contentedly for so long, however, I saw clearly how stressed and scared they were. Their movements and voices shifted up a register, as they acted and sounded like any group of refugees being torn from their home. I stood with them for a long time, attempting to convince the workmen that this was a bad idea, especially since the rainy season had already started. Where would they go? What if there were nests? After a while, knowing that asking for help from my university would be a lost cause, I sat by my car and sadly wondered what the pigeons were saying to each other. This was one of many times when it was clear to me that animals were communicating with each other and what they were saying was of utmost importance to *them*.

When I returned to the garage a day later, all the spikes had been installed, and the pigeons were nowhere in sight. Now, it was just another concrete structure, cold and dark and silent, empty of the iridescent and softly murmuring birds who had greeted me each morning.

2

Communication Unlimited

Do Not Ask What That Prairie Dog Is Saying about You

For us, the idea that other animals have language is a bridge
back to the natural world. We can begin to cross the vast
chasm that we have set up between "Us" and "Them," and
start to see that we are not very different after all.
—Con Slobodchikoff, *Chasing Doctor Dolittle*

When Lewis and Clark first set eyes upon a prairie dog colony about 25
miles north of the Nebraska River, they estimated that it "covered about
4 acres of ground on a gradual descent of a hill."[1] Lewis had been tasked
by the US president in 1804, Thomas Jefferson, to explore and survey
the land west of the Mississippi River purchased from France, called
the Louisiana Purchase. France owned very little of the 827,000 square
miles the United States purchased since it was not actually a tract of
land they had bought. Almost all that land was still owned, occupied,
and ruled by Native Americans, so what the United States had actually
bought was the imperial rights to the land.[2] Prairie dogs outnumbered
everyone.

Just below the mouth of the Marias River in what is now Montana,
Lewis passed along the edges of the largest prairie dog community they
had seen thus far. In his diary, he described it as stretching 20 miles out-
ward while lining the river for seven miles. Even 100 years later, in 1906,
an employee of the US Biological Survey, Vernon Bailey, reported a prairie dog village in Texas that was an astonishing 25,000 square miles, containing as many as 400 million prairie dogs.[3] In contrast, today's prairie
dog populations have declined by over 95% during the last century.[4]

These are facts that Con Slobodchikoff is painstakingly aware of since he knows prairie dogs probably better than anyone else on earth. Over the last thirty years of studying them in the wild, the animal behaviorist and evolutionary biologist, now professor emeritus at Northern Arizona University, has learned a great deal about the lives of these small but important ecological engineers and how they communicate. Spread over the plains and grasslands of twelve American states and a small area in Mexico, the five species of prairie dogs have what Slobodchikoff considers a language. Given the prairie dog's history, it is not surprising that the key for Slobodchikoff and his students to deciphering this language has been the prairie dogs' alarm calls. Sounding very much like chirps, these calls are often mistaken by first-time visitors to a prairie dog town as coming from birds. They function just as their name implies, as calls to others, sounding the alarm that some kind of danger is approaching or is even within the immediate vicinity.

As Slobodchikoff explains in his book *Chasing Dr. Dolittle: Learning the Language of Animals*,[5] traditional animal behaviorists believed that alarm calls from any animal were just expressions of fear or some other internal emotional state rather than a meaningful communication alerting others to danger. Slobodchikoff's research, however, proves that the variations in prairie dog alarm calls, even if they sound similar to the uninitiated, contain a great deal of meaningful information, something linguists prefer to describe as semantic information. Prairie dogs are not just yelling out a cry of fear similar to the loud gasp or expletive I might make when the car ahead of me slams on its brakes. Each alarm call contains important information about which predator is near and warns other prairie dogs whether it is a coyote, dog, hawk, snake, or human. A call also might label the size, shape, and color of the intruder and how rapidly it is approaching.

The prairie dog, a furrier, taller, and chubbier version of a squirrel with a shorter tail inked white or black at the tip depending on which of the five species it belongs to, is a social animal. Living in large, highly populated, and complex towns with hundreds or thousands of deep and multiroomed burrows for smaller social groups made up of relatives or friends, prairie dogs meet their relatives and friends with a "greet kiss"—a phrase that describes exactly what it is. At the entrance to each family's home is a raised mound of dirt and stones atop which the sentry of the family, often the mother, can have a 360-degree view of the surroundings. From here, her wide-set, luxuriously large, black eyes perceive any threat that might approach. When an alert prairie dog sounds the alarm, others understand the meaning and begin calling too. The original caller might send out a single-note call specific to what kind of predator is in the area and whether it is approaching rapidly. That way her neighbors understand whether the predator is approaching from the sky, as in a hawk, or from the ground, as in a coyote. Slobodchikoff and his team of research students have been able, over the years, to discern that prairie dogs have what they think is a grammar.[6] Their alarm calls are made up of varying parts: some noun-like, indicating which type of predator is approaching; some adjective-like, indicating the color, shape, and size of the predator; and some verb-like or adverb-like, indicating the speed at which the predator is approaching. In prairie dog language, a single alarm call might convey something like, "Heads up! A large gray coyote is approaching rapidly."

Slobodchikoff explains that anyone can tell the difference between the calls for each predator if they are introduced to the differences and do not only rely on their own assumptions. During one of their research stints, he and his team began glancing around expectantly for the coyote that the prairie dogs were already describing. As usual, the prairie dogs had identified the coyote at a distance before anyone in the team had noticed it. But, as the coyote came closer, the humans were sure it was a German Shepherd dog, not a coyote, and became excited about the possibility that the prairie dogs had made a mistake. This had not happened before, and scientists get very excited about mistakes since discrepancies in data might reveal some new bit of information. As the German Shepherd came closer, however, he morphed into what the prairie dogs knew him to be, a coyote. The prairie dogs had made no mistake about that.[7]

Slobodchikoff, through analyzing endless sound recordings of prairie dog alarm calls with the help of his team, explains,

> We think that each prairie dog has a unique vocal quality just like humans have different voices and different voiceprints, but though each prairie dog might differ, all the prairie dogs have a common call for a coyote even within those individual voiceprint differences. So we think when an individual is calling for a coyote, they [the prairie dogs] know who that individual prairie dog is that is calling in just the same way we can hear a person on the telephone and immediately recognize it as a person that we know.[8]

That each prairie dog has a unique timbre and tone to their voice is in itself illuminating. Contrary to beliefs about the infinite sameness of this species, this fact conveys something we have been slow to associate with animals in general, and wild animals specifically—their individual identities. The unique quality of a particular voice offers us a window into the peculiar perspectives and personalities of the being who owns that voice. The sound of your child's voice is one that you would not mistake, even after years of separation. Once, when I had my wildly curly hair straightened, much to my surprise, my son did not recognize me. Until I spoke.

What is so intriguing about Slobodchikoff's research is that in documenting the prairie dog's unique language, he also has recorded the prairie dog's ability to discern the behavior of other species. This ability is ample evidence for the recognition that animals, in this case prairie dogs, grasp the feasibility of other minds. A long-standing philosophical difficulty, the question of other minds, is the fundamental issue of what entitles us to our basic belief that other beings have inner lives. Even if they cannot be found at their desks, smoking their pipes, and arguing with other prairie dog philosophers about whether they can ever know the thoughts and feelings of others, these wild conversationalists express daily their particular method of answering that question.

For prairie dogs, those other minds include those of humans, almost always in the category of a predator. Slobodchikoff's team found that the response to humans was unlike any of the responses to other predators; a human, even at the edge of the colony, demanded that all the prairie dogs in the colony run as fast as possible and jump inside their burrows. Hawks, a frequent prairie dog predator, receive this kind of instant response only from the prairie dogs directly in their flight paths. Others "stand up and gawk at the hawk—like spectators at an accident site," Slobodchikoff comments.[9] Prairie dogs describe humans by their general shape, fat or thin, tall or short, and by the color of their clothes. If a human appears with a gun, this too is described via a unique sequence of chirps and remembered by the group. Once a particular human appears with a gun, even if he does not use it on the prairie dogs, that label is his for all time to come.[10] Having long been on the receiving end of humans using guns, prairie dogs appear to never trust a human with a gun. This is a telling example of how an animal perceives other minds, specifically human ones.

One surprising example for the research team, and yet in hindsight a revealing example of creative communication among animals, was the ability of prairie dogs to describe a new object in their midst with a new alarm call. Using flat plywood cutouts of a coyote, a skunk, and a coyote-sized oval painted a flat black, the researchers treated the prairie dogs to what must have resembled a puppet show. Pulling each cutout from behind camouflage material by a set of pulleys, the team recorded the reactions of the prairie dogs. The coyote cutout elicited a call that was similar to the usual coyote call but was surprisingly different. This was not unexpected, Slobodchikoff comments, since coyotes are not two-dimensional and are not jet black. The oval was something strange to the prairie dogs, and as Slobodchikoff reminds us, "There aren't any oval silhouettes creeping through the prairie dog colonies waiting to pounce on a prairie dog."[11] The prairie dogs, however, used their store of descriptive terms to create a new term for this unique object, much as we use familiar, everyday words to evoke an imaginative verbal response. Describing something new or previously unseen by combining two or more known words or images laden with meaning is a common creative activity.

When I interviewed Slobodchikoff, I asked him if he considered the generation of new terms to describe something not seen before as a creative behavior. He enthusiastically agreed and referenced the prairie dog's term for the black cutout to explain why:

> It was definitely something we hadn't heard before, the way that they put it all together. The different elements were similar to what we had heard before, going back to my analogy of humans using words to describe something they hadn't seen before. The words we've heard before, but the description has not occurred before.[12]

Coyote Language

Similar examples exist in other animals, coyotes, for instance. I interviewed wildlife ecologist Robert Crabtree, chief scientist at the Yellowstone Ecological Research Center in Bozeman, Montana, and a research associate professor in the Department of Ecosystem and Conservation Sciences at the University of Montana. He told me,

> The more that we look we can see the tip of the iceberg of what is going on with coyote communications. I think it is much more in-depth and personal in contact with slight differences in timbre and cadence. There is so much more we don't even know yet. And that is just vocalization. What about their nose? That probably works a lot better and maybe could relay more information. So it is probably extensive.[13]

As an example, Crabtree shared an experience he had when wolves were introduced into Yellowstone National Park after he had been studying coyotes there for six years. The researchers were not allowed out in the park for a month when the wolves were first released from their cages. There were worries about people's presence disturbing the wolves, causing them to run out of the park, leading to the possibility of them being shot. He continued,

The day that we were allowed back into Lamar Valley and on the Northern Range—we had gotten the call the night before—we got up early to go out the next day. We were sitting at the Tamar Valley Ranger Station. It is called Buffalo Ranch. Several of us heard this weird vocalization, and I thought, that is a coyote howl but it is a really high pitch. We kept hearing it off and on for about an hour. And I thought that is really weird. We thought we would go over and check it out. And we actually saw at a distance the magpies and eagles flying around and we thought maybe it's a kill and then, oh gosh, maybe it's a wolf kill. Sure enough, it was the first wolf kill documented in Yellowstone. So when we got there, there was this coyote doing this bizarre high-pitched yip howl we had never heard before. And from that day forward we have heard it commonly now when a wolf approaches their territory, especially in the spring when there are pups in the den. So it is a coyote alarm call specific to wolves.[14]

Slobodchikoff agreed with me that these two examples, his and Crabtree's, of animals creating new terms for something hitherto unknown were similar examples of a creative use of language:

Absolutely. There is no reason to suppose that animals can't do this, except that animal behaviorists have supposed that animals can't do this. If you postulate that animals have language and you see the parallels between our language and their language: we can do this, why can't they do this? So to me that makes perfect sense.[15]

Slobodchikoff submits that there is a difference between what we call communication and what we call language. He sees language as a subset of communication. After studying animal communication for over forty years, Slobodchikoff believes that language is part of a biological system that evolved in humans and animals, based upon the need to function individually, but also as part of a community in a particular context. Animals, like humans, rely on memory to help them do this. Remembering who is an enemy, who is a friend, where one fits among others in the social group hierarchy, where the best food is located, where predators often lurk, and other important bits of intelligence that make life run more smoothly are the basics of what languages have developed for.

Languages also have the power to engage the imagination, but how can we understand whether an animal is communicating creatively if we dismiss even the notion that they possess a language unique to them and their world? Unlike some other animal researchers, Slobodchikoff thought it was imperative to understand their communication in context, not in the lab but in the wild. His method is to understand the language of a particular animal species rather than attempting to teach animals (usually primates) human language. The history of attempts to teach animals human language is long. Starting in the 1920s with the Kellogs' efforts at raising a female chimp named Gua along with their ten-month-old son Donald,[16] these efforts have involved other chimps, gorillas, bonobos, dolphins, and dogs, among other animals. Slobodchikoff does not want to detract from the extensive work done in these studies and thinks they have been useful—though, I might add, at a price to the animals involved. Slobodchikoff points out that it has been difficult for these studies to fend off skeptics who have continued to point out problems with these methods that, in their minds, prove that animals cannot learn human language. He feels, given his success with what he has learned about prairie dog language, that studying animals within their wild environments and communicating with their languages is a better approach, given the continuing bias in the scientific community that only humans can grasp the intricacies of a verbal language. Slobodchikoff argues that this predisposition in the science community towards not even considering the possibility of animal languages has even curtailed some animal communication researchers from calling what they are studying a language. As he summarizes the problem, "If something doesn't exist, why study it?"

The Discourse System

Slobodchikoff insists that the opposite perspective is true. He has given a name to his proposal that we think of language not as a product constructed only by humans but as a biological system shared with other species: he calls this the discourse system theory. This system is made up of physical parts that have a specialized, vital function—to receive, process, and produce signals that contain information about our internal and external conditions—signals that may affect the behavior of others in ways that increase our fitness. When he uses the word "our," he means it in the broadest way possible, including vertebrates, and perhaps invertebrates as well. There is support for Slobodchikoff's thinking in the finding of what is called the FOXP2 gene in both humans and animals.

Known as the "language gene," FOXP2 was originally discovered in 2001 through molecular investigations of an unusual family who suffered from a mutation in that gene causing severe speech and language insufficiencies. Half of the family members across three generations were affected. Since then, researchers have found the FOXP2 gene in song birds, chimpanzees, elephants, bats, and mice, among many others, and with varying versions in each species. The ensuing research has shown, like most research in genetics, that pinning a trait on one gene does no service to the complexity of genetics.

There is some consensus that FOXP2 plays a broader and more essential role in the brain, not only in humans but also in animals. FOXP2, a protein, is expressed in at least three major brain circuits that have to do with sensory processing and sensorimotor integration. So while one of those circuits is essential for learned vocal communication, the protein's expression is not limited to that circuit but influences the development of the head and face, motor skills, the growth of cartilage and connective tissues, and the development of the nervous system, all of which are important for speech and language. Variations in this scenario in humans have been found in other species and support Slobodchikoff's contention that human language was not something that emerged suddenly in the human species. Language is fundamentally based on our biological and genetic similarities and shared evolutionary histories with other animals.

I asked Slobodchikoff if he thought the ability to be creative might have evolved similarly to the discourse system. He said,

> I have no doubt about that. We have been very limited about body systems of us and animals in general. Look at all the things in terms of physiology that people are finding out, for example, that we have neurons in our stomach that are kind of like an additional brain. We have something in our heart that is kind of like an additional brain. We have three of these things, we have the brain, the heart, and the stomach, and they all have to work in concert with each other; otherwise, we get sick. Look at what people are finding out just in the last few years, so I think that there is certainly plenty in terms of psychological systems, in terms of anatomical systems, and in terms of behavioral systems that we have to find out about ourselves and animals in general.[17]

This comment speaks to Slobodchikoff's contention that most people rely on assumptions to explain something that is not well understood, shutting out the possibility that another view is possible, or that a new understanding might replace an assumption.[18]

While Slobodchikoff's conclusions concerning prairie dogs having a complex language have been both critiqued and supported by other scientists,[19] one only has to remember the criticisms Karl von Frisch endured regarding his theory that bees communicate the direction and distance of food sources through a symbolic dance language. In my experience, the discovery of bees' waggle dances as a language is one of the most popular pieces of animal intelligence knowledge in North America. While I was writing this book, most people were aware of this research and accepted it as fact. Why that would be is worth another book-length study, but von Frisch's winning of the Nobel Prize in 1973 for this work helped to silence his critics and to encourage similar ethological research to develop. Tania Munz, science historian and author of *The Dancing Bees: Karl von Frisch and the Discovery of the Honeybee Language*, summarizes the enormous influence this had on the turn away from behaviorism to a more open understanding of the complexity of animal life:

> The dispute over the bee dances was never just about whether the bees locate foods by means of a dance language or simply by reacting to odor cues. At stake were competing visions of animals, their behaviors and how science could best come to know them. . . . Indeed, von Frisch's case was picked up by a range of scientists reacting to the overly restrictive behaviorism that had dominated much of the century's American studies of behavior. As it turned out, the bees could dance to a variety of tunes.[20]

Slobodchikoff's work has all the hallmarks of a similar discovery, one that points to rethinking our assumptions about language as only possible in humans. Is it possible for us to rid ourselves of a narcissism so innate we find it hard to even imagine alternative ways of being? For Slobodchikoff, the alarm calls of prairie dogs have been what he calls the Rosetta Stone for understanding their language. For those of us who are a bit rusty on linguistic history, the Rosetta Stone is a three-and-a-half-foot-tall polygonal piece of granite inscribed with Egyptian hieroglyphs, the visual language of early Egypt. First discovered by Napoleon's soldiers in 1799 near the town of El-Rashid, Rosetta, it was unable to be wholly deciphered until French scholar Jean-François Champollion was able to translate the hieroglyphs through the two other forms of inscriptions, including Greek. His careful matching of the Greek language to the little he knew of Egyptian hieroglyphs on tombs began the extensive work of understanding the otherwise lost language of ancient Egyptian hieroglyphics and consequently the culture of a major ancient human civilization.[21]

Like all useful metaphors, Slobodchikoff comparing his work on prairie dog alarm calls to the Rosetta Stone reveals layers of meaning and is a sly but unqualified directive by Slobodchikoff to treat animal language as carefully as we have done with at least some extant human languages. Imagine that the Rosetta Stone had been destroyed and thus never translated. Losing the opportunity of translating one of the oldest written languages in the world with its use of hieroglyphics may have obliterated forever the history of an ancient and influential civilization. Slobodchikoff's work similarly builds a model for engaging with languages and the animals who speak them. Allowing those animals and their languages to disappear would be as lamentable as disregarding the richness of the Rosetta Stone. Unlike with the Rosetta Stone, however, the languages that we would lose if we ignore research like his are those of animals of the here and now, animals that we value, such as the elephant, and the ones often seen as pests, such as prairie dogs.

Communication Unlimited

Humans are gifted with a fairly limited number of channels of communication compared to other animals. While we have used discoveries of natural forces, such as electromagnetism, to enhance our vocal, aural, and gestural modes of communication, animals are plugged into what seems like unlimited forms of conversation. Across species, animals make use of chemical, visual, acoustic, vibrational, sonic, bioluminescent, electric, and tactile systems of communication in unlimited combinations. Desert iguanas, for example, use scent marks to reflect ultraviolet light that other iguanas can see and that tells them who has been in their territory. Some male red-sided garter snakes have developed the ability to produce a female pheromone that allows them to mislead other males while jockeying for a position to mate with the same female.[22]

A male cuttlefish applies a similar, though more visual, tactic by mimicking the coloring of a female on one side of his body to fool rivals into thinking he is just one of the girls. At the same time, he displays typically male coloring on the other side so that a nearby female recognizes him as a possible mate.[23] Any number of older films from *Some Like It Hot* to

Mrs. Doubtfire come to mind, but the inspired inventiveness of this ploy by cuttlefish is hard to match. Researchers have documented individual cuttlefish matching their immediate vicinity, often to camouflage themselves from predators. One cuttlefish may match the sand of the ocean floor while another may blend into the coral or rock ten feet away. They do this in seconds, and sometimes in total darkness.[24]

Cuttlefish manipulate their chromatophores, organs in the shape of elastic sacs, to display red, yellow, brown, and black. Contracting or relaxing bands of muscles spreading in a circle from each chromatophore (up to 200 chromatophores per .001 square inch), cuttlefish can layer those four colors and their corresponding dark-to-light values to make whatever colors they need, much like painting in a digital software program. Also, contracting bands of circular muscle allow them to sculpt little nodes, or spikes, changing their skin in fundamental ways.

Consider that cuttlefish do not do this innately, but by consciously choosing what colors, values, shapes, and textures they need to use to disappear into the environment or to best woo their chosen ones. Culum Brown, a biologist at Macquarie University in Australia who studies fish behavior and cognition, is the first researcher to establish how cuttlefish simultaneously communicate with both the chosen female and the other male by combining both female mimicry and a split visual display. Brown insists that this form of tactical deception is on a par with the abilities of primates and suggests that "cuttlefish cognition is sophisticated" since they only choose to behave in this way when they can be sure one other male is present.[25] After all, keeping the female mimicry stable while attempting to stay between two other cuttlefish, one female on one side and one male on the other, must be difficult, but add a second male and the orientation calculations for our amorous but sneaky cuttlefish would be staggering. As well, the possibilities of a rival male recognizing the deception might be grounds for a rumble. Never a good thing, especially if the other male is larger.

Vibration as a form of communication among animals is one of the newest areas of research in animal communication. Previous research focused on humanly focused communication forms such as the acoustic and visual and, until recently, the ability to "hear" the vibrations. In the past ten years, however, new instruments for locating and listening to vibratory communication, such as laser Doppler vibrometers, have been added to earlier recording technologies like geophones.[26] Vibration is, however, one of the oldest forms of animal communication. It is used by the tiny Panamanian red-eyed tree frog who vibrates tree branches to send messages to rival males and by elephants who can detect infrasonic (inaudible) vibrations through pressure-sensitive nerve endings in their very large feet. In motion, the Panamanian red-eyed tree frog, one of the most photographed animals on the planet, appears to be a hopping painting. Small enough to fit in a teacup, these frogs have bright green skin with blue and yellow markings, blue upper legs, blue and yellow striped flanks, orange feet with suction on the toes, and bright red eyes. These colors play varying roles in both camouflaging these frogs and protecting them from predators. With their legs tucked in, their eyes closed, and their feet attached to the bottom of a leaf, they melt into their green surroundings, allowing them time to sleep. Their intense red eyes often startle a predator and give them a second or two to jump out of harm's way.

These tiny creatures vocalize, using what are called "chacks" for advertising their presence and "chuckles" for indicating aggression. Their "release calls" tell another frog to let them go if they are male and have no eggs, are female and have already bred, or simply to indicate that they are another species of frog. These tiny frogs use vibrations asserting warning and aggression. Michael S. Caldwell, a doctoral student at the time of the study, and a team of researchers at the Smithsonian Tropical Research Institute in Panama[27] were interested in understanding more about the vibrations of plant-dwelling vertebrae, including the red-eyed frog. They wanted to find out if the vibrations instigated by what are called "tremulations" played a role in eliciting a response from the intruder frog sitting on a leaf or branch. But let's back up. The word "vibration" is somewhat self-explanatory, implying that something is vibrated or exhibits a repetitive oscillation. But the word "tremulation" makes it sound as though the frog is trembling, and his trembling shakes the branch or leaf the other frog is on. Trembling rarely indicates aggression.

Exactly the opposite. Here is another example of why it is important to study animals in their natural context if we are to understand them at all. The trembling frog is trembling in a frog rage of aggression. He is saying, "This is my branch, get off this branch, or I will hurt you." And as with most altercations between animals in the same species, the whole idea is to have one party back down so that no actual bloodshed is needed. In this case, if the intruder does not back down, however, the defender will rise to the occasion and leap upon him with what looks like a full-body wrestling hold called the Saturday Night Ride. The aggressor is atop the intruder and locking him in place with various limbs. These matches may last a few seconds or up to four hours, and they end when the loser absconds to another and presumably more distant branch. The vibrational communication preceding these bouts provided Caldwell and his team with important information about this vibrational communication: "The further study of vibrational communication among arboreal vertebrates presents important unexplored opportunities to improve our comprehension of the behavioral ecology of these species, and of animal communication as a whole."[28]

Though red-eyed frog tremulation was originally described by William F. Pyburn in 1970, it was not until Caldwell began using an infrared camera to record the frogs at night that the importance of this shaking behavior was recognized as essential to the frogs' communicating their intentions. Male frogs tremulate by raising their body off the plant they are clutching, then thrusting their hind ends in the air, contracting and straightening their legs, all the while shaking those hind ends for all they are worth. What is at stake is reproduction. The intruder frog hears the plant shaking at only one sound frequency, 12 Hz. Caldwell experimented with several ways to document that frogs only responded to that frequency and that it is only heard by another frog on the same plant (this frequency is not in the human range either). According to

Caldwell, this vibrational message targets a particular receiver, a kind of telephone call for the intruder frog, who gets the message and must leave immediately or try to duke it out with the aggressor.

At the other end of the size spectrum, elephants also use a form of vibration to communicate. When the legendary South African conservationist Lawrence Anthony died of a heart attack, his family reported that two herds of elephants walked 12 miles to his house.[29] Arriving two days after his death, they stayed near his home without eating for several days and appearing to grieve. Years before, Anthony had rescued the elephants in these herds from certain death and had lived with them for weeks so that they might trust him. How did they know he had died? Was their visit to his home for that reason? Researchers and others have observed elephants seeming to mourn over their dead, even visiting and handling the bones of their dead relatives. In light of these findings, the coordinated funeral procession by these elephants to the home of a valued friend seems anything but "mysterious," as several news agencies dubbed it. I would describe it as downright courteous and expected. According to anthropologist and author of *How Animals Grieve*, Barbara King, the behavior of grief is similar in many animals and humans: "My definition of grief requires that an animal's normal behavior routine is significantly altered, and that she shows visible emotional distress through body language, vocalizations, social withdrawal, and/or failure to eat or sleep."[30]

Anthony's wife, Francoise, and son, Dylan, asserted that the elephants whom Anthony had previously saved from certain death had not visited the compound where Anthony lived for a year and a half, even though he would often visit them in the bush. Their account of the two groups of elephants suddenly appearing on their doorstep from two different directions and then quietly staying for two days and nights, not eating, matches King's definition of what mourning looks like. They altered their normal routine by converging on the compound and continuing to stay for two days and nights, something they had not done before, and by not eating. Dylan estimated that each herd had traveled about 12 hours to reach the farmhouse. What kind of communication might have played a role in their knowledge of Anthony's death, and more to the point, in their reaction to it? When he was alive, Anthony was baffled by the ability of elephants to sense circumstances across distances. It is obvious to anyone who watches elephants what a communicative species they are. Large-brained, intelligent, and socially complex, elephants use almost every communication channel available in the natural world: auditory, visual, gestural, tactile, chemical, and vibrational.

They use low-frequency forms of sound mostly below the human hearing range, called infrasound, as one means of communicating with other elephants. Animals, such as toothed whales, rhinos, dolphins, crocodiles, and some birds, such as pigeons, also perceive infrasonic sounds as vibrations. Able to communicate over two miles with their deep infrasonic rumbles through the atmosphere, elephants gain the advantage of these rumbles generating seismic waves traveling up to three times that distance through the ground. They pick up these vibrations through pressure-sensitive nerve endings in their trunk and feet.

Katy Payne, after spending a week with elephants in the Portland Zoo in 1984, was the first to consider, and then, with others, to prove that elephants communicate through infrasound.[31] If this sounds like a serendipitous discovery, it was more than likely not. Payne had been doing whale research with her biologist husband for the previous two decades. The Paynes and their collaborators, while recording and analyzing whale songs, in 1970 produced a best-selling nature recording entitled *Songs of the Humpback Whale*.[32] The intense interest and concern generated by that recording were influential in galvanizing the public into action against the continued killing of whales for industrial use. Dr. Peter Marler, professor of neurobiology and behavior at the University of California at Davis, explains the contribution Payne made to the project through her painstaking analysis of the spectrographs—a means of visualizing the energy and pitch of a particular sound—of whale songs: "She really was the one who worked out the most extraordinary findings about whale songs: the fact that they rhyme and the predictable ways in which the whales change their songs each season."[33]

According to Payne, her musical background permitted her to write out a score of the songs after listening repeatedly until she could recognize individual voices in a whale quartet. The songs themselves are made up of notes, or units, of the song arranged in a very structured way. Cycling in periods of up to thirty minutes, whales may continue singing these songs for hours in which up to about eight themes emerge in a particular order in what Payne describes as "a round in which some of the singers leave out some of the lines."[34]

With Linda Guinee, Payne also found that the more thematic material was in the song, the more likely theme substructures were to have repeating refrains that made up rhymes.[35] This finding suggested, though it did not prove, that the whales were using rhyme the way people do: as a mnemonic device to help them remember complex material. Citing several sources that refer to the everyday use of rhyme and its use in the oral transmission of long narratives (epic poems, for instance), the researchers explain,

> We are not convinced that multi-theme sub-phrases actually serve a mnemonic function for whales. Nonetheless, we wish to call attention to the structural and contextual similarities between whales' multi-theme sub-phrases and human rhymes, which are widely accepted as a mnemonic device.[36]

Aside from Payne's training in the creative art of music, her openness to disparate ideas, and her willingness to follow hunches that might be dead-end paths were also key to her considering that what she was experiencing in the elephant house were low sounds made by the elephants that could be felt, but not heard. Using a tape recorder that picked up infrasound, Payne returned a second time to the Portland Zoo elephant house with biologist William Langberger and anthropologist Elizabeth Marshall Thomas.[37] Reviewing a printout of the recording, they saw the visual evidence of the elephant noises they had not heard but felt. Payne and her cohorts realized that elephants use low-frequency sounds, something that up to that time had not been considered for any land mammal. Payne and Langberger, along with Joyce Poole and Cynthia Moss, who were studying the behavior of elephant families in Amboseli National Park in Kenya, introduced a new way of understanding elephants.[38] That elephants were definitely communicating over long distances with infrasonic sounds led to new questions about what they were saying and why.

Then, in 1992, ecologist Caitlin O'Connell-Rodwell, while living with and studying elephants in the Caprivi Park in Africa, realized that elephant vocalizations called "rumbles" produced seismic waves that spread through the ground as well.[39] It took her many tests and years to prove that they spread over distances through not only the air but the ground itself, increasing the distances from which other elephants could detect these seismic communications. Although Payne and others' research had established that under optimum air conditions elephant infrasonic rumbles could travel six miles, O'Connell-Rodwell's research on ground-borne seismic waves proved that they travel double that number of miles. Elephants often freeze in place and seem to be sensing their environment, sometimes with one foot raised. Elephants' feet contain pads of acoustically sensitive fat with similar tissue in their heels and their trunks. O'Connell-Rodwell explains, "We think they're sensing these underground vibrations through their feet." She adds, "Seismic waves could travel from their toenails to the ear via bone conduction, or through somatosensory receptors in the foot similar to ones found in the trunk. We think it may be a combination of both."[40]

Elephants' large diaphragms, less bony larynx, and large nasal cavities, coupled with the greater integrity of ground surface compared to atmospheric fluctuations, drive the calls across a greater distance. These ground-borne sounds may help keep herd members in touch with one another across a dozen or more miles.

"They are talking through the ground. It's not just elephant-to-elephant noise. It's a richer system of communication than we'd thought. They can discriminate very subtle vibrations through their feet," O'Connell-Rodwell told a reporter at the *Boston Globe*. She and several other researchers documented elephants' ability to discriminate between the alarm calls of familiar and unfamiliar herds:

> Given that the local herds would have interacted with the herd that origi-
> nally made the familiar alarm calls, they would be in a much better posi-
> tion to evaluate the reliability of those calls. They would know from prior
> experience whether or not the signaling herd was likely to be correct in
> its assessment of the level of danger.[41]

And perhaps, growing knowledge of the multiple and extremely sensitive channels of elephant communication may help to explain how
and why the two Thula Thula elephant herds assembled at the Anthony
compound soon after his death. Michael Garstang, a meteorologist who
accomplished pioneering work on the role of the various effects of atmospheric conditions on the theoretical distances over which elephants can
communicate, offers one of the more complete and scientifically based
explanations of this well-observed experience:

> The social structure of elephants, combined with their capacity to inter-
> pret multiple signals, would suggest that they are both highly sensitive
> to emotional signals from other elephants and signals from other spe-
> cies, including humans. . . . News of Anthony's death would have reached
> Thula Thula within minutes of the event on Friday. Dismay, translated
> to grief, would have spread rapidly amongst the people on the farm. . . .
> Equally, we could argue that through these mechanisms both herds had
> in fact made what can only be seen as a sophisticated interpretation of
> the observed activity and did in fact go to the farmhouse to express grief
> and compassion.[42]

I have spent a few summers in the Eastern Townships of Quebec on
a friend's land. The contrast between urban and rural life there is so
stunning, at least where I make my home for those months, that I end
up having a hard time returning to my home in what is a slightly more

urban area. One night in July as I was getting ready for bed, an insistent hum drew me to the open windows of the small bunkhouse I inhabit while there. The night sounds grew more noticeable and continued to grow to a raucous level, demanding complete attention. For an hour, the trees behind the field were host to a cacophony of songs from birds, crickets, tree frogs, katydids, and owls. Soon, the underlying structure of the sound unified the whole into an earthly symphony. And just as suddenly as it had started, it stopped, leaving a profound silence. I woke up later that night when the rain started.

All around us the world is singing and talking, though we have no small amount of trouble hearing it. Tuned into our exclusively humanly constructed soundscapes, our ears are full of high-pitched sirens, thundering airplanes, pounding construction, screeching traffic, drones, and insistent human voices. The sounds of other beings have become inaudible. Listening only to the hum of telephone lines, wi-fi, appliances, and the constant demands of our phones and computers, we have little extra aural energy left even if we do occasionally try to listen to those other voices.

Bird Song

Bird song is a rich area of study, and the amount of research by ornithologists and others in just the past decade is formidable. Songbirds make up almost half of the world's 10,000 bird species, including warblers, thrushes, and sparrows, among others. Songbirds sing to defend their territories, to attract mates, and sometimes just for reasons we do not know, perhaps for practice, for showing off, or for joy. Researchers and birders distinguish between calls and songs, and each species and individuals in those species have their specific repertoires. While often the songs you hear will be from males, females also sing, especially in the tropics, where the female song is more common.

The bird voice box, called a syrinx, is located between the trachea and the bronchi, and both branches are controlled individually. This enables birds to sweep through many notes without stopping by switching between the two sides of the syrinx. It also allows some birds to sing two notes at once. Some birds learn songs, but some birds are known for their invention and improvisation. Like humpback whales, they also have dialects found in different geographic locations that they pass down through generations.

Over the last 35 years, however, certain people have made it their life's work not only to record and try to understand the communicative singing of other species but to entertain the idea that what they were listening to is singing, composed and structured in ways similar to our own songs, but created by the animals themselves. Since 1968, ornithologist Donald Kroodsma, now professor emeritus at the University of Massachusetts at Amherst, has been studying the vocal behavior of birds in North and South America, and he has appreciated the vocal ability of birds as both a scientist and a music lover. The individual themes of particular species are exceedingly diverse and are enhanced by the ability to improvise different tunes within these themes. But this range of ability is a continuum, with some species of birds confined to the songs encoded in their genes while others, such as the northern mockingbird, whom Kroodsma calls "the ultimate song-learner, the ultimate mimic," have a repertoire of 100 to 200 songs.[43] This is not the upper limit of birdsong repertoires. The Brown thrasher, improvising but seldom mimicking, as the mockingbird does, offers more than 2000 songs in his song cycles, which can last for hours.

This numerical richness is just one indication of the creativity involved in bird song. While Kroodsma agrees that bird song shares some similarities to human music, he also insists that those similarities are not the answer to how and why birds sing. His vast knowledge of bird song, obtained not just by long hours of recording one bird of each species but by years of recording and then analyzing many different individuals of many different species in multiple field locations, tells him that birds are composers of their music. Attempting to match the notes in bird song to the Western musical scale has allowed several other bird researchers and musicians to imply that bird song uses that same scale. An influential paper in science whose authors include Patricia Gray, Bernie Krause (the author of *The Great Animal Orchestra*), Roger Payne, and Luis Baptista describes the commonalities of whale and bird song with human music:

> An examination of bird song reveals every elementary rhythmic effect found in human music. There are interval inversions, simple harmonic relations, and retention of melody with change of key. Many birds regularly transpose motifs to different keys. Some birds pitch their songs to the same scale as Western music, one possible reason for human attraction to these sounds.[44]

Kroodsma disagrees and points out that this conclusion is not supported. As he says, "The thrush isn't really using the Western musical scale, but we can match its notes, like any note produced by any means, to notes used in Western music."[45]

We will come back to disagreements about comparing bird song to music, but Kroodsma's descriptions of bird songs are unique, combining his expert knowledge with the passion that comes from spending one's life committed to the comprehension of another species from their point of view. The Brown thrasher is known in North American bird circles for their enormous song repertoire, at least up to 2400 songs. Kroodsma explains that the thrasher both improvises and copies:

> I now believe he is highly skilled at acquiring new songs for his performance. Some songs are no doubt improvised at his leisure, as he sings all alone from the treetops, the general form of the song dictated only by the need to conform to thrasher twosome. But other songs are added to the performance on demand, as when he mimics the exact couplet that a neighboring bird has just sung.[46]

The "twosome," a precisely guided breath of air through a double voice box, produces the dual-frequency sounds as if the thrasher had four hands on a piano or was singing a duet.

Another observation about the thrasher that Kroodsma makes is one we will hear more of later in the book. It speaks to the role of females in the making of these magnificent songs. Noting that the Brown thrasher sings far less once he has a mate, Kroodsma suggests, "Something that the male thrasher is doing is 'right' in her ears, because these females, by choosing to mate with some males and not others, have very likely been the creative force behind why males sing the way they do."[47] Kroodsma also wonders, Is the bird enjoying himself when he sings?

Birds have dialects similar to those of humans, except that, as Kroodsma explains, young birds often leave their homes and move into a location with a new dialect and learn those songs. According to Kroodsma, each songbird has a basic theme, the one that identifies him or her as an individual and a member of a species. He offers two examples: the Hermit thrush's "sustained whistle followed by a flourish," with nine to ten variations of that theme;[48] and the Brown thrasher's theme—the couplet, as described above, and his over 2000 variations. Kroodsma comments, "I think of creativity, or the ability to improvise different tunes, and the range of this ability among birds." For him, "how the songs are arranged during a performance" is another instance of creativity.[49] The choruses of birds, the variety and contrasts between successive songs, their varied pacing, and the range of songs from simple to complex Kroodsma lists as the reasons that have kept him coming back to record their songs.

While working on this chapter I interviewed Kroodsma, and though I enjoyed our exchange a great deal, parts of the conversation surprised me. I have read three of his books, and was inspired by his liberal use of the word "creativity" in the longest and most detailed book, *The Singing Life of Birds*. Yet when I was talking to Kroodsma about creativity, he was very hesitant to use that word. Why? I wondered. He explained,

> We could go to the word "creativity" and I cringe a little when I use that word, just as I cringe when I use the word "performance." I don't cringe quite so much at "performance" because I know that there might be something that other birds are listening to that we might judge as per-

formance, how well males are singing for example, and performance is a loaded term. But I can see where it might apply biologically. But as soon as I get the language, "creativity," these are human things that I hesitate to impose on birds.[50]

I countered by agreeing with him, since there is a large literature on creativity in humans. I explained that the concept of creativity as it plays out within evolution, however, is not limited to those definitions. I am human, so I am using a particular word, "creativity," to speak to my species, but I am trying to get people to see that we lose a great deal if we limit the concept of creativity to only human definitions.

During a conversation about the newer research on bird song performance, I asked him about the influence of females on males' songs. He suggested that they might be listening for consistency, for example. Since young birds show a great deal of inconsistency in their song, the lack of it would tell a female the singer's age. He stipulated that it could very well be something the females are listening to, something that we might call performance. But to be sure of this, Kroodsma argued, was unknowable:

> We can't crawl inside the head of another, let alone another human being, and then we have another species. Let's go to catbirds. I have done some developmental work with them and they are closely related to thrashers. If you take catbirds in captivity and you train them for a large repertoire of songs, it turns out they don't come up with very many. It turns out the fewer songs you play to them, the more they improvise or create on their own. As birds improvise, are they creating?[51]

I assured him that I think they are. Again, he reiterated that he could not get past the word "create" and all its human-related meanings:

> I can tell you I am pretty confident that these gray catbirds are making songs up and I did raise a couple of thrashers once and they were making

songs up, they are improvising in order to generate. The result is to generate a large repertoire of songs. So, I can say they "improvise" and that is a
more neutral word than "creative."[52]

I told him that it is good that he is uncomfortable with that word. My
goal for this book is to argue that animals are creative, and so he was
adding to the list of all the other things that we have found that we
thought only humans did, such as improvise, but then found animals
do in their own way. That is, in my mind, a good thing for animals. He
answered, "We humans have always felt that there were certain things
only we do. Only we use tools and then we point to what certain animals
do and then we have to qualify what certain words mean so we can keep
our platform well above the animals."[53]

We talked for a while about the list of words I am using to describe
cross-species creative abilities, and some he could get on board with,
others not so much. He said that it was a wonderful list, and I felt a little
like one of my students before I critique their work after I have said
something positive about it. About intelligence, we agree:

> Each species is equally successful, we are all equally intelligent to survive,
> the drive for individuals to reproduce, lineages being traceable back to
> primordial soup. Not in the human way, but in the evolutionary sense.
> But, by definition, all species are equally intelligent given their own
> standards.[54]

About curiosity, he cautioned that since we cannot document it, he did
not know where to fit it into bird song. Inventiveness and flexibility
passed the test, but complexity would require him to know what birds'
standards are. He explained,

> I have about a forty-minute singing sequence from a Berwick's wren on
> two successive days. And he uses seven different songs, maybe sings thirty
> or forty examples of each of those songs over those two days. He gets to

choose which songs he is going to sing. . . . Is this a level of creativity, too, what he puts together and the sequence he puts together? There are all kinds of things birds do where they clearly have to make choices. And I don't think they are robots in what they do. They are reacting to what is around them. They are choosing the appropriate sound for a particular context. You know some people would call that language. There is a fair literature comparing bird song to human language. I just shy away from it all, because it seems to me like comparing bird song to human music so much of it just seems to be shoehorned into the human definitions. . . . And I just want to know what the birds do.[55]

My discussion with Kroodsma is important because although he felt he could not use the word "creative" when talking about birds, it was for reasons that had little to do with their lack of intellect, agency, or consciousness. Kroodsma's desire to stay with them in their world to understand who they are, what they sing, and why they sing is impressive, and unusual in this day of computer modeling, statistics, and reliance on laboratory experiments. It speaks to that ability to keep an open mind, to understand animals where they are and who they are, instead of attempting to fit them into our cultures and our needs.

In Slobodchikoff's and Kroodsma's approaches, there is an underlying respect for the animals they have spent the better part of their lives trying to understand. Each has particular views on the best ways to go about that, but both have spent their time out in the field listening daily to the details of a speaking and singing world. Both researchers have decided that rather than comparing what they find to the details of only one other species, humans, they have endeavored to allow the individuals, families, and groups of animals they spend time with to teach them what it is they need to know.

3

Play as a Creative Source

Finding Your Inner Kea

One does not dream with taught ideas.
—Gaston Bachelard, *The Poetics of Reverie*

In the forests south of the Congo, an adult female bonobo sits alone, languidly trailing first her foot and then one hand in the water. Surrounded by trees and branches, she gazes around her in an unfocused way with an inward look that might be a prelude to what might be called an "aha!" moment. After a few minutes of concentrated rhythmic water play, she reaches down into the water and dredges up large clumps of damp leaves. Shifting into a better position for pulling out more leaves, she surveys the wet and sticky masses, investigating each cluster for something she cannot find.[1]

This vignette is from a research video taken by a primatologist during her studies of play in wild habituated bonobos. This example is one of the thousands of bonobo play events collected by Isabel Behncke in the Democratic Republic of the Congo (DRC) in the three years she was collecting data for her doctoral dissertation through the Institute of Cognitive and Cultural Anthropology at Oxford University. Behncke is now an associate professor in the Social Complexity Research Center, Universidad del Desarrollo, Santiago de Chile, and a visiting researcher in the Social and Evolutionary Neuroscience Research Group at Oxford. This example links solitary water play, one of the many forms of play she witnessed in bonobos, with the generation of novelty, a key component of creative behavior. Behncke describes adult females' slower and more rhythmic water play as sometimes giving "a sense of aesthetic exploration of water's properties and blurs the transitions between exploration and play."[2]

Water is not a necessary element of bonobo life since the fruit and vegetable matter they eat keeps them appropriately hydrated. They avoid sitting or wading in the water, and they meet rain with subdued activity until it clears. Aside from collecting water lilies, a bonobo delicacy, the main interaction bonobos have with water is in play. A theme Behncke has identified in bonobo play is how exploration often leads to the generation of novelty. Water play is a prime example of the pleasurable emotion underlying this kind of play, and according to Behncke, pleasure is motivation for "individuals to interact with novel elements that would otherwise be extraneous to their lives. This can sometimes generate further novelty, with new variations on a game."[3]

Mihaly Csikszentmihalyi, in his book *Creativity: Flow and the Psychology of Discovery and Invention*, outlines what he considers the core characteristics of creativity. After considering many domains in which creative people work and individual idiosyncrasies they might possess, he proposes five periods in the creative process: preparation, incubation, insight, evaluation, and elaboration. These five general parts of the creative process seldom happen in linear order, and often one or more segments are neglected or appear recursively throughout the process's evolution.[4] Having watched and encouraged this process in many individuals and groups in varying areas of interest in my classes, I have found Csikszentmihalyi's open-ended description particularly helpful for considering the creativity of other animals.

The inward look on the female bonobo's face is one of pre-exploration or an "aha-I-could-do-that" moment that might fall somewhere in incubation before the insight period. Her investigation of the submerged leaves is exploratory behavior, one of the key elements in the evaluation period of the creative process. Searching for something interesting and worthwhile to engage with, in this case, among the leaves, is the goal. The reverie brought on by her solitary water play—a good example of incubation, described by Csikszentmihalyi as "a period . . . during which ideas churn around below the threshold of consciousness"[5]—may have allowed her to consider what might lie beneath the surface underneath her fingers.

Intelligence is an important condition for creativity, but the ability to play is essential in encouraging openness, flexibility, curiosity, and inventiveness, all characteristics found in creative behavior. The creative process as described by Csikszentmihalyi does not include play as one of its categories. However, the freedom of behavior and openness to experience found in play offers a uniquely rich context in which creativity flourishes. The founder of the field of human ethology, Irenäus Eibl-Eibesfeldt, who initially studied animals for twenty years, supports this view of the importance of play to the entire creative process.

When Eibl-Eibesfeldt was a new student of mammalian behavior studies at a field station near post–World War II Vienna in 1947, he adopted a badger. Living daily with the badger allowed the budding ethologist to note the profound differences between the badger's serious fight behavior and his play behavior. When playing, the badger was free of anxiety and invented new movement patterns. He taught himself to somersault, something he had not done before. The badger's quick changes in movement and behavior included playfully chasing the ethologist or running away from him, play hunting, or exploring light-heartedly. It was clear, however, to Eibl-Eibesfeldt that these fast shifts of behavior were never visible in a serious mood: "With the badger, and I have observed similar behaviors in animals and humans, the animals in play act free from the tension which besets them in the non-play situation and this behavior is at the root of what we consider to be the specific freedom of man."[6] About his subsequent work focusing on the cross-cultural documentation of human rather than animal behavior, he admits, "My observations about the play of the badger and true freedom remain firmly entrenched in my mind today."[7]

Freedom from stress is the last of five criteria that well-known animal play researcher and evolutionary biologist Gordon Burghardt has listed in his definition of play. His book, *The Genesis of Animal Play:*

Testing the Limits, lays out five criteria that when used together may distinguish play from other activities, one quagmire of previous animal play research, at least for scientists. They are (1) behavior is not fully functional; (2) play is spontaneous, voluntary, pleasurable, or engaged in for its own sake; (3) play differs from serious performance of normal behavior, either structurally or temporally; (4) behavior is repeated but not stereotyped; and (5) behavior occurs when the animal is in a relaxed state (e.g., well fed, safe, healthy).[8] One of Burghardt's goals is to extend the circle of species who are deemed playful. Burghardt willingly admits that he has collected the data from the activities of his fellow scientists in Europe, Russia, North America, and Australia and the massive body of evidence on play in hundreds of species accumulated since 1960. But, he specifies about his book, "The packaging is new, and that provides the added value."[9]

The added value Burghardt mentions is helping to define animal play as a rich field of study in its own right. Much like the study of creativity in animals, studies of animal play have suffered from lack of research across a wide array of species. Play has been viewed as an anthropomorphic conceit or a nonserious endeavor and as an enigmatic and ultimately impossible area of study. Burghardt's five criteria have helped to synthesize the varied and useful knowledge on animal play and have encouraged a mushrooming amount of play research across many groups of animals, including primates, rodents, carnivores, ungulates, elephants, cetaceans, fishes, birds, reptiles, spiders, and wasps.

How to Have Fun

Bonobos are one of our closest relatives. Once we look more closely at bonobos' social behavior, we can see clearly the differences between theirs and ours. The matriarchal society in which bonobos live relies on peaceful cooperation, altruism, and trust. Compared to our often-aggressive way of dealing with each other when conflict arises—and when doesn't conflict arise?—bonobos more quickly solve those kinds of problems with creative and playful activity, frequently sexual. This happens between females, between males, between males and females, and between the young. According to Brian Hare, a professor at Duke University, "There has never been a recorded case in captivity or in the wild of a bonobo killing another bonobo."[10]

Hare and his wife, Vanessa Woods, have spent time with bonobos in the DRC. Hare, Woods, and their colleagues have run noninvasive experiments with bonobos, endeavoring to fathom why the level of violence in bonobos is so low when compared to chimpanzees, who more closely mirror human aggressive behavior. They found a higher level of tolerance in bonobos towards other bonobos. This resulted in more flexible cooperation in solving problems with their families and friends. They even share resources with other bonobos they might not know when that may cost them part of their share of food. These characteristics of bonobo culture create a relatively peaceful society. Bonobos play constantly as infants, juveniles, and adults. They use play as social currency to soothe over any aggression, but they also play because they enjoy playing. As with many species, bonobo play includes solitary play with objects, movement play, and social play. Playing may lead to creative solutions to any number of problems, but it also offers the joy of experiencing the problem-solving process, whether it involves sex, tickling, food, or affection. Play is practice for being able to handle new and changing experiences, and it is visibly obvious that it is enjoyable in itself. We can recognize that "universal" indicator of fun, laughter, in bonobos.

While researching bonobo play, I came across a study that has opened the doors for researchers to describe laughter in the great apes as just that, rather than a "play-face" or the "pant-pant" descriptions that were used previously. The human laugh was thought to be unique in that the laughing sound came out with the exhalation. Say "ha ha" and you will hear the out-breath of air. But this study, in which the researchers recorded bonobos, gorillas, chimpanzees, and orangutans while they were being tickled, found all also exhaling on the laugh sound, or "voicing," as they describe it in the study. Their findings suggest that rather than laughter being a unique characteristic of human fun, we inherited our laughter from the last common ancestor from which humans and great apes evolved.[11]

Not only do great apes laugh, but mice and rats giggle, birds tease, octopuses like to play hide and seek, crocodiles give each other rides on their backs, and according to ethologist and author Jonathan Balcombe, fishes are among the most playful beings on the planet. In Balcombe's book, *What a Fish Knows*, he describes the impressive leaping of mobula rays whose wingspans are seventeen feet and bodies weigh a ton. Nicknamed "flying mobulas," they hurtle themselves ten feet out of the water, with an enormous and explosive splash landing. In schools of hundreds, they most often land on their bellies, but sometimes land on their backs. Since this behavior is most often initiated by males, courtship may play a role, but other scientists suggest that leaping is a way to remove parasites. As in the leaping of dolphins and whales, however, Balcombe recognizes the obvious playfulness and sense of fun. He says, "Whatever the function, I posit that the rays are enjoying themselves."[12]

No less than the late Patrick Bateson, zoologist and former biological secretary and vice president of the Royal Society, argues that play and playfulness lead to "radically new approaches to challenges set by the physical and social environment"[13] in both animals and human animals. In his book *Play, Playfulness, Creativity, and Innovation*, Bateson and his coauthor, Paul Martin, differentiate between play and playfulness, describing the former as observable behavior and the latter as an "underlying mood state." While they see the two as overlapping sometimes, they point to play behavior that verges into competition or aggression as lacking the light mood of playfulness—consider football. Playful individuals may not be playing—think political comedy.

They also separate creativity and innovation, something discussed in the introduction. Bateson considers the generation of a novel behavior or idea by any species to be creative regardless of its practical value or application. Innovation exploits that creative idea or behavior to achieve a useful benefit. Sometimes the creator and the innovator are one individual, and at other times, the creator and the innovator are distinct.

Bateson and Martin suggest that while some novel problem-solving abilities in animals emerge both from trial and error and social learning, those abilities might arise from experience in other contexts, such as play. They propose that "individuals discover properties of their environment that prove crucial when they are later faced with a new challenge."[14] Considering studies of the novel behaviors of rooks, chimps, and humpback whales, Bateson and Martin point to the known playfulness of all three species as a plausible driver of their early exploration of how the world works and its role in adult creative problem solving.

Christopher Bird and his colleague Nathan Emery of Queen Mary University of London found that rooks, given some stones and a flask full of water containing a mealworm, could figure out how to get the worm out of the flask in one try. They calculated how high the water in a flask had to rise and how large and how many stones would accomplish the task more quickly. They did this without stopping to reach the worm after dropping each stone into the flask.[15]

According to Bateson, young rooks, jays, and magpies are particularly playful and spend a great deal of time manipulating objects, including stones, just as young chimps animatedly play with sticks. In an experiment, a chimp who had prior playing experience threading a smaller stick through a larger hollow one could solve the problem of accessing out-of-reach food with threaded bamboo sticks. Bateson notes that chimps who had not had experience playing with sticks failed to solve the problem. Playing with sticks opened up possibilities for the chimps who had played with them before.

Bateson suggests that the use of bubbles by humpback whales to catch fish as a common feeding technique may have initially resulted from playfully blowing bubbles and learning that fish do not swim through a bubble screen. Who was the first humpback to start the trend of what are now elaborate cooperative foraging behaviors of humpbacks blowing bubble nets? Humpbacks use the bubble-blown nets to corral prey into a small area so they can more efficiently scoop them up in their large baleen-filtered mouths. Research by Fred Sharpe on bubble-net feeding variations by small groups of humpbacks in southeast Alaska documented an even more intricate way to use this technique. This involves several humpbacks. One spirals upwards in trapping the fish, usually herring, above in a tower of bubbles while several other whales call loudly from the bottom of the cylinder, forcing the trapped fish upwards. The whales on the bottom then move upward, opening their mouths to catch as many fishes as possible in their jaws.[16] Bateson and Martin suggest that given the uniqueness of this feeding technique to the humpbacks of the waters of southeastern Alaska, "at one point, it was a creative discovery."[17]

Since bubble netting only occurs when humpbacks are about two years old, whale researchers think that the whales do not learn this behavior from their mothers, but within different contexts, such as play and feeding. Bubble netting and its novel variations are passed on through "social learning"—learning from members of the social group in which the whale, or any animal, travels. So for this group of humpbacks, what was once a novel idea generated through play and then used for a unique way to eat more herring is learned through hanging out with other whales.

Who was the first humpback to bubble net? We will never know, but research done over a 33-year span on a variation on bubble netting suggests that playful behavior was a precursor of this innovative feeding method. Hal Whitehead and Luke Rendell, experts on the social behavior and culture of whales, propose that whales' learning over a generation a variation on bubble netting called "lobtail" feeding makes a strong argument for this kind of feeding being culturally based. Watching a humpback raise their massive tail high out of the water and then smack it down on the water's surface, one immediately assumes that the whale is playing, much like the big kid in the pool who makes the loudest and most far-reaching splashes when they cannonball. While that may be the case, certain cultures of humpbacks have added lobtailing to their bubble nets to catch a fish called a sand lance. The disturbance caused by whales' lobtails increases the sand lance's confusion and makes it easier for the whale to scoop many of them up as he lunges up into the bubble cloud he has created for just this purpose. Whitehead and Rendell surmise,

> At some point, one bright, or lucky, humpback figured out that hitting the water with his or her tail did something to the sand lance (perhaps causing them to bunch together more, making the shoal easier to enclose with a bubble net), and since then this trick has been spread and maintained in the population by cultural transmission.[18]

Johan Huizinga, often mentioned as a founder of modern human cultural history, wrote in 1938, "Animals have not waited for man to teach them their playing."[19] Huizinga focused on play as a human cultural phenomenon, not just one of many cultural activities, such as sport, music, art, or performance, but a fundamental aspect of culture itself. He saw play as a necessary support for cultural activities and as an innately universal activity. Whitehead and Rendell's research on the cultural lives of whales and dolphins suggests that play is an integral part of the transmission of cultural behavior for those animals besides providing the impetus for the initial creative behaviors.

A Bit of Playful History

Darwin recognized the similarities between humans and nonhumans across a broad range of emotions, happiness among them. Offering play in puppies, kittens, and lambs as examples of animals' pleasure of playing together just like human children, he adds, "Even insects play together as has been described by that excellent observer, P. Huber, who saw ants chasing and pretending to bite each other, like so many puppies."[20] Artists, authors, and various thinkers recognized animal play, long before the mid-1800s.

Montaigne, at the beginning of his most widely read and admired essay, "Apology for Raymond Sebold," in describing the human "presumption" of superiority when compared to animals, describes playing with his cat in this way: "When I play with my cat, who knows whether I do not make her more sport than she makes me? We mutually divert one another with our play. If I have my hour to begin or to refuse, she also has hers."[21]

Montaigne, as he does often in his three books of essays, offers, for the mid-sixteenth century, a unique leap of imaginative empathy into the mind of an animal. Here, he levels the assumed inequality between his desire or refusal to play and his cat's intentions. Being invited to play by those animals who live intimately with us is always a lesson in humility. Are we so uninspired with life that we don't feel a strong sense of gratitude wash over us when a favorite toy is brought to our lap, or the sharp pang of a lost opportunity when we turn down such an invitation? Children and young animals never seem to want to stop playing. It is usually the adults who find a reason to halt the festivities in order to return to a reality that makes sense only to them.

In fact, until the 1980s much of existing play research involved animal (and human) youngsters, not adults. One of the most frequently recurring explanations for play in both humans and animals has been that of play as practice. Karl Groos, a psychologist and philosopher, took animal play seriously enough to devote an entire book to it. He constructed the theory that youth is the time when young animals perfect the instinctual behavior of adulthood. Combining ideas about instinct and imitation, he describes play not as one of youths' many activities but as the major reason there is a period of youth. "Animals can not be said to play because they are young and frolicsome, but rather they have a period of youth in order to play."[22]

Play as practice for adult behavior is still a popular explanation for play in young animals, but adult animals also play—one reason for more robust and wide-ranging investigations in play research. As with research in animal intelligence and communication, it has been a long road in defining criteria and methods for observing and verifying examples of play in animals, even though observing play is often a more direct experience than observing intelligence, communication, or emotion in animals. Two baby bobcats romping, rolling, and rubbing together as their mother watches is more than likely easier to label as play than, for instance, labeling the male toadfish's underwater droning in A-flat an emotional, intelligent, and communicative process all directed at securing a mate.

As early as 1974, ethologist Robert Fagen summed up the link between play and creativity in animals this way: "A novel behavior originating in play and propagated via observational learning could move a cohort of animals into a complex of new selective pressures, under which gene frequencies would begin to shift, affecting morphology, physiology, and behavior itself."[23] Fagen's work is seminal in play research. Fagen sees play as an important universal trait in both humans and other animals, but he also suggests that playfulness is a path to creative behavior, not only in individual animals but in evolutionary selection.[24] Fagen, who along with his wife, Joanna Fagen, studied play in brown bears on the Admiralty Islands, Alaska, for eight years, argues that "a cognitive-level description of what humans might do when they create serves equally well to describe what animals might do when they play."[25] We may see the iterative nature of the creative process in animals' recombinations, functional reuses, and new associations of species-specific behaviors in play. Combined with experience and environmental relationships, one result of play in animals is an openness to discovery, and according to Fagen, it may lead to creative behavior.

No animal demonstrates this quite like the kea, an endangered, omnivorous parrot that lives on the South Island of New Zealand. Known for their intelligence and playfulness, they also have gained a reputation for mischief or worse. At least that is what humans might say if they have had their car's rubber tires ripped apart or their passports stolen by a kea. In December 2016, a one-way tunnel CCTV camera on a popular tourist route caught a video of keas dragging highway cones onto the road, stopping traffic coming out of the tunnel. Initially, highway workers were mystified to find the cones constantly in the middle of the traffic lanes, but upon seeing the video footage from a camera located at the tunnel, they realized who the culprits were. The flow of traffic alternates between either end of the tunnel so that each direction of cars stops for a few minutes as the drivers wait for the change-over. Highway workers in this area of New Zealand are familiar with keas and concluded that the birds are mindful that stopped cars contain humans bearing food. Kevin Thompson, a road manager, added, "We think the keas listen for the cars in the tunnel and move the road cones between the streams of traffic."[26]

In their book *Kea, Bird of Paradox: The Evolution and Behavior of a New Zealand Parrot*, scientists Judy Diamond and Alan Bond conclude after years of studying the bird that behavioral flexibility is the primary function of play for the kea. It has afforded them the ability to modify their behavior or ecology to survive in their original difficult alpine environment and in the more recent devastation of much of that original ecosystem. Diamond and Bond describe playing for the kea as "less a set of ritualized behaviors than an attitude to the world at large."[27]

Recognizing Play and Playfulness in Many Species

Gordon Burghardt has been writing about animal behavior since 1972, publishing his first research article on play in reptiles in 1974. Burghardt alludes to the paucity of play research because of the early attitudes towards the topic as, ironically, a "nonserious" research area. Fagen clarifies this relationship between play and behavior such as mating, hunting, or foraging, in this way: "Previous definitions failed to recognize that play relates to serious behavior as creativity to innovation."[28] New and useful behaviors are not possible without an open-ended environment in which the imagination is unrestrained. When I was teaching in a large urban high school during the eighties, it took many weeks of encouragement to convince some of my students that making art was about far more than being able to draw or paint well. Reframing the goals of art making to include freedom and play seemed to make an enormous difference. Rather than a classroom where grades depended on the students accomplishing some specific thing, I fostered a studio atmosphere, where students were responsible for their own response to assignments. It worked. For many of my students, some of whom recently had come from war-torn countries such as El Salvador, Guatemala, and Cambodia, grasping that the paper or canvas was a safe place for them to do whatever they wanted without constraint was a life-changing experience. Over time, playing with the forms and techniques of art making led to a place of refuge, and many students stayed to take more advanced art and art history classes. On paper or canvas, students formed new ways of viewing personal emotion, knowledge, and experience. For many students, this process became a way to learn how to deal with the world, its difficulties and joys, in a personal way, something that many students had not experienced before. Play and creativity mesh in emotional, cognitive, and neurophysiological ways, depending on the environment in which individuals, both nonhuman animals and human animals, find themselves.

How do researchers recognize play in animals we think of as more unlike us—amphibians, reptiles, spiders, and insects, for instance? Play in animals is now considered a serious form of scientific investigation, as documented by a twentieth anniversary special issue of *Current Biology* entitled "Biology of Fun." The editor of this issue, Geoffrey North, tells us, "Playfulness, by encouraging new forms of behavior and ideas, is a great stimulus to creativity."[29] If we can recognize play in many animals, then might we be able to recognize their creative and innovative behavior as well?

Let's start with a kind of social spider, commonly known as a communal spider, who indulges in sexual foreplay long before females are ready to mate. Male communal spiders mature earlier than females, so they spend their time in the webs of juvenile females and guard them until they mature, too. During this interim period, males and females engage in "nonconceptive (play)" sexual behavior, or mock copulation.

While both males and females gain sexual performance experience in this way, the researchers also examined personality types of both male and female spiders to determine what this sexual foreplay might mean for individuals.[30]

Insect researchers also have been aware of continuing skepticism towards insect play. Dapporto, Turillazzi, and Palagi begin their article on play behavior in paper wasps with this bit of coaching: "The idea that insects play has often aroused skepticism. Nevertheless, the authors investigated the occurrence of a play-like behavior in young individuals of a paper wasp."[31] Up to six months before young adult female paper wasps found their own colonies, they practice dominance interactions with other females and, much like mammals, engage in play fighting. The researchers surmise that this play behavior allows the female wasps to assess their dominance potential before it is needed.

Gordon Burghardt undertook one of the first official studies of play behavior in a reptile, a Nile softshell turtle, in 1996. Pigface, as the turtle was called, was bored and stressed in captivity. Zookeepers at the National Zoo worried about Pigface's reaction to boredom, which was to continuously scratch himself to the point of pain and infection. Burghardt's group not only documented how Pigface played with his enrichment toys but also created an energy budget for Pigface's typical day. Playing tug-of-war with his keepers over a garden hose was his favorite game, but he also enjoyed "nosing a basketball around the enclosure, bouncing a hula-hoop through the water, and positioning the water hose so that it sprayed him in the face."[32] The group found that Pigface played twice as much as even young mammals do.

Zoologist Vladimir Dinets, having published several research articles and a book on crocodilian behavior, found that while knowledge of play in crocodiles was common among zookeepers and crocodile farm personnel—a rather chilling thought—nothing had appeared in the scientific literature. He found that the lack of knowledge resulted from their rare appearance in the wild and the fact that they are nocturnal predators. With play observation, however, "an additional problem appears to be that people witnessing such behavior consider their observations unworthy of publishing or unlikely to be taken seriously."[33]

Based on over 300 hours of personal observations and reports from other crocodilian biologists, Dinets documented 17 separate incidents of play, most matching all five of Burghardt's criteria listed earlier. So, what have we been missing about crocodiles? Well, for one thing, they have more fun than we have given them credit for. Crocodiles surf waves, slide down slopes into the water, and ride the current from an inflow pipe in a pool. Dinets, however, asserts that observations predominantly based on motor activities are rare due to crocodiles' status as ambush predators with low metabolism levels. Object play, the most frequently observed play behavior in crocodiles, is another thing entirely. Zoo caretakers now regularly provide various objects, such as balls, as habitat enrichment. According to Dinets, streams of water seem to be a favorite object of play. American alligators have been reported playing with drips from a faucet for 45 minutes, slowly swimming by only to veer off at the last minute. This progressed into biting at the drip as the alligator cruised by. Dinets observed another alligator "moving its head horizontally back and forth across a stream of water falling from a pipe and making snapping movements as if trying to bite the stream."[34] I have often seen this biting water play in dogs. Dinets reviews crocodiles playing with balls, some as if attacking the ball and others as if in courtship. One particular crocodile played with the same ball for 15 years without destroying it. Dinets explains that while adult crocodiles can often be seen pushing twigs, grass, or other floating material through the water while swimming, he observed two different crocodiles playing with pink objects. He reports,

> In both cases, the objects were pink *Bougainvillea* flowers that were floating in the pools where the animals were kept captive. Adult male Cuban crocodiles in Zoo Miami (Florida, USA) manipulated such flowers repeatedly over seven days of observation, picking them up, pushing them around, and carrying in the teeth or on the tip of the snout. An adult

West African dwarf crocodile in Madras Crocodile Bank (Tamil Nadu, India) behaved in exactly the same way.[35]

In both cases, Dinets explains that although there were many other objects in the pools, all but the pink bougainvillea were ignored. Social play, he explains, is rarely reported, although he documented other kinds of play fighting or chasing between young crocodiles he observed and photographed. One rare behavior he documented was of a pair of adult Cuban crocodiles at Zoo Miami performing an unusual behavior at the time of courtship: "The female would get on the back of the larger male, and he would give her a few rides around the pool."[36] Since this kind of courtship behavior had never been seen before, Dinets surmised that it might have been devised by the crocodilian couple who had been together for many years.

The example of alligator play that stuck with me most of all, however, was the play between an alligator and an otter. While in Big Cypress National Preserve in Florida, USA, Dinets witnessed a surprising outcome to what was play behavior between the two species. Eight to twelve subadult alligators were camping out in a bayou over five days and were often visited by four to six otters. The otters often harassed the alligators by nipping their tail tips and splashing water onto their heads. Most of the alligators merely submerged themselves during these teasing bouts, but one alligator responded by lunging at the otters whenever they got close. According to Dinets, the otters then focused most of their attention on this one alligator. At one point, one otter slipped on a steep bank and the alligator grabbed him and pulled him under, and you think you know where this is going, but no, not so fast. The alligator raised his head out of the water and let the otter go, unharmed. These games between this alligator and the otters continued for two more days, without the faux drowning, until the bayou dried up and both the alligators and the otters decamped for more watery locations. The otters continuing to tease this alligator even after the faux drowning says something about the perception of whether or not this was play for both the otters and the alligator.

Pretend Play

I was delighted to find a volume edited by Robert W. Mitchell entitled *Pretending and Imagination in Children and Animals*[37] in the university library near my home. Thirty-three neuroscientists, cognitive psychologists, and anthropologists discuss and argue the nuances of pretense and its relation to imagination, imitation, and theory of mind in these three groups. The book is full of examples of wild and captive animals engaging in pretend play. The book makes the point that make-believe is an important component of our childhood imaginative life. This volume and other more recent research clarify that like children, some animals pretend about daily life, such as food-related behavior, social activities, tool and object use, unusual or stimulating behaviors or events, and often the imagined presence of babies. Animals may carry a stick or other object for hours or days as if it is a newborn. Pretense in play, though still under-researched when it concerns animals, builds on years of thought and experience of Jean Piaget, the French child development psychologist, and Lev Vygotsky, the Soviet psychologist who stressed the role of social interaction in cognitive development. Researchers in this book apply knowledge of pretend play in children to their work with animals while noting differences and similarities.

Some of the most poignant examples in the book come from "crossfostered" primates who from infancy were treated like human children: drinking from cups, eating at the dinner table with silverware, dressing themselves, using a toilet, and playing with children's toys. The original cross-fostering experiment began with Winthrop and Luella Kellog's nine-month trial of bringing up the infant chimpanzee Gua along with their infant son.[38] The method of cross-fostering primates was used to study the impact of environmental and genetic factors on cognition. In later experiments, testing whether primates could learn human language became equally important.

The details of the 1950s experiment by Keith and Kathy Hayes, who adopted an infant chimpanzee and named her Viki, deeply affected me.

At about 16 months Viki imitated her adoptive mother in all her daily activities, including kitchen chores, dusting, and vacuuming, even personal care, like eyebrow tweezing and putting on lipstick. Every day, Viki ran to get the morning newspaper, proceeded to sit on the couch, and then, "settling back she would turn the upper corners a hand's breadth, one by one, as though she were looking for the sports page or the comics. Occasionally she would grin and open a page partway as people do when some fascinating tidbit catches the eye."[39]

The most famous example of Viki pretending was her month-long creation of an imaginary pull-toy. Trailing her hand holding an imaginary string behind her, she "pulled" her invisible toy through the house until her adoptive mother asked her what she was doing. Viki became embarrassed, stopped her pulling motions, and began investigating every detail of the toilet flush handle. Hayes's description of what happened when she also invented a "pull-toy" is heart-rending.[40] Initially, Viki was captivated, but "then became frightened, leapt into her mother's arms, and never played with the imaginary pull toy again."[41] Two thoughts occurred to me while reading this. The first concerns Viki's enormous trust in her adoptive mother. Like any young being, she was exploring the world and creating meaning in it for herself. But also like any child, sometimes that can be very scary and only Mom can assure one of the stability of the physical world as opposed to one in which parents also have invisible toys. My second thought is how clearly Viki's presence as an intelligent, imaginative, and emotional being lights up the pages of this book. Though the Hayeses attempted to teach Viki English, she was only able to say "mama, papa, cup, and up."[42]

Viki proved, and the Hayeses were smart enough to support this, that primates do not have the physiological equipment to handle vowels, but possess the cognitive qualities for supporting a language of their own. Viki lived with the Hayeses until she died of viral meningitis at age seven. While the shortness of her life is upsetting, at least she did not have to go through losing yet another mother, as many of the cross-fostered chimpanzees did when they grew too big and too physically powerful to continue living in a human home. Many cross-fostered chimps captured from the wild during the killing of their original mother then endured the loss of their human adoptive parents or family, doubling their grief, loss, and loneliness.

This became all too clear when I visited the only chimp sanctuary in Canada on one of my summer visits to eastern Quebec. The Fauna Foundation is located in Carignan, 18 miles east of Montreal. As in other responsible animal sanctuaries, the animals are not on view for the general public, but the foundation offers educational and service programs. Through a friend, I was invited to visit the foundation to interview Gloria Grow, the founder and director of the foundation, and Mary Lee Jensvold, the foundation's associate director and primate communication scientist for the foundation and Friends of Washoe, and a senior lecturer at Central Washington University. They invited me to meet the chimps.

The Fauna Foundation is now home to fourteen chimps who live in the sprawling outside areas, impeccably designed skywalks, cozy nesting rooms, fertile islands, and common areas, all of which each chimp can decide to stay in or leave. Begun as a sanctuary for farmed and domestic animals who have been abandoned or abused, the sanctuary is home to animals used in entertainment, education, or research. Sixty-six other animals also make the foundation their home. In 1997 the Fauna Foundation expanded its mission when Grow answered a plea to take a group of 15 chimpanzees who were being retired from the now-closed Laboratory for Experimental Medicine and Surgery in Primates in New York State. Eight of these 15 chimpanzees were HIV positive, making the Fauna Foundation the first sanctuary in the world to offer retirement to HIV-infected chimpanzees. Only one of those chimps, Sue Ellen, is still alive. In 2002, Toby arrived from the Zoo Sauvage de Saint-Félicien, followed in 2007 by Maya, Sophie (who died soon after arrival), and Spock from the Quebec City Zoo. All three were cross-fostered as children until they were five, when they were sent to the zoo. Loulis and Tatu, both signing chimpanzees, were welcomed in 2013 from the Chimpanzee and Human Communication Institute in Ellensburg, Washington. The last two chimpanzees, Dolly and Blackie, arrived at Fauna from Parc Safari in Hemmingford, Quebec, on November 28, 2016.

Grow talks eloquently about the life stories of each chimpanzee in her care, both present and gone, emphasizing her ultimate goal: to end chimpanzee research. Whether born in a lab, cross-fostered, or wild caught, many of the chimps suffer from severe posttraumatic stress disorder. Grow collaborated on two papers published in peer-reviewed journals concerning the traumatic effects of invasive research on chimpanzees that continued for years while they were housed in solo cages in sterile and stressful medical research lab environments.[43] The life stories of these chimpanzees are painful to read, and the scars and the sadness from their abusive past lives are often visible on their faces and bodies, if not always in their behavior.

One of the most important gifts and rehabilitative aspects that Fauna has offered is the freedom to choose. During our discussion before meeting the chimps, Grow explained that there are so few things you can offer them in captivity that choices about door closings, options on where time is spent, and alternatives as to what food to eat become important. Slider doors opened even a fraction allow the chimps to know that they still have the freedom to choose to stay in or go out. While that difference might not be significant to us, to anyone who has spent time incarcerated, the difference between an open or a locked door is immense. Grow's affection for the chimps is apparent as she relates what happens when one of the nonsigning chimps finds a door closed because of cleaning or inclement weather:

> Banging on a door usually means, "I want it open." Trying to lift it means, "I want it open." Trying to pull it means, "I want it open." Trying to jiggle the lock at the top means, "I really want it open."[44]

When I was in the central kitchen at lunchtime, the importance of food choice became apparent. The staff offers each chimp an ample selection of deliciously nutritious food from which to choose, including food saved for later. As Grow says, "We aren't ever going to make them better. We have to learn to be the right people in their lives." And Jensvold adds, "My son just graduated from high school and he is going to college, and then you come back here and they aren't going anywhere. There is only one ticket out of here." Grow, Jensvold, and the staff I met while at Fauna have committed to making the remaining years for these fourteen chimpanzees as comfortable, free, and love-filled as possible.

Jensvold's published research during 30 years of working with chimpanzees includes pretend play in signing chimpanzees. Two chimps she has worked with previously were Tatu and Loulis, who were once part of the Washoe Project, named after the first chimpanzee in the ASL (American Sign Language) signing project started by Beatrix and Allen Gardner and then taken over by Roger and Debbie Fouts. Loulis, who became Washoe's adopted son, was born at the Yerkes Regional Primate Research Center in Atlanta, Georgia, in 1978. Tatu was born in the Institute for Primate Studies in Norman, Oklahoma, where the Washoe Project operated during that time. Tatu and Loulis, while showing behavior that comes from being institutionalized at their former locations, are calmer and adjusting more quickly to sanctuary life. Before living at Fauna they were treated with respect and sensitivity by Roger and Deborah Fouts, who founded the Chimpanzee and Human Communication Institute on the campus of Central Washington University in Ellensburg, Washington, where Roger Fouts was a faculty member. Jensvold served as director before Tatu and Loulis were moved to Fauna after the death of Washoe. Jensvold joined the Washoe Project in 1986 and coauthored with Fouts an early paper on pretend play in signing chimpanzees in which they analyzed 15 hours of videotape recorded over three weeks.[45] More recently, Jensvold and Tennyson E. Egan analyzed over 67 hours of videotape recorded during an 18-year period when Jensvold worked with the Washoe Project.[46]

Four of the five chimpanzees involved in this project, Washoe, Moja, Tatu, and Dar, were cross-fostered and taught ASL by caregivers. Loulis, however, when adopted by Washoe, was not taught ASL to determine whether he might learn it from other chimpanzees. All human signing was prohibited in his presence, except for seven signs: WHO, WHAT, WHERE, WHICH, WANT, SIGN, and NAME. Loulis, however, signed in seven days, and combined signs into phrases in five months. He acquired his signs in conversation with the other chimpanzees. Jensvold describes pretend play in the chimps in the same way pretend play in human children is described:

> The chimpanzees signed to dolls and stuffed animals. For example, Dar put a stuffed animal to his side and signed TICKLE. They used toy objects as if they were real. In one instance Moja held a phone to her ear and moved her mouth and pressed buttons as if dialing. They pretended one object was another. For example, Moja put a purse on her foot and signed SHOE.[47]

Jensvold's work with chimpanzees includes conversational behaviors, private signing, phrase development, chimpanzee-to-chimpanzee conversation, imaginary play, and artwork. She provided me with a transcript from one of her recent presentations on the last item, this one at the University of Indiana at Bloomington.

> The chimpanzees paint and color. These images show evidence for individual style, and aspects of aesthetics such as balance, center marking. The signing chimpanzees also name their paintings. There is evidence for consistent schema in the chimpanzees' named artwork. The schema varies between objects. For example, drawings of Moja's cups look similar to each other, but look different from drawings of other objects, like bananas.[48]

Jensvold and Egan suggest that researchers working with signing apes may use the symbols to understand the situation. A cultural overlap of objects and routines between captive apes and their researchers means that more behaviors are recognizable to the researchers. However, language is unnecessary for pretend play in animals. Studies done on wild chimpanzees have also documented pretend play. None other than Jane Goodall recounts an instance of pretend play in a young chimpanzee named Wunda:

> Once a four-year-old Wunda watched intently from a safe distance as her mother, using a long stick, fished for fierce driver ants from a branch overhanging the nest. Presently, Wunda picked a tiny twig, perched herself on a low branch of a sapling in the same attitude as her mother, and poked her little tool down into an imaginary nest.[49]

There are several cases of captive Indian Ocean bottlenose dolphins acting as other animals might. For example, a female bottlenose dolphin frequently imitated the behavior of a fur seal and the postures and swimming behavior of fish, turtles, and penguins.[50]

Play as Joyful Freedom

Lyanda Lynn Haupt, in her wonderful book *Crow Planet,* tells of the creative destruction of her garden by four fledging crows. Since young crows initially cannot fly, they remained on the ground during the few days her garden was their home. The four amused themselves by eliminating a low willow fence and uprooting all the seedling carrots she had planted. She describes their approach to this destruction as not wild but slow, neat, and "with concentration, as if working on their knitting." When they went after the pole beans, Haupt decided enough was enough and "very gently turned the garden hose on the chicks. Instead of showing fear, all four of them gathered under the spray, flapped their wings, and opened their bills, in what appeared to be absolute joy."[51]

Play is often joyful. Ideally, it allows for immersion in a world that needs no reason or motive but offers instead sheer, uncomplicated pleasure. The word "ideally" should be noted, since the lives of animals are every bit as complex as ours and so is their play, even play that brings them joy. Ethologist and author Jonathan Balcombe offers a wise view of pleasure when he says, "It is one of the blessings of evolution."[52] That description also may explain joy, the most intense form of pleasure, just as well. He says, "Pleasure helps animals maintain a stable state."[53] It also rewards adaptive behavior. The flight of birds, for instance, is an adaption that allows for escaping predators, exploring new territories, and a unique view of food resources. But from below, a seagull cruising through the air seems to be as pleased as I am lazing on a raft in calm water. As Balcombe and others before him insist, many behaviors that enhance survival are not seen as such by the animals themselves.[54] Just as many a human baby emits peals of joyful laughter while in the bathtub, so do baby crows relish a good soaking on a hot day. Neither the human babies nor the baby crows care how sensible that bath or soaking might be for their survival.

One of the foremost experts on play, the evolutionary biologist and cognitive ethologist Marc Bekoff, has written extensively and evocatively about the play of animals. His groundbreaking work with philosopher Jessica Pierce on what they call "wild justice" is significant for its influential perspective on the evolution and existence of empathy, justice, cooperation, and morality in social animals.[55] Bekoff says elsewhere, "There's also incredible freedom and creativity in the flow of play. This is easy to see and amazing to watch. I refer to this as the 'Six F's of Play': its Flexibility, Freedom, Friendship, Frolic, Fun, and Flow."[56] This list includes several terms we have been using to describe creative behavior, flexibility, freedom, and flow. Mihaly Csikszentmihalyi describes the state of flow as "being completely involved in an activity for its own sake. The ego falls away. Time flies. Every action, movement, and thought follows inevitably from the previous one, like playing jazz. Your whole being is involved, and you're using your skills to the utmost."[57]

Bekoff echoes this description of flow as he describes how during play "animals re-create a mind-boggling array of scenarios and social behaviors. It's difficult to believe that when animals are deep into play they can keep track of what they are doing, but they can."[58] Bekoff explains that it is not unusual to see documented mating behaviors intermingled with fighting behaviors or behaviors more attuned to being prey. "In no other activity but play do you see all of the attributes and behaviors occurring together."[59]

Immersion in an activity for its own sake while using "your skills to the utmost" describes the flow of creativity as much as Bekoff's characterization of the flow of play. Combining over forty years of long-term detailed studies of play in social carnivores with his deep love of animals, Bekoff supports the claim that some animals are moral. This might seem far afield from the topic at hand, but I find Bekoff's and Pierce's case helpful in considering the creativity of animals. Their arguments are supported by other cognitive ethologists in addition to ideas from psychology, such as cooperation and altruism, and research from neuroscience, such as neurological evidence for empathy and fairness. Pierce, as a bioethicist and philosopher, adds the essential ability to rethink assumed concepts of morality in reconsidering the evolutionary continuity between humans and other animals and the uniqueness of particular species. So how is morality involved in play and what does that have to do with animal creativity? To answer that question, let us first review the kinds of examples and ideas found in Bekoff's and Pierce's case for animal morality.

Imagine you are watching two dogs play. Perhaps one is the dog you live with, so you know his physical behaviors fairly well. Over time, you have learned to intuit his emotional states from these behaviors. (To be fair, you think he does a far better job recognizing your emotional states.) As the two dogs are playing, you see a repeated behavior, but it happens so quickly that you are not sure what it means, if it means anything. It looks very much like what your dog does when he wants you to get the heck up from the computer and play with him. Bekoff's work with wolves, coyotes, red foxes, and domesticated dogs informing his many books and interviews have helped people now recognize this as the "play bow." It looks simple enough. Stick your butt in the air while you stretch your arms in front of you on the floor. The yoga pose,

Downward Dog, appears very similar to what a play bow in the canid family looks like.

The play bow, one of many play signals among animals in the canine family, announces to the chosen playmate, "Hey, I want to play with you." If the playmate accepts, it also is an indication that what will happen after this is play, not fighting, though at times it may seem like fighting to the humans watching. Bekoff explains how a playmate may initiate the bow several times during a play session, either before a behavior that might seem dangerous, or after a playmate becomes overly rambunctious in biting the play partner too hard, for instance. In these contexts, the play bow indicates, "I am going to do something that might seem like real fighting, but I am really just playing" or "I am sorry I bit you too hard, I didn't mean to. Let's keep playing." Playing animals use other techniques to put their partners at ease, such as self-handicapping and role reversal. According to Bekoff and fellow ethologists, "Animals can actively seek and create unexpected events in play through self-handicapping; that is, deliberately relaxing control over their movements or actively putting themselves into disadvantageous positions and situations."[60]

When older male red-neck wallabies (marsupials related to kangaroos) play with younger, smaller, and usually gentler play partners, they sometimes clumsily but gently paw their partners when in low-intensity bouts. They spend little time in these frequent low-intensity bouts in what is called the high-stance posture—standing on the tips of toes and tail with the back held vertical or inclined back from the vertical. Most tellingly, they do not take advantage of their greater size to overcome their partner. While the younger partner takes opportunities to spar more vigorously than when play fighting with their peers, the older wallabies never respond aggressively to these fighting tactics. They simply avoid the other's attacks. Ethologists Duncan Watson and David Croft, who accomplished this oft-cited study, conclude, "These observations suggest that not only did older partners in mixed-age class play-fights self-handicap, but that they were highly tolerant of the tactics used by their partners."[61]

Through play, immature animals learn how to respond to new situations, how to cooperate, resolve conflicts, and play fair. Play is a place to test out behaviors they are unfamiliar with, like playing with an older, wiser, and supportive family member. Trying out new physical and emotional behaviors in a safe situation such as play can serve as training for the unexpected in more dangerous situations. Bekoff and Pierce point out that play is a learning laboratory for qualities such as trust, cooperation, fairness, empathy, punishment, and forgiveness, words often used when talking about morality. There is a strong evolutionary selection for these traits.

Play is rarely unfair or uncooperative. Those who deceive or prove they are not to be trusted are excluded and risk not doing well on their own. It is often argued that the qualities listed above make us the only moral species. Yet current research, such as that of Bekoff, Pierce, and Frans de Waal, indicates that we are not unique in these qualities. What does justice have to do with creativity?[62] And weren't we talking about play? If play is essential in offering the freedom to make mistakes, try out new behaviors, and at the same time learn and use egalitarian components of social systems, might the common denominator be judgment?

How does an animal decide how to choose their playmates or how to treat a playmate that does not play fair? How do birds choose what songs to sing to court a possible mate? How do elephants decide how to mourn a beloved human friend? Judgment is an essential ingredient of social behavior of all kinds, and necessary for making decisions on how to act. Perhaps this seems redundant information. If animals are intelligent and able to communicate in ways that work for their needs, of course they are making decisions. I agree, but just to prove the point more fully, here are some results from recent research on decision making in animals, and what role judgment might make in those decisions. African wild dogs have a unique method of making their decisions known. They sneeze. Researchers found that in the rest periods after hunting, sneezes among wild dogs indicate individual votes to hunt again. If higher-ranking individuals are sneezing, only three or more sneezes are needed to start the group moving for another hunt, but if lower-ranking individuals are sneezing, often those who have not had as much to eat, it takes ten or more sneezes to get everyone to move. Others who have eaten well must be convinced that sleeping is not the better option. The researchers say, "Our findings illustrate how specific behavioral mechanisms (here, sneezing) allow for negotiation (in effect, voting) that shapes decision-making in a wild, socially complex animal society." Just to be clear, the sneezing itself is not creative, but the wild dogs are making decisions; they are making a judgment call.[63]

Compelling research in recent organizational scholarship has questioned the assumed links between intrinsic or internal motivation and creativity. It has been thought that creativity only emerged from an individual's motivation. Employing meticulous use of both field and lab data, researchers Adam Grant and Adam Berry have proposed that psychological processes, particularly those focused on the needs or desires of others, enhance creativity. What biologists call prosocial motivation and perspective taking (seen as a component of empathy) are identified as "important contingencies that strengthen the effects of intrinsic motivation on creativity."[64] What this research tells us is that rather than looking at creativity emerging only from an individual with a unique idea all their own, creative behavior is also influenced and enhanced by emotions that involve care for others. The researchers are keen to mention that while prosocial behaviors may involve altruism, the two concepts should not be equated. Prosocial motivation can serve multiple goals. "Thus, prosocial motivation can involve, but should not necessarily be equated with, altruism; it refers to a concern for others, not a concern for others at the expense of self-interest."[65] African wild dogs voting to hunt again by sneezing is a clear example of a creative form of decision making involving negotiation of the differing hunger needs of pack members. According to Grant and Berry, perspective taking (simply, taking the perspective of another) "is an important influence on creativity."[66] At some point, members of the pack had to be able to take the perspective of a hungry dog lower on the hierarchy to feel enough concern for others to agree to this form of negotiation. Deciding to accept this form of self-government involves a sense of what is just. As Bekoff and Pierce argue, "Caring about the interests of others, and comparing these interests to your own, is the essence of justice."[67] Within the freedom of play, one learns a great deal about negotiating others' interests and one's own. These lessons on empathy also offer important experiences guaranteed to enhance creativity.

Back to Joy and Fun

There is nothing so delightful as watching children of any species playing. If one is honest, there is nothing so freeing as playing for any of us. A recent article in "Society and Animals" is entitled "Role of Joy in Farm Animal Welfare Legislation."[68] In it, agricultural researchers Philipp von Gall and Mickey Gjerris analyze the role joy plays in farm animal welfare and then argue that economic reasons are responsible for failure to recognize the importance of that role. "It is argued that overlooking elements of joy cannot be justified from any ethical perspective that claims to take animal welfare into consideration."[69] "Joy" is a neglected term in science and, like boredom in pigs, described in the first chapter, is indicative of how we have ignored a wide range of both emotion and ability in animals of all kinds. Psychologist and neuroscientist Richard Byrne would add curiosity to that list. According to Byrne,

> To find how and why questions interesting, an animal would need to be able to compute mentally, on the basis of known facts, whether or not something was likely to happen. This means that some kinds of curiosity have the potential to tell us about the ways in which animals understand their world: specifically, cases in which nothing the slightest bit abnormal is present, superficially, but the configuration is improbable and surprising to those who have a causal understanding of objects or a mental state understanding of individuals.[70]

In another essay on play, Byrne asks, "What do animals find fun?" Aside from all the fun things that also are training for adult life, what things do animals find fun in their daily lives? Observations made by Byrne and others make one pause: some baboons like to pull the tails of cows if they are behind a fence so the cows cannot retaliate, and baby elephants find fun in chasing other species, even those whom they would not have to practice evading.[71] Mischievousness offers detours around the conventions that stifle creativity. One has to look no further than animals we may live with to find instances of their playful mischief.

Chimpanzees use objects as tools, so it is not a surprise to Byrne that they often play with objects as well. Still, he asks,

> But when an adult chimpanzee, slowly consuming the brain of a monkey it has helped hunt, carefully places small pieces of the skull onto a nearby liana, one-by-one in a neat row just like we might place plum stones on the edge of a plate, it raises a question: how does a chimpanzee think about objects, such that this neat pattern is fun to make?[72]

While some readers may find this behavior abhorrent, I find that this observation fits into what I know of the obsessiveness of creativity. Obsessive behavior is not a substitute for creativity, but it can be linked to a zealous curiosity and exploration phase involved in the creative process and may be involved in the evaluation and implementation phases. If we combine the previous discussion on justice with this example of obsessive behavior when eating one's prey, it is possible for us to see that justice for some animals may be species or small-group specific. I do not need to point to war or slavery as examples of the noninclusive quality of our human sense of justice.

4

Creating Built Environments

Nests, Lodges, Bowers, Avenues, Tunnels, and Hives

A tree becomes a nest the moment a great dreamer hides in it.
—Gaston Bachelard, *The Poetics of Space*

A nest becomes a home for the bird who builds it, as does the lodge for the beaver, the mound for the termite, the web for the spider, the shell for the snail. Sometimes hidden, at other times overtly visible, animal architecture provides shelter, protection, food, and thermoregulation, among other less obvious functions, across many species around the globe. Each species, however, builds their home in their singular way. Originally, I had thought to begin this chapter with the elegantly constructed and beautifully decorated arbors made by bowerbirds of Australia and New Guinea, but something changed my mind. A beaver kidnapped me.

I moved to Oregon while writing this book. At first, I rented a place next to the Delta Ponds in Eugene, a restored 150-acre wetland that is part of a braided channel of the Willamette River. While I made breakfast, I watched Great Egrets, Canadian Geese, and families of several kinds of ducks move back and forth across the pond closest to my back door. The geese, usually taking off and landing in the ponds with urgent and raucous cries, were sometimes strangely quiet on the little stone island in the middle of the pond. A truce had been struck, perhaps, between the geese communities who squabble all day over territorial rights to various sections of the ponds.

I found the people in Eugene friendly and welcoming, but it was the inhabitants of the Delta Ponds that offered much more life and interest.

Those first months I was too busy exploring the ponds to feel lonely having moved to a new area where I knew no one. Each morning the wind's breath rippling the surface of the water and gently swaying the leaves of trees also stirred the geese into beginning their noisy introduction to the day. When the air was still, Great Egrets would stand for what seemed like hours of contemplation. Sometimes I would come to the back door to find the same egret in the same position as an hour before. On daytime walks around the ponds with Copernicus, my canine companion, we saw osprey bringing food to their enormous chicks in their gigantic nests, in this case resting on wooden platforms built specifically for this purpose by the park workers. The chicks, almost three-quarters of their mother's size, emitted loud and impatient calls until she returned to the nest with food. Longer walks revealed Great Blue Herons and pond turtles. At dusk, the light was a burnt orange that melted the trees and ponds into a warm glow. On one of those nights I spotted a beaver in the water fixing a part of his home. I think that is what he was doing. We were only privy to his swimming and diving at the edges of his lodge. We came back regularly just to check on him and were sometimes gifted with a good view of his head above water. I became completely besotted with him. Copernicus humored me.

Learning Hydro-Engineering from Beavers

Donald Griffin, in one of his groundbreaking books, *Animal Minds*, says of beavers, "When we consider the kinds of animal behavior that suggest conscious thinking, the beaver comes naturally to mind."[1] To many, beavers may not be the first animal vying for attention in that context, but that is only because for hundreds of years beavers were hunted and trapped for their luxurious fur. Consciousness was the last thing humans thought this "pest," "varmint," rodent might have. Hat and garment felting made use of their fur as early as the fourteenth century, depleting the European beaver population during the seventeenth century.[2] By 1900 the North American beaver was almost driven to extinction due to hunting, trapping, and the impact of agriculture and building within their habitats.[3] Thirty-two years before, Lewis Henry Morgan published *The American Beaver and His Works*, considered for the following century to be the seminal writing on the beaver.[4] The first to write about the North American beaver in detail, Morgan presented personal knowledge of their building of dams, lodges, and canals, and their "lengthy and even complicated process of reasoning."[5] He also remarked on the "capacity in the beaver to adapt his constructions to the particular conditions in which he finds himself placed," basing his observation on the differences in canals built by beavers living in the Upper Missouri River and Lake Superior.[6] In this behavior, he argued, was the clearest evidence for the beaver's and other species' "free intelligence" and their possession of capacities of memory, reason, imagination, will, passions, and appetites. He even offers a section on animal madness.[7]

Today, after species-preservation work in North America brought the numbers up to 15 percent of their original count, the beaver is again gaining respect. Conservationists, ecologists, and biologists are now documenting how beavers' dams protect against climate change in their historical habitat. Their dams are uniquely constructed to raise the water table alongside a stream, preventing erosion as the trees and plants there become stabilized. The dams also contribute to a vastly improved fish and wildlife habitat, while promoting new and rich soil. Beaver dams do everything human-made dams do but better and for free[8] or, as a recent study on the building methods and results of beaver dams by engineers explains, "It must be considered that beavers and their dams have existed in rivers for more than 15 million years and that the river ecosystems and species evolved around them."[9] As an instance of ecosystems and other species needing what individual animals create, the building process of the beaver offers a model for the creative process in animals.

Our interest includes beavers' ingenious construction methods as well as their flexibility in changing those methods as needed. Griffin includes a sizeable portion of a chapter on constructing artifacts in his book *Animal Minds* on beavers, as have other biologists. James L. and Carol Gould, in their book *Animal Architecture: Building and the Evolution of Intelligence*, point out,

> Less is known about these large aquatic rodents than we might expect. Beavers are shy, mostly nocturnal, and live much of their lives hidden in lodges; even when outside, they are generally swimming, with little more than the tops of their heads or a bit of broad sleek back showing. At the same time, they ought to be one of the most interesting of all species for our purposes.[10]

Beavers are elegant animals in and under the water, with large, webbed feet and a substantial paddle-like tail helping them to effortlessly glide along as if motorized. On land, their svelte shape disappears and is replaced by the shape and movement of a waddling mass of fur, but they have strong, agile, hand-like front paws with five fingers, one of which is semi-opposable. What beavers lack in grace while on land is more than compensated for by their deeply creative architectural talent.

Beavers live in monogamous pairs with one or two litters of kits born each year. Family life can be a bit crowded since the kits stay for at least two years, sometimes three, before going off to make their own families. Supplied with orange iron-clad gigantic front teeth that never stop growing, the beaver fells trees by gnawing them. This is possibly the best known of their activities because the results are highly visible in areas where beavers have decided to live. Munching on the bark of cut trees and branches, beavers use whole trunks, dead trees, and trees with inedible bark for dam- and lodge-building materials.

Both Griffin and the Goulds offer numerous examples of what they see as beavers' obvious intelligence, self-awareness, and extreme flexibility in changing strategies to achieve their desired results. As Griffin so adroitly responds to an anthropologist of the time who insists that a beaver *does not* and *cannot* know what he wants to build before he builds it,

Proving a global negative statement, that something never happens under any circumstances, is notoriously difficult; but Ingold and others deny that beaver might be aware of the results of their actions, without presenting any convincing evidence to support such a sweeping and dogmatic assertion.[11]

Griffin asks us to consider the actual behavior of beavers and then make up our minds. While the intelligence and self-awareness of beavers and other animals may be more accepted today among the sciences, the creativity of what beavers do has yet to be widely appreciated.

The Goulds agree:

> They build elaborate dams and canals to control or create water flow, establish desirable water levels to ensure the safety of their communal family lodge, and generate essential transportation arteries for finding food and moving building materials. Because no two situations require the same set of designs to solve the hydraulic problems at hand, perhaps no other species outside humans have such an opportunity to display the creativity it may possess.[12]

Limiting discussion of creativity to only one animal species is not where this book is going. The Goulds, however, articulate specifically just how evident beavers' creative processes are when one looks realistically and closely at their behavior and their architectural and engineering prowess. This kind of close inspection may be used as a model for understanding the creative components of other species' creative lives.

There is no single beaver habitat, putting to rest any argument that beavers innately know how to build nests, or that they only learn a specific building plan that can be used in any situation.[13] Beavers need several nonoptional items: hardwood trees to eat, a burrow with a predator-proof underwater entrance, and a dry nest above water for living. Whether or not a dam or even a pond is necessary depends on the beaver's choice of habitat. To meet these needs, beavers must understand what they entail and devise appropriate strategies to meet them in the chosen habitat. When discussing how beavers dig into the slope of the bank of the stream or lake they have decided to make home, Griffin considers the implications of their unerring choice of slopes in which to dig. They do not dig into slopes that are too gradual to provide space for a tunnel above the water level. He points out, "This implies they recognize that some shores are too low to make burrowing worthwhile. As far as I have been able to learn from published accounts of beaver behavior or from my own observations, beavers do not start useless burrows."[14]

As the family grows, beavers will often enlarge the lodge upward or begin to dig a tunnel to a higher living room. Eventually, the family may have multiple lodges differing in both location and style. To accomplish these continuing goals, beavers will dig a deep canal into the sloping bank to add another lodge to the first. Or, they might construct a mounded peninsula out in the pond with a tunnel dug up into it. Other lodges may be installed on an island built by the beaver family by hauling and amassing large stones as a foundation just below the waterline. The floor, the roof, and the comfortable and dry inner chamber are all finished with appropriate materials of sticks, branches, mud, shavings, and grasses. Interestingly, many beaver families live happily and peacefully in their lodges with muskrats, mice, water voles, and flying insects. Perhaps, after all that work, they want to share the perfection of their labor. The Goulds sum all this up by saying, "Imagination, an ability to plan, and a ready willingness to learn from experience seem the most realistic combination of cognitive faculties to generate this aspect of the beaver's life. And this is just the burrow."[15]

The beavers' ability to also build dams and canals relies on all the creative characteristics listed so far, and then some. Beavers, when necessary, build dams to stabilize water levels, keeping their homes safe from intrusion by predators or other dangers. The largest beaver dam recorded is in Alberta's Wood Buffalo National Park and is 2,790 feet long and only discovered by researchers using Google Earth in October

2007. The second-longest beaver dam in the world is 2,139 feet long and is located in Three Forks, Montana.[16]

Beaver dams vary in height from three feet to twelve feet in most situations, and beavers build them to efficiently manage the flow of water in any situation. Some are constructed so that the right amount of water permeates the dam and sediment is filtered out. Larger dams contain carefully crafted spillways to moderate water flow as well as stair-step pools, making life easier for the beavers carrying branches and other building materials in their mouths.

The Goulds highlight two ways in which beavers have been known to innovate. The first occurs when beavers encounter man-made dams. Beavers recognize them as dams and modify them to meet their needs. This ability to recognize an opportunity when one sees one is key to the creative process, and beavers are constantly demonstrating their willingness to do so in this way.

The second way is how beavers willingly modify and even damage their dams to ensure a layer of air across the entire pond between the water and winter ice. This layer is crucial in providing the family of oxygen-breathing mammals a definite supply of air when the ice is too thick to break holes through. Since the beaver is all about repairing any breach in the dam, it is even more interesting that previous biologists assumed that both seeing and hearing running water "triggered" what was considered an instinctual urge in beavers to repair. The Goulds relay a test used to prove this assumption. Researchers used a speaker to play a recording of trickling water sounds, though not matched with any real leak. The beavers showed mild interest at first, but then ignored it. After a time, seemingly tired of listening to the sound of leaking water coming from the speaker, the beavers attempted to bury the speaker. The beavers distinguished between real and recorded leaks. Those deemed to be hazardous were dealt with immediately.

Beavers build canals for navigation and transportation of materials. They are not as agile on land as in the water, so in their incessant need to repair the lodges or dams, self-built canals float the branches and tree parts to wherever they are needed. Stepped canals extend into the forest and sometimes have burrows for hiding, just in case. At other times, the canals, rather than following the curves of a river, are built so that more efficient travel can take place by building lodges into these detours.

Given the many challenges beavers face in building their homes, the Goulds suggest that beavers regularly employ abstract concepts and reasoning in their daily life with innovation and insight emerging as they encounter especially difficult challenges. One of the most important moments in the creative process is the realization that an accident can be used to propel the process further. Consequently, if a mistake dissuades one from following a misleading path, it also may reveal new options of approach. What at first seems like an error in craft or judgment may open up new avenues of consideration, new questions, or concealed opportunities that forethought and planning might miss. The Goulds insist, "Their cognitive abilities have broadened their range of habitats, and that increased range has selected for yet more flexibility and creativity in dealing with the challenges that face them."[17] The ability to recognize possibilities for something new emerging out of what others might consider as an obstacle, a piece of trash, or an aberration is a cornerstone of the creative process, and beavers and other animals are masters at this process.

After dedicating over three-quarters of his book *Animal Architecture* to the building talents of anthropods and vertebrates other than mammals, Austrian ethologist Karl von Frisch notes, "On the whole, the architectural achievements of mammals are not very impressive. The order of rodents is, however, an exception in that it contains, comparatively speaking, quite a number of clever builders."[18] He discusses the tunnels of moles, the burrows of badgers, woodrats, and marmots, the nests of harvest mice, dormice, and squirrels, and of course the elaborate building of beavers. Writing in the mid-twentieth century, von Frisch was able to describe the longevity of some dams; however, the destruction of beaver dams and their habitat at that time was not as common as it is now: "Large dams are maintained by generations of beaver families over a period of many years, perhaps even centuries, and are constantly adapted to changes in the water level. . . . A skilled hydro-engineer could not regulate the water level any better."[19] It is difficult, then, for anyone studying beavers firsthand to dismiss their behavior, and that of other members of the order Rodentia, as simply instinctual. Across species, animals exhibit creativity. Even those animals we, as humans, generally find dispensable.

Insect Architecture and Bee Democracy.

From ants to spiders to beavers to birds, the practice of architecture, grand and minimal, extends throughout the animal kingdom. The idea that humans exclusively use tools or are the only ones able to construct intricate and long-lasting artifacts has been proven wrong so often that to see the idea come up in serious creativity literature is laughable. Mike Hansell, professor emeritus in animal architecture at the University of Glasgow, has been studying animal architecture, a field in itself, for the last forty-seven years. His research has amassed an intriguing collection of examples, and these have helped reveal that animals too possess a sense of beauty.[20] The aesthetic sophistication of examples he and other researchers have collected opens up a rich area of animal creativity that has been in front of us all the time.

From ant lions and caddisflies to Weaver birds and bowerbirds, establishing a place in the universe that one can call home or, for bowerbirds, more of a bachelor pad, is particularly important. The details of how each animal approaches the construction of their home or another piece of architecture within a particular context, such as geography, temperature, or human encroachment, may vary considerably even though the general species needs may be similar. Building in some species may be genetically programmed, but this does not prohibit great cognitive ingenuity in their building methods. Even builders who use simple behaviors to build their homes collect materials they are able to standardize in order to build what are impressive tiny structures. Caddisflies develop through four stages: egg, larva, pupa, and adult. When they are in the underwater larva stage, the larva constructs an ornate protective case around itself using sticky silk threads expelled from its head. Carefully choosing just the right material, such as plant fragments, sand grains, wood fragments, pebbles, or small shells, they construct the exquisitely intricate cases in which they live for up to two years until they shed them as adults.[21]

The Goulds point to other species of caddisfly who fabricate free-standing funnels to filter food and inorganic matter directly to the larva or the more advanced two-chimney filtering system the larva builds and attaches to its protective tube. The flexibility needed to respond to both the possibilities and the unforeseen eventualities of this kind of structure fascinated Griffin as well:

> It has been customary to view such artifacts as caddisfly cases in much the same light that biologists view the elaborate structures of animal bodies—patterns regulated primarily by genetic instructions. But on close examination, it turns out that even simple creatures such as the caddisfly larvae adjust their building behaviors in ways that would seem to be aided by simple thinking about what they are doing. . . . The fact that a central nervous system operates in a certain way because of genetic instructions does not necessarily mean that its operations may not also lead to cognition and perceptual consciousness.[22]

If an individual insect can think flexibly about their building behavior, and the caddisfly larvae are one of many insects who do, how then might we approach the possible creativity of what is often called the "hive mind"? In the study of social insects, those that live in colonies with group integration, division of labor, and an overlap of generations have provided researchers with data that have indicated high intelligence. The social brain hypothesis, theorized by the neuroscientist Lesley Brothers (1990), was based on primate research by Allison Jolly, followed by psychologist Nicholas Humphrey's research. This theory connected living and thriving in social groups to the development of intelligence, at least among primates. Related theories associate larger group size with larger brain size (and more brain power), and other studies connect group size and neocortex volume. More recently, there is a move towards thinking of social complexity and accompanying group size as only part of what influenced the evolution of intelligence. The connection to brain size, particularly, has taken a back seat. Multiple influences, foraging per-haps, may have stimulated a more complex intelligence. Challenges out-side group social dynamics may have added other levels of complexity needed to solve those challenges. Intelligence, remember, is not homog-enous.[23] Bekoff and Pierce in their book on the moral lives of animals, *Wild Justice*, explain,

> We defined intelligence as how well an individual adapts to his or her particular environment. There is no general intelligence. Intelligence is not a universal and measurable entity. . . . Intelligence is context-specific. And to reiterate, cross-species comparisons or even within-species com-parisons, are fraught with difficulty.[24]

This brings us back to the "hive mind." Sometimes called a superorgan-ism, it describes a colony of insects acting as a single organism. The assumption here is that intelligence, if it exists, resides in the resulting group action, not in judgments of the individual bees (or as the case may be, wasps, termites, or ants). The term originated in the 1950s with both beekeeping and science fiction vying for the first use of the term.[25] Living and negotiating with up to 9,999 other honeybees in some colo-nies has had some influence not only on the intelligence of the honeybee but also on its creative abilities to make various social decisions that might affect the group as a whole. One of those decisions has to do with where the hive will live.

Just as beavers' architecture is an essential component of river health, honeybees, protected and nourished by the hives they build, are a principal contributor to growing the world's food. More than 90 percent of the leading global crop types are visited by bees.[26] Their hives are built of combs of hexagonal cells hanging vertically. For millions of years, according to fossil records found in Europe, the honeybee has been employing the hexagon, a perfect hexagon with all six sides equidistant, to build their hives. It took humans quite a while to use the hexagon as a structure for architecture. The ribbing and hidden chambers of the Pantheon's dome are an early example.[27] Why is the hexagon so special to bees? Bees store the honey they have made in each of the hexagonal chambers. The walls of the chambers are made of wax from the honey, and the wax also holds the honeycomb together. Bees are extremely diligent and spend enormous amounts of time and energy finding nectar and then transporting it back to the hive in their honey stomach, not the same stomach that they use for food. Once at the hive, they pass the nectar through their mouths to other worker bees, who after chewing on it for a time, pass it to other bees. All this chewing causes the nectar to slowly convert to honey. The hexagonal cells act as jars for the honey, ones that can store the maximum amount of honey that the bees have worked so hard at making and use the least amount of wax. Darwin, who called the honeycomb "absolutely perfect" in economizing labor and wax, also wondered if the bees initially constructed circular cells, which subsequently turned into hexagons.[28]

Recently, arguments in this direction were given a boost by a team study led by Bhushan Karihaloo. Initially, the bees make circular cells. The wax, softened by the heat of the bees' bodies, is pulled into hexagons by surface tension at the junction where the three walls meet. Rather than concluding that bees are not managing this process, Karihallo and his colleagues specify that the kneading and heating of the wax flakes of the "specialist 'hot workers'" near the triple junctions enable these walls' maximum state of stress, thus forming the individual hexagonal shapes. The researchers state, "We cannot but marvel at the crucial role played by the bees in this process: they knead, heat, and thin the wax exactly where it is needed."[29]

Similar perspectives, including those searching for more specific information about a particular biological process while acknowledging the intelligent planning of the individuals involved, have multiplied in fields such as ethology, evolutionary biology, psychology, and neuroscience. The early work of von Frisch on bees' color vision and dance language opened up new avenues into animal language and cognition.[30] Research on what neuroscientist in animal behavior Tom Seally calls "swarm intelligence" reveals a side of bees one might not expect. One of the least appreciated aspects of architectural design is the choice of location. An individual human architect may find it easier to make decisions based on her concerns, but allow a committee to help with the decision, and suddenly the task of getting everyone to agree seems monumental. Honeybees have solved the tricky problem of group decision making in what amounts to a creative brainstorming process.

In late spring or early summer, colonies of honeybees *swarm*. The swarming entails the queen bee and approximately half the worker bees leaving to establish a new colony. This allows a daughter queen and the rest of the workers to continue living and working in the old colony. The new colony must find a new and advantageous site to call home. In the 1950s, Martin Lindauer, a German postdoctoral student studying with Karl von Frisch at the University of Munich, noticed that the bees on the surface of the swarm he was watching were performing waggle dances. Unlike those foragers bearing nectar and pollen, whose dancing indicated the location of valuable food sources, these bees seemed to be scouts. He wondered, Were they waggle dancing to advertise choice sites they had found?

After a great deal of painstaking observation, including dotting recorded dancing bees with a blue paint dot, Lindauer made several discoveries. The first was that only a few hundred of the thousands of bees in the swarm were active during this early phase of the decision-making process. These scouts flew from the swarm, finding and then inspecting potential nest sites. They then returned to the swarm to perform waggle dances. The second remarkable finding was that initially, the bees pointed to many sites, but in a matter of hours, the number of sites advertised by the scouts shrank to one site, which was then reported excitedly by dozens of bees. To Lindauer's delight, once the dancing bees focused on one site, soon the entire cluster of bees would suddenly fly towards this site. He knew that the dancing bees had scouted and reported the final site, but he still did not know how the scouts had agreed on this particular site.[31]

In the mid-1990s, Seeley and his colleagues decided to revisit Lindauer's research to find out exactly how the scout bees implemented the very precise wish list for the perfect honeybee colony location. According to several investigators since Lindauer, "A first-rate home for a honeybee colony has a cavity volume greater than 20 liters and an entrance hole that is smaller than 30 square centimeters, perched several meters off the ground, facing south and located at the floor of the cavity."[32] No small list for these home seekers, and one whose precision requires both memory and intelligence to fulfill.

Implementing video equipment, Seeley and his colleagues worked with smaller swarms of about 4,000 bees, identified each bee, and recorded each dance performed by each bee scout (Lindauer's solo and nonvideotaped reports of each scout's first dance closely matched those of Seeley's team, a tribute to Lindauer's tenacity and commitment in initiating this research). At first, the researchers considered the "tempting" hypothesis of consensus—an agreement of dancing scouts—forming among the bees. Two details, however, began to chip away at that conclusion. No evidence for the scout bees polling their fellow dancers was visible, and occasionally the swarm launched into flight when there were still two strong nest-site contenders left. What if a quorum—a sufficient number of scouts—was used? The bees' behavior after the quorum is reached, called "piping," is understood. This special high-pitched sound signaling the nonscouts to begin warming their flight muscles takes over an hour. Because of this, usually, there is enough time for the quorum to shift to a consensus before the entire swarm takes flight. How the scout bees *know* there is a quorum is still not understood, but how the best nest is chosen is. The bees fly to the new nest in unison. Seeley and his colleagues, however, affirm that a quorum "is the essence of the bee's group decision-making process."[33]

I can hear you asking, How is this creative? Is voting creative? Well, it depends on how one comes to cast one's vote. How do bees collectively choose the best home? For humans, collectively making good decisions is often fraught with dissent. Compromising may involve only a few requirements to make a successful decision. More often, the process results in a complete stalemate. If you have sat on a committee, you will know this to be true. But there are times when things seem to flow. Members appear more open to innovative strategies, or they listen and try to understand others' positions. The resulting decisions are sizeable improvements over those emanating from committees where discord rules the day. Thinking of creativity as a wide-angle perspective through which to consider various intentions is what the creative process is all about. Today's business culture has embraced creative process theory, or at least its version of the theory, to boost sales. Seeley, after years of studying honeybees, suggests, "Bees' nest-site selection behavior can provide guidance on this topic, for it is clear they are successful at making collective judgments."[34]

His descriptions of the honeybees' successful decision-making process to find the best nest reads like a how-to for creative decision making. He offers three significant factors bees rely on to make a successful decision. The first rests on how the group of scouts, up to several hundred members, is organized in a decentralized way. There is no individual or small group of leaders; rather, each scout is a free agent able to search independently. This allows for the collection of a profusion of alternative nest sites from which to choose. The scouts share all their suggestions through waggle dancing, from those suggestions that are poor to the few that seem to fit the bill. This ensures that the best possible site will be considered.

The second factor is the competition that ensues among the scouts advertising for their particular alternative. Soon there are adherents to some of the sites, and these small-group alliances recruit new members by performing waggle dances varying in enthusiasm for the quality of the site. One particularly important indicator of the value of this process is that when an uncommitted scout is recruited to a site, she first examines the site herself, and if she deems it worthy, only then does she dance to recruit more bees to the cause. This independence of judgment is essential for such an important decision.

The third factor is how the quorum-sensing process, which Seeley admits is still a puzzle, provides a balance between the independent opinions of the scouts and the need to limit the time the colony is homeless. As Seeley explains, "Thus, the quorum-sensing method of aggregating the bees' information allows diversity and independence of opinion to thrive, but only long enough to ensure that a decision error is improbable."[35]

Knowing when to stop, when you are done with a creative project, is often one of the most difficult steps in the creative process. A poet friend of mine says she seldom finds satisfying the endings to the novels she reads. I know she means satisfying to her sense of what is excellent writing, but I can't help but think that life itself has so few satisfying endings. Perhaps novels, if the author is writing about the reality of life, are unable to offer an ending that mollifies our desire for "closure," a term that has come to mean the necessity of ending the grieving process so that one is able to move on, something that is often not even possible or healthy. Somewhere between my friend's need for a satisfyingly written ending and my need for the reality of an unsatisfying, but astute, last page is one example of a novel whose author knew when she was done. Somewhere between the bee scouts' search for the perfect home and one that was found within the constraints of bee reality is a bee colony that found a good-enough home just in time.

Honeybees meet their creative architectural demands collectively, accepting what is a good-enough home, while other species go it alone. The caddisfly larva, a leaf-rolling caterpillar, individual spiders, and carrier snails rely on their sense of what the perfect shelter looks like. But some, such as the male bowerbird, only know if what he has built is successful when the female bowerbird gives him the nod. That fact is essential to understanding why 20 different species of male bowerbirds build, well, their bowers.

The Architecture of Birds

Male bowerbirds of New Guinea and Australia are the avian architects of courtship. Carefully constructing thoughtfully planned and lavishly decorated bowers of several types, they also dance and sing, charming and seducing their possible mates. Increasingly expert and effective at their art over time (sometimes undergoing seven years of training before their methods work), some bowerbirds indirectly cultivate a particular type of berry plant. They use these particular berries not as food but as contributions to the decoration of their bowers, just as other kinds of bowerbirds add particular colors of glass shards to their seductive bowers.

You will notice that I have used the word "art" to describe this activity of male bowerbirds. I hear the catcalls (these may sound like the caws of catbirds, a genus of birds in the bowerbird family, so to be fair I should have found another description) from several battlements protecting the uniqueness of human intelligence and creativity. Even so, and being careful not to give ammunition to the skeptics perched on those battlements, asking whether it is appropriate to use the word "art" for what bowerbirds construct is a good question. Four of the scientists we have been leaning on in this chapter spend time with this quandary, and my sense is that we should as well.

Hansell, an evolutionary biologist, gives over the last chapter of his most recent book on animal architecture to bowerbirds, and his answer to the question of whether or not these are art is yes.[36] In *The Descent of Man and Selection in Relation to Sex*, Darwin discusses bowerbirds and their elaborate and beautiful bowers. He decides, "The Bower-birds by tastefully ornamenting their playing-passages with gaily-colored objects, as do certain humming-birds their nests, offer additional evidence that they possess a sense of beauty."[37] But, he wonders, usually "the taste for the beautiful" is limited to the attraction to the opposite sex. Darwin offers this example along with many others in proposing his theory of sexual selection through female choice, and, as it turns out, that theory is emerging as "Darwin's *really* dangerous idea."[38]

Griffin spends eight pages on bowerbirds and their constructions, summarizing research from Alan John Marshall, Jared Diamond, and Gerald Borgia, among others. In a few lines towards the end of the section he alludes to the birds' pleasure in the beauty they have made. He references von Frisch's observation: "It would be difficult to deny that impressing females motivates much human artistic creation."[39] The Goulds devote an entire chapter to "the ultimate example of architectural show, unconstrained by the need for conventional utility,"[40] the bower. They too ask whether bowers are an example of the aesthetic sense of delight shared by humans and animals, and answer positively.

You may think all this talk of art and aesthetics makes me happy. After all, it seems to prove my point that animals too are creative. Well, yes, but art and creativity should not be conflated into one category. Art and aesthetics are subsets of the creative process. The creative process emerges from and for countless endeavors. I recall a question Kroodsma asked: "If males are creative when they create songs, does that mean females are not creative?" For him, the word "creative" connotes humanly construed artistic activities that fit the creativity of animals neatly into our restrictions surrounding that concept. Is it art? Can animals feel aesthetic pleasure, defined here as pleasure at either making or recognizing something beautiful? Does that prove their creativity? My answer is that that kind of pleasure may be present in the creative process, but its inclusion is not a necessary ingredient. The creative behaviors of all animals are still not completely documented or understood. Creative behavior may emerge as a solution to a difficult problem, one not involved with pleasure at all. I reiterate my metaphor of creativity as a fluid process able to fill infinite containers.

In any case, Alfred Russel Wallace, Darwin's contemporary and colleague in evolutionary theory, lays out a crucial caveat about the building of bird nests in his essay "A Theory of Bird's Nests":

> The very general belief that every bird is enabled to build its nest, not by the ordinary faculties of observation, memory, and imitation, but by means of some innate and mysterious impulse, has had the bad effect of withdrawing attention from the very evident relation that exists between the structure, habits, and intelligence of birds, and the kind of nest they construct.[41]

At the time, these claims were controversial but now are evaluated much more sympathetically. The nests of Sociable Weaver birds and Baya Weaver birds are two of the more complex and structurally intricate nests made by birds.[42] Sociable Weavers, only found in southwest Africa, construct enormous structures over time—25 feet long, 15 feet wide, and five feet high. These last for many seasons; the longest known has been in use for 100 years. Each pair of weavers builds their own nest, not attached to their neighbors' nests but connected to the overall structure. All the birds share responsibility for the thatched roof.[43] Baya Weavers' elegant nests hide their intense stability and capacity to withstand tropical storms. The entrance to the nest is a delicately interwoven tunnel leading to the main chamber, allowing the birds to live in luxury while guarding against predators.[44]

Male bowerbirds' nests, however, are concerned not with nesting but with display. The males who build them are concerned with the details of seduction, and the bowers they build are where they practice these skills, eventually turning all those specifics into the fleeting permission from a female to mate. The unique twenty species of bowerbirds build essentially three different kinds of bowers.[45] The first and simplest is the stage. Only two species build stages, and that word hardly fits when compared to the other kinds of construction. The Tooth-billed Bowerbird, one of two species that build stages, is found only in the tropical forest of northeast Queensland, where he clears debris from a level area of the forest floor. There he carefully arranges large, pale leaves, shiny side up, after he has cut them with his notched bill. He will replace these as their sheen and color fade. He also chooses a perch where he will sing his mix-tape of both harsh and melodious songs all day.

The avenue is probably the most written about and videotaped kind of bower. The Western Bowerbird, who inhabits the outback of the Northern Territory and Western Australia, builds two parallel walls of thin sticks that curve gracefully at the bottom towards the avenue itself. Western Bowerbirds are only about 11 inches in length from beak to tail, but the bowers reach 12 to 15 inches in height. The walls of the bower are lined inside the avenue with dried grass. Within and on both ends of the avenue, the male has amassed and organized all kinds of decorative (at least to him) materials, such as bones, pieces of glass, colored berries, shiny pebbles, shells, man-made materials like straw, buttons, bottle caps, spoons, coins, and glass eyes (trying to imagine how that happened gave me hours of fun) in pleasing arrangements. Sometimes the decorations surround the bower as well. The bird paints the straw-colored grass of the base of the avenue with a mixture of saliva and finely chewed particles of grass. Some bowerbirds use twigs to apply this paint, an example of tool use in birds.

Male Satin Bowerbirds, found only in the forests of Queensland and Victoria, Australia, also build an avenue bower by first making a round platform with sticks and then attaching two parallel walls of sticks, forming an incomplete arch in graceful and symmetrical sweeps on both sides. Since the bower avenue aligns in a north-south direction, the display platform at the north and sunny end allows his incredible decorating ability to shine along with his song and dance talent.

This platform is decorated with mostly blue objects. Red is never used. Shards of blue glass, blue paper, blue bottle caps, blue plastic straws, blue toothbrushes, as well as blue tail feathers from the crimson rosella parrot are carefully placed by the male. At times he stands back to consider his placement choice only to move it to a more appropriate location.[46]

The Satin Bowerbird favors snail shells in their more muted brown and yellow casts, however, and yellow leaves are sometimes added. One theory links the choice of blue ornaments to the blue iridescence of the Satin Bowerbird himself.[47] Other theories look to the increased contrast between the decoration collection and the platform, while the UV-reflecting subset of bottle tops and feathers may increase contrast within the decoration collection itself. Either way, the Satin Bowerbird appears to understand color contrast. Like the Western Bowerbird, the Satin paints the lower quarter of the inside of the bower walls. Saliva mixed with crushed bark, ground-up charcoal, and blue Dianella berries that eventually turn black is painted on in fibrous wads. The females nibble on the dried paint when spending time in the bower.[48]

The Vogelkop Bowerbird is the best-known maypole builder. Living in the mountains of the Vogelkop Peninsula of Western New Guinea, Indonesia, the Vogelkop weaves sticks and orchid stems into a tower that surrounds one or sometimes two leafless saplings. He then constructs a circular canopy of interlocking sticks reaching up to six and a half feet tall, quite a feat since males are only ten inches long. The entrance to the canopy is a gracefully curved arch entrance in front of which the Vogelkop assembles groups of unique and color-grouped items, including colored fruits, black beetle wing cases, black bracket fungi, deer droppings, and flowers of all kinds. Recent bowers have included all kinds of human trash, again grouped into piles of similar kind and color.[49]

The male's commitment to his mission and his vision is admirable, as he spends up to nine months on the gardening phase of the bower. Discarding wilting flowers or rotting fruits, trimming fungus from deer droppings, and then traveling to retrieve novel replacements keeps the male busy until the females are ready to visit. One of the reasons why so much time and attention is spent on the bower and decorations is that the Volgelkop is very plain and doesn't dance or sing well. Since this is true for Vogelkops in general, the competition to dazzle females with colorful and unusual decorations on their massive and well-built bowers is very high, with males often raiding their neighbors' bowers for stolen decorations.[50]

Bowerbird researchers Laura Kelly and John Endler have done extensive work on male Great Bowerbirds' use of forced perspective to create illusions with their bower decorations. These avenue bowerbirds favor large piles of grey stones and white bones at either end of the avenue. The birds arrange the objects in the entrance courts so that they increase in size as the distance from the bower increases. Since the female sits within the bower while the male Great Bowerbird plies his seductive wares, what she sees is what is called "forced perspective." In other words, the males are violating the assumption that objects in the distance appear smaller. What is particularly fascinating about this, other than that birds can tweak assumptions about distance in their arrangements, is that the males who create the higher quality of these kinds of illusions mate with more females than males whose illusion-creating abilities are not quite so expert.[51]

In another example of male bowerbirds' commitment to their art, animal behaviorist Joah Madden and a team of researchers have determined that Spotted Bowerbirds living in Tauton Park of Central Queensland use fruits from the potato bush not as food but as decoration for their bowers. While this is the first instance of an animal directly or indirectly cultivating a plant for a nonfood use (ants cultivate fungus to eat, for instance), Madden considers this in the indirect category. Plants appear at bower locations after the males have installed themselves there, and the fruit of these plants differs visually from the fruit of plants further away. The mutual benefits of cultivation between Spotted Bowerbirds and potato bushes provide the male bowerbirds with more fruit to exhibit in their bowers, and the plants gain better germination sites when they are used as decorations.[52]

We have been focusing on the male bowerbirds and their building and decorating abilities. But what about the females? What part do they play in all of this, besides birthing the babies and then taking on complete responsibility for their survival? On the basis of Darwin's thoughts, Griffin, Hansell, and the Goulds initiate a discussion about what role female preference plays in the male's building and decorating, and sometimes dancing and singing activities. The Goulds' phrasing concerning art would rankle many artists I know:

> And yet, if any aspect of human behavior can be divorced from utilitarian purpose—if, for instance, art may be said to be simply a useless sensory or neurological extravagance, a pleasure-inducing stimulus whose roots in natural selection are obscure at best—then the ontogeny, individual variation, construction methods, and preferences associated with bowers may be very close to crossing some important line between the mental experiences of humans and other animals.[53]

In the end, they insist that evolution selects for smarter birds. In other words, the females are making mating choices on the basis of signs of intelligence. A male's response to the constant raiding and destruction of competitive bowers is also a factor, the Goulds contend, as is how well the bower shields the female from the sometimes-aggressive displays of the male.

While the writers mentioned here and others have similar questions about bowerbird architecture, many answers rely on, frankly, outdated definitions for those two terms, "art" and "aesthetics." While I cannot go into the profuse details of the history of this change, suffice it to say that humans have enlarged the boundaries of what constitutes art and aesthetics over the past century to include qualities other than beauty, such as justice, ethics, politics, identity, evolution, environmental aesthetics, and computation, to name only a few. Even so, those terms still relate to human standards of what those words mean. Trying to understand the creative lives of animals only through constantly shifting human notions of art and aesthetics is not particularly helpful. However, the concepts of pleasure and desire seem to be more universal. What is desired and gives pleasure comes in all kinds of packages. The recognition of cognitive abilities and creative abilities of both male and female bowerbirds has opened up the understudied area of how species use cognitive abilities in mate selection to researchers Gerald Borgia and Jason Keagy, among others.[54]

For male bowerbirds to meet the aesthetic requirements of female bowerbirds—and their ability to reproduce centers on this—they must be able to understand what it is a female wants. What colors will draw her in? Will the bower allow her to feel secure and protected while watching the male sing, dance, throw things around, and make a fool of himself? Will the bower itself impress her? Will she hang around long enough for a bit of shagging?

Other recent evolutionary-biology thinking recalibrates how aesthetic judgment might work for animals. One of the most interesting and contentious ideas comes from Richard O. Prum, a Yale ornithologist and evolutionary behaviorist. He has taken Darwin's original sexual selection proposal, that mostly female animals choose their mates based on their evaluations of male display traits, very seriously. Prum insists that the really revolutionary meaning of Darwin's theories lies within his use of aesthetic language to describe how these capacities in various species "evolved differences in mating preference that could be merely pleasing for their own sake and without any other value, meaning, or utility."[55] Prum realizes that sexual selection is accepted as an evolutionary driver but calls the arbitrariness of these choices "Beauty Happens." He insists that the pleasure animals take in their choices of what is "beautiful to them" is the driver not only of their evolution as a species but of biodiversity itself. That idea is crucial to my argument that animals are creative in individual, species, cultural, and biodiverse ways, and we will come back to it in more detail later.

Creative Tool Use

But first, I want to touch on creative tool use. Like language, tool use was once thought of as one more reason why humans are not only different from animals but also better. However, just as new research has increasingly shown many instances of animal language, so has new research grown around identifying tool use in multiple species. Most research articles detailing tool use in animals still start with a roundup of various perspectives on what constitutes a tool and what forms of cognition and experience are linked to using it. The fact that animals across kingdoms use tools, however, is no longer a shock to the human sense of self. In the foreword to the revised and updated version of *Animal Tool Behavior*, Gordon Burghardt defines tool use as "a major cognitive and behavioral component of 'mental evolution,'" referring to the titles of George John Romanes's late-nineteenth-century works comparing the cognitive processes of human and nonhuman animals. Burghardt sees tool manufacture and use less as what he calls "progressive creativity" and more as ad hoc solutions to novel problems. I see his point, but again, if we are searching for evidence of the creative process, some of these examples seem to fit. Also, if the behavior catches on in a larger group, we may use it as evidence of culture, as in the case of the Indo-Pacific dolphins of Shark Bay detailed below.

Our closest relatives, chimpanzees, have used long stripped twigs to insert into termite mounds to "fish" for termites. Termites clung to the twig in the case of David Graybeard, a chimp whom Jane Goodall named while in Gombe, as he picked them off with his lips and ate them up. Chimps, it turns out, use a variety of tools they make, including using stones as hammers or anvils to break open fruit, branches to make spears, or leaves to drink with. Ancient stone tools used by chimpanzees dated 4,300 years ago have been found, leading to questions about cultural transmission of tool use by chimpanzees through millennia.[56] Lest we assume that these innovations are accomplished by only the males of the species, research by Jill Pruetz and colleagues on savannah chimpanzees at Fongoli, Sénégal, has documented unique tool-assisted hunting of vertebrate prey, done mostly by females. Adolescents of both sexes learn to use tools from their mothers.[57]

While tool use is not thought of as universal among animals of all species, at least as far as our knowledge and assumptions about tool use have taken us, examples are found in mammals, fish, birds, amphibians, reptiles, cephalopods, and invertebrates. New Caledonian crows craft hooked tools from branches, both in captivity and in the wild. A recent study on these crows discovered that the depth of the hook was directly related to both the properties of the plant material and the technique crows used for detaching branches. Carefully controlling cutting with their sharp beaks, crows are able to craft deep and more useful hooks than are used by chimpanzees, leaving more wooden material at the tip of the stick to "sculpt." It was also found that older, more experienced crows often use what the lead researcher called "a quick and dirty" technique that did not produce the deepest hook. These hooks got the job done but in half the time, while not breaking off in narrow holes and crevices.[58]

Elephants use branches to swat flies, chew branches into balls to plug up a waterhole for future use, move items for standing on to reach food that is out of reach, and as Joyce Poole relates in *Coming of Age with Elephants*, have used large rocks to drop on an electric fence to cut off the electricity.[59]

A community of Indo-Pacific bottlenose dolphins in Shark Bay, Australia, place conical sponges over their rostrums to protect themselves when foraging for fish that burrow in the ocean floor. This behavior, which researchers have dubbed "sponging," seems to be culturally transmitted, perhaps from mother to offspring. The same community of dolphins occasionally uses conch shells to scoop up fish from the sea floor, carrying them back to the surface where the fish can be retrieved.[60]

Corolla spiders place seven or eight small stones in a single-layered circle around the entrance to their burrows. The carefully selected stones are affixed to the burrow by silk threads and serve as foraging tools since they allow the spiders to extend their sensory range by monitoring the vibrations passed through the stones.[61]

We know that crocodiles not only are good hunters but are also playful. They have been added to the list of reptiles who use tools after recent research found that they used lures, such as sticks, to catch nesting birds. Granted, that list is short, but researchers see this example as more insight into the complexity of reptiles we have previously ignored.[62]

The archerfish's ability to shoot water spouts at targets such as insects, spiders, lizards, bits of raw meat, man-made models of appropriate prey, observers' eyes, and lit cigarettes, all done with great aplomb and careful aim preparation by older, experienced archerfishes, guarantees that they almost always meet their target.[63]

Unfortunately, amphibian tool use has not been widely seen or reported, though horned frogs have been known to use vegetation to cover themselves in preparation for the advance of a predator, and if the vegetation doesn't do the job, then kicking little mounds of dirt over themselves with their feet seems to do the trick.[64]

Octopuses have been seen hiding in shells by researchers and divers before, but in 2009 Julian Finn and his colleagues videotaped a veined octopus spreading his soft body over coconut shells he had neatly stacked. He then made his eight arms rigid. In this way, he was able to carry the whole stack above the sea floor by stilt walking long distances to use the shells later as shelters or lairs. Spending 500 diver hours deep off the coasts of Northern Sulawesi and Bali in Indonesia, the group studied more than 20 veined octopus individuals, some of whom had traveled great distances (up to 20 meters) while carrying stacked coconut shells. Finn and his group concluded that since the octopus is exposing his head and body while carrying the shells, the future use of the shells as shelters or lairs must seem worth it.[65] This obvious use of foresight distinguishes this activity as tool use for Finn and his group, as well as other researchers who see this as a clear signal of the ability to plan. The continuing debate about future-oriented cognition revolves around whether or not animals, like humans, mentally travel in time and see themselves in the future. Tool use, and I would add building, offer profuse examples of animals who plan for the future, whether or not we can prove somehow that they project images of themselves into the future. Imagining oneself in the future is not prophecy, but a mental construction, often visual, and based on memories of the past. So knowing that animals plan future actions relating to past experiences would seem to be valuable information about the ability of certain animals to do just that in their creative process, even if the goal is revenge.

Imagine that you are an intelligent and creative being. Well, of course, you are. I knew that. But, imagine that you are intelligent and creative and you have been kept captive in a zoo enclosure for twenty years. Half the year, there is snow covering your outside enclosure, and so the humans who come to stare at you for the rest of the year are gone. You love this part of the year for that reason, but then you hear the birds chirping, you feel and see the snow melting, and before you know it, there are those humans again who laugh and point at you and generally make your days miserable. They make you so angry that at night you begin to plan how to get back at them, make them move away, and force them to treat you with respect. They seem to know nothing about your position as the highest-ranking male in the troop with which you share the enclosures, one of the few things that make your life as a captive chimpanzee bearable.

Santino, a captive chimpanzee, whose motives I have imagined, has been observed for a decade by three senior chimpanzee caretakers and Mathias Osvarth, a cognitive zoologist at Lund University documenting real-life reactions to zoo life.[66] Keepers noticed that Santino, also the dominant male chimpanzee, began an increased program of stone throwing across the water moat surrounding one end of his outdoor enclosure. He consistently aimed these projectiles at zoo visitors gathered in front of the moat, evoking reactions from the crowd and often getting them to move away. The zoo staff decided to check his enclosure and found five caches of three to eight stones each, most located along the shore facing the public view. One of the caretakers, hiding in a blind for five days, watched Santino gathering stones from the water before the zoo opened for the public and then later in the day using those same stones as weapons in his daily war of repulsion.

One of the more interesting discoveries was Santino's exploitation of the concrete rocks located at the center of the island. Osvarth explains that in subarctic zoos, such as those in Sweden, surface layers of concrete structures may detach due to water entering and freezing and causing micro-cracks only detected by knocking on damaged areas to listen for hollow sounds. Santino gathered up his concrete fragments by gently knocking on these areas to find where he might hit harder to break off the detached concrete. No one had shown him how to do this. He had detected this method himself and creatively incorporated it and its results into his overall plan.

For researchers who attempt to decide whether an animal's behavior indicates planning for a future state, "the predominant mental state during the planning must deviate from the one experienced in the situation that is planned for."[67] Santino was always calm while collecting his arms, in contrast to his male-chimp-typical aroused state when throwing the stones at visitors. Knowing that the zoo staff did not like this behavior, he began hiding his stones under heaps of hay as well as pretending to be calm and disinterested in front of visitors until it was too late for them to back away.

This particular example of future planning and tool use encapsulates a fair number of rebuttals to still-existing critiques of the possibility of future-oriented cognition in animals. Osvarth and Gemma Martin-Ordas, in an article about research on future-oriented thinking in animals, offer copious examples of this kind of thinking in animals, concluding,

> No one today would ask whether animals have physical cognition, or—for social animals—whether they have social cognition. What one finds instead in these areas is a variety of theories, paradigms, and evolutionary accounts. We suggest that future-oriented cognition should best be understood as referring to a research interest rather than any singular skills or real state of the world.[68]

Osvarth and Ordas add an astute philosophical speculation to the concluding paragraph, which speaks to the continuing resistance not only to understanding animals' inner lives but also to misapprehending our own:

One cannot help but wonder whether researchers themselves get fooled into thinking that it is actually possible to think about the future, owing to our cultural constructs of time and our remarkable skills in affecting future outcomes, thereby coming to believe in a distinct type of cognition that deals with the future in a way detached from the current moment.[69]

Gifts from Crows

Staying in the present moment is not a state of being many humans are adept at. My friend and colleague, artist Julie Andreyev, has written about her relationship with the crows that live in her neighborhood and how their creativity has impacted hers. Staying in the present moment with the crows and her interactions with them has opened up a deep well of creativity for her and, as it turns out, for the crows. Andreyev thinks of this as an interspecies art-making process. But, unlike many of the summaries about the aesthetics of animals discussed above, Andreyev's conclusion is a unique perspective on an aesthetic sense that might be shared in animals and humans. In a discussion with her, Andreyev described the changes her experiences with the crows have encouraged: "The creativity of the crows has had a significant impact on my own creativity; in my day-to-day relatings with the crows, in my relatings with the rest of the world, and in how I approach art making."[70] Interestingly, though the action is not unheard of, a crow left a pebble on her roof balcony in Vancouver, British Columbia, where Andreyev lives.[71] Having been in the practice of leaving plates of stones filled with water for the crows, Andreyev realized that the pebble had been left exactly where she would notice it when sitting on the deck chair overlooking distant Grouse and Seymour Mountains on the other side of Burrard Inlet. A growing comfort emerged on both sides as they collaborated in a playful but meaningful game with stones. Arranging and rearranging the stones, Andreyev began to sense a change taking place in herself and her relationship with the animals in her immediate surroundings.

The unexpected gifts from the crows, particularly the first pebble, and the subsequent stone play interactions, affected me in a way I wasn't expecting. For instance, just realizing that the crow had left the initial small pebble as a gesture of appreciation created a whole new feeling for me in relation to other animals around my home. I realized how playful and generous these birds can be, and how important it is to think about kinship with other animals in the neighborhood.[72]

The crow began to leave other kinds of gifts, for that is what Andreyev began to see them as: a pair of earplugs, a beautiful piece of lichen-covered tree bark, a nail, a deck screw, a set of barnacle shells, a pine cone, two pieces of white beach glass, set somewhere on the rooftop where they would be noticed, often next to the food or water Andreyev was leaving out for the crows. What I find particularly striking in Andreyev's comments about this process is her admitting, "Excitement and doubt alternated in my mind."[73] At work here is the doubt that has been instilled in most of us that animals do not have their own sense of gratefulness, or that somehow they cannot communicate with others, including humans, in other ways than through speech. The functionalist view that permeates our observations of animals' behaviors is so ingrained that we have a difficult time allowing our senses to perceive what is actually happening. Andreyev, however, continuing to develop her attentiveness in her growing relationship with the crow, came to a discovery, one that I have not found in any of the scientific literature I have been reading, but I argue that it is just as valuable an observation.

> Some of these items we can imagine coming across in the urban environment and considering them trash, and just ignore them. But with the crows, I came to understand that each item had meaning. . . . The commonly held view that birds do not use objects to communicate closes down any possibility of noticing how birds may use objects, and how their use of objects generates meaning.[74]

We do not give meaning to the lives of animals; they are able and willing to do that themselves. They plan their future, build their homes, fabricate bowers for their beloveds, defend themselves from predators they fear, take revenge on humans who anger them, leave gifts in thanks, and in doing so create all kinds of tools. Their lives have meaning for them. To their detriment and ours, we have until recently dismissed and neglected the critical importance of that knowledge.

5

Sexual Exuberance

Ratchet-Pointing, Water Dancing, and Same-Sex Enjoyment

Throughout the living world whenever the opportunity has arisen, the subjective experiences and cognitive choices of animals have aesthetically shaped the evolution of biodiversity.
—Richard O. Prum, *The Evolution of Beauty*

I will skip all the gnarly comparisons with human sexuality I might have written about when describing the mating of leopard slugs; their coupling is so spectacularly choreographed and unique that it needs no metaphorical depiction. Leopard slugs, so called because of their leopard spots, possess male and female sexual organs. Mating begins by circling each other in a slow, sometimes two-and-a-half-hour dance. It continues as the two slugs climb into a high place, perhaps a tree, and secrete a thick "rope" of mucous approximately a meter long. Both using their mucous ropes to lower themselves, they gracefully entwine their bodies as they move down along the rope. They then turn their sexual organs—for mating they use their penises, which emerge from their heads—inside out from the back so that the organs, blue, white, and glossy, can meet and entwine, producing a beautiful flower-like structure that enables each slug to insert a sperm sac into the body of its mate. This incredibly sensual and elegant performance ends with one leopard slug crawling up the slime thread while eating it, so that the other one drops to the ground.[1]

The sheer ebullience of this example of animal sensuality is one of the countless instances of what biologist Bruce Bagemihl has called "biological exuberance." Extravagantly diverse natural processes that could have been accomplished more conservatively instead result in uncounted numbers of examples of sexual variety and choice.[2] The limits of the profusion of obviously pleasurable sexual activity have in no way been reached, nor have all its progeny been accounted for. While this kind of activity might be categorized as examples of evolutionary patterns, Bagemihl's phrase points to the extraordinary variability and sheer inventiveness of a universal creativity in which both animals and humans exist. This emerging view is supported by research in which animals are seen as sophisticated decision makers creatively involved in their own sexual choices.[3] Serving as a taste of this larger and more communal sense of creativity we all share as creative sexual beings, the following examples provide glimpses of how animals use their creative impulses to drive variation in sexual behavior and individual choice. Let's begin with a pocket-sized overview of just how varied animal sexual lives may be.

Blue Penises and Anti-Aphrodisiacs

In just that one description of leopard slug sex on a rope, we find a slew of possibilities for creative sexuality. "Hermaphrodite" is a term once used disparagingly for humans who are born with a reproductive or sexual anatomy that does not seem to fit the typical definitions of female or male. The current preferred usage for humans is "intersex" since the word "hermaphrodite" is considered not only misleading but stigmatizing, as well as "scientifically specious and clinically problematic."[4] In the animal kingdom, true hermaphrodites are the proud owners of both female and male reproductive systems. The largest group of pure hermaphrodites is found in invertebrates, such as slugs and worms, but can be found in fish species, such as lantern fish, hamlets, and deep-sea lizardfish. "Simultaneous hermaphroditism" is another term used to describe individuals who mate as both male and female, exchanging both sperm and eggs. After their acrobatic coupling, each leopard slug lays up to 200 eggs that look like a small bunch of soap bubbles. Some hermaphrodites do fertilize themselves, but many species prefer the mutual exchange of eggs and sperm. When I first read about those relatively giant blue slug penises, I wondered if they had perhaps influenced Margaret Atwood's description of the blue Crakers, the biogenetically engineered new species of humans crafted by one of the characters in her MaddAddam trilogy.[5] Unabashed delight in what would have been considered a transgressive sexual experience among humans is the attitude Atwood seemed to be going for.

But wait. Other kinds of hermaphroditic sexual activity need to be explored. Just as Virginia Woolf's Orlando—the character in Woolf's *novel of the same name*—changed sex for each lifetime, some hermaphrodites begin their lives as one sex, but then later switch to another. In contrast with simultaneous hermaphroditism, this is called "sequential hermaphroditism," in which animals can develop first as male and then switch to female or vice versa. An example would be the clownfish, around which the story of Pixar's *Finding Nemo* was written.[6] At the very beginning of the film version, Nemo's mother is killed by a barracuda while his parents are watching their eggs. He is raised by his father until he explores too far past the anemone where they live and is lost. In the real lives of clownfish, if Nemo's mother was killed, his father would turn into a female since he must now raise the eggs alone. Nemo would be born a male and when grown a bit would mate with his father, now a female. This is a decidedly different reality from the narrative of the Pixar version.

Virgin birth, or parthenogenesis, predates cloning and the religious variety by a hundred million years or so. All members of a parthenogenetic species are female, and so can produce eggs, but do not need sperm for fertilization. While there are a few deviations from this simple definition, a few examples lend a more subjective tint to what might seem an asexual activity. While it is true that most parthenogenic species do not have sex with each other, same-sex trysts do exist among some species. Bagemihl tells us, "In some species, such as the Amazon Molly and the Whiptail Lizard, females actually court and mate with one another, even though no eggs or sperm are exchanged in such encounters."[7]

Sometimes, virgin births indicate a more prudent attitude towards same-sex involvement. Facultative parthenogenesis (FP) is a type of virgin birth in which a female can reproduce both sexually or asexually. In a recent study of spiny leaf stick insects of Australia, females that were able to mate with a male chose not to do so. It was thought that females may transition to virgin births, or parthenogenesis, because of the scarcity of males, but in this study Nathan Burke and his colleagues tested the hypothesis that virgin births may happen when same-sex interactions are costly. The research team found this to be the case, as predicted by what is called the "sexual conflict" theory:

> Females resisted matings by curling their abdomens and kicking their legs during copulation attempts, pre-reproductive virgin females produced an anti-aphrodisiac that repelled males, and parthenogenetic females made themselves inconspicuous to males by altering their pheromonal signals.[8]

Virgin births in captivity have been studied since the 1800s, when it was found that domesticated female turkeys produced unfertilized eggs that produced live young. A parthenogenetic strain of turkeys was then developed, producing males that appeared normal and reproduced successfully. Since then, virgin births have been documented in captive sharks, Komodo dragons, fishes, and lizards. In 2012, biologists Warren Booth, Gordon Schuett, and their colleagues discovered the first cases of FP in wild-collected pregnant females and their offspring of two closely related species of North American pit viper snakes—the copperhead and the cottonmouth. The authors were particularly interested to find support for their view that the origins of parthenogenesis, such as FP, are more common in snakes and lizards than previously thought. With this confirmation, FP can no longer be viewed as a rare curiosity outside the mainstream of vertebrate evolution. In 2015, an ongoing study by Andrew Field and colleagues documented virgin births in a normally sexually producing wild vertebrate, the smalltooth sawfish, a large, critically endangered ray.[9] Virgin births: that phrase has less of the baggage that has caused other kinds of sexual behavior in animals to be ignored, censored, or misinterpreted over much of the last two hundred years.

"Explaining (Away) Animal Homosexuality"

That is what Bagemihl entitled the fourth chapter of his 700-page seminal book. Researchers, naturalists, and almost anyone who has watched captive or wild animals at length have reported same-sex sexual behavior. While same-sex behavior does not fall into the creative category in and of itself, Bagemihl highlights the fact that same-sex-behavior activities have often been classified as dominance or aggressive behavior, as a form of play, as tension reducers, or even as greetings by researchers, thereby negating any interpretation of these behaviors as fundamentally sexual. In many cases, these categorizations were more about the researcher's inability or unwillingness to engage with the sexual nature of the behavior itself. Even if, Bagemihl argues, animal same-sex sexuality may have elements of any or all of these other forms of activity, those possibilities do not eliminate or cancel out its sexual aspect:

> Astounding as it sounds, a number of scientists have actually argued that when a female Bonobo wraps her legs around another female, rubbing her own clitoris against her partner's while emitting screams of enjoyment, ... this is almost anything, it seems, besides *pleasurable sexual* behavior.[10]

As in playing simply for the pleasure, engaging in sexual activity simply *because* it feels good is a reason that seems to have eluded the majority of researchers when it comes to asking why two animals of the same sex might engage in any number of nonprocreative but sexually stimulating activities. As Jonathan Balcombe says in his wonderful book, *Pleasurable Kingdom*, while same-sex sexual behavior is clearly a bad idea from a strictly procreational standpoint, 300 species of vertebrates are known to practice it.[11] According to a more recent article, five research biologists place that number at 1500, and that is a low estimation.[12]

What does this have to do with creativity, you might ask? What both Bagemihl and Balcombe are alluding to, as did Darwin, is that many animals are capable of choosing sexual behavior that does not necessarily rely on "fitness" or, for that matter, the need to procreate. Economically based explanations have obscured our understanding of how animals make individual choices. Like play, sexuality is often a driver of creative behavior. If we want to understand how creative animals are, we need to admit that individual animals can choose what gives them sexual pleasure, and sometimes, emotional connection as well. Individual animals exhibit creative behavior in many ways, and for many reasons. Including sexual behavior is an important step in understanding not only the creativity of animals but also, as we shall see later when discussing the work of Richard O. Prum and sexual selection, just how important those individual choices are for the evolution of biodiversity.

Saying that animals engage in many sexual activities is a bit of a vague understatement. The profusion of inventive sexual activity in animals may result in reproduction, but also in sexual activities given various names by scientists: serial polyandry, sexual trios and quartets, self-sex changing, cannibalism, incest, masturbatory tool creation, beak-genital propulsion, and same-sex bonding, to name just a few examples. Take the Red-Necked Phalarope. She is an example of serial polyandry in which one female gets exclusive mating rights with multiple males. The female is larger, is more brightly colored, and is the dominant partner who courts the male, fights off other females, and establishes the breeding territory in the low Arctic. While these birds prefer to copulate in water, often out at sea, the male is happy to be the one to incubate the eggs and feed the young in scrapes on mounds or tussocks near inland water. Once the clutch is laid, the female flies off to mate with someone else.[13]

Angler fish are another example of female polyandry. In comparison to what male angler fish endure, the fathering life of male Red-Necked Phalaropes is quite pleasant. The male angler fish, who is quite small, searches for a female so that he can latch onto her using his tiny sharp teeth to dig into her skin. Over time, other males latch on as well, with females connected to as many as six males, all of whom begin to fuse physically with the female, connecting to her skin and bloodstream, first losing their faces and then all internal organs, but not the testes, which is all that is left. Her eggs need to be fertilized, after all.[14]

During the breeding season from January to March, male walruses are solidly heterosexual, courting and mating with female walruses. Come summer and early fall, however, males gather together on haul-outs to court, having sexual and affectionate activities as they float in the water, buoyed by special inflatable sacs in their throats that act like life vests. Rubbing their bodies together, embracing with their front flippers, touching noses, and generally lolling about together, males sometimes even sleep together in long chains, each spooning the next from behind. Males display for other males using the same behaviors as when court-ing females. They bob their heads, using those throat pouches for court-ship "songs" made up of knocks, bells, and whistles. Sometimes older males will sing their courtship songs to a group of younger males, ac-companied by a single young male who dives in synchrony with him.[15]

Simultaneous same-sex sexual behavior (SSB) and different-sex sex-ual behavior (DSB) exist in many species of mammals, birds, waterfowl, and marine animals.[16] Timing plays a role in this kind of sexual behav-ior. Same-sex and opposite-sex activity may happen in small groups, as in pile-up copulations, in which a male is mounting a male who is mounting a female, or in larger group activities. At the other end of the spectrum, individuals may both court and mate with same-sex and different-sex partners in short bouts of time. Between those extremes are a multitude of variations. Bagemihl clarifies, "Each individual within a population generally exhibits a unique sexual orientation profile, con-sisting of his or her own particular combination of same- and opposite-sex activity."[17] Each individual within a species may fulfill the overall preference of the species, but individually exhibit varying degrees of same-sex enjoyment. For instance, all female bonobos engage in both SSB and DSB. According to data collected in one of the hundreds of peer-reviewed journal articles used by Bagemihl to support his landmark study, "The proportion of same-sex behavior exhibited by each of the females in one particular troop, varied between 33 percent and 88 percent (averaging 64 percent)."[18] Individual choice plays an important role in these variations. The females in another troop might fall into a higher or lower range.

Bagemihl lists averages for documented same-sex activity in female red deer, male bonnet macaques, pig-tailed macaques, and kob females that run from averages of 11 percent to 49 percent.[19] In other words, individual animals may engage in mostly same-sex behavior for only a few instances out of the year. Those numbers come from studies in which those behaviors were not only recognized but also counted, and as Bagemihl argues throughout his book, we are only now more willing to learn about DSB, SSB, and the variety of sexual behaviors listed above by unique names, existing across the animal kingdom. Bagemihl's book was published in 1999, yet a recent article by five biologists felt the need to propose an alternative theory for sexual behavior in animals, in contrast to the prevailing "heteronormative world view in which 'heterosexual' behaviour is framed as the 'natural order' for sexually reproducing species, and 'homosexuality' is viewed as a recent aberration whose existence must be explained and justified."[20] Instead, they propose that SSB is a widely spread ancestral behavior in selecting mates, rather than the costly sexual behavior it often is still assumed to be.

> Thus, we predict the astonishing diversity of sexual behaviours present in animals to be the result of varying degrees of adaptive and non-adaptive processes (including drift) acting on existing continuous variation in the extent of DSB or SSB expressed across individuals, populations and species.[21]

Same and Different

One of my favorite examples of the variations found in the use of self-sex-change ability is the rusty angelfish. According to coral reef ecologist

Marah J. Hardt in her insightful book, *Sex in the Sea*, female rusty angel-fish can transform themselves into males when need be. During the breeding season, males guard their harems of one to six females, pleasuring them nightly just before sunset. This is all delightful until another harem shows up and the male goes off to check out the new neighbors. Too much of this gallivanting about and the largest female in the first harem sometimes decides she has had enough. Since she is not using up her energy in pleasure, it shifts into growth, and in a few weeks, "she bursts forth in all her masculine glory and swims off with a number of her former harem."[22]

Another gripping example comes from the evolutionary biologist Olivia Judson in the form of one of the many letters she has received from the natural world asking for sex advice from her nom de plume, Dr. Tatiana. In Judson's book *Dr. Tatiana's Sex Advice to All Creation*, one letter, from "I Like 'Em Headless in Lisbon," asks, "I'm a European praying mantis, and I've noticed I enjoy sex more if I bite my lovers' heads off first. It's because when I decapitate them they go into the most thrilling spasms. Somehow they seem less inhibited, more urgent—it's fabulous. Do you find this too?"[23]

Cannibalism, Dr. Tatiana explains to the mantis, is just not her cup of tea, but then biologist Judson chimes in to explain that females in more than eighty species have been known to eat their paramours before, during, or after sex. Spiders have the most infamous reputation for this, but midges, those tiny flies sometimes called "no see-ums," also are notorious for their horrific idea of fun sex. A female captures a mate, stabbing his head with her proboscis while their genitalia link, using her spittle to turn his insides to liquid, which she drinks. She then drops his husk aside as if she never knew him, except for the fact that his male part has broken off inside her.[24]

What of incest? While diverse sexual activities between related individuals occur, Bagemihl explains that taboos against incest do exist, and while these have often been given as evidence of the biological basis of bans on incestuous sexual activity in humans, animal bans indicate that there is a cultural or social aspect in these decisions in animals.[25] Recent findings from research in Gombe National Park conclude, "We provide evidence that chimpanzees breed with genetically dissimilar mates and that inbreeding is uncommon even where opposite sex adult relatives reside together."[26] While researchers are unsure of how chimps can distinguish genetic closeness—perhaps smell, sound, or appearance— female chimps were able to tell which possible unfamiliar males were far removed from their family tree. They chose males unrelated genetically for their sexual partners during the part of a female's cycle when she is most likely to conceive.

While the following example of sexual creativity might have belonged in the chapter on creative architecture and tool use, only while working on this chapter did I learn that primates' ability to use tools extends into the sexual sphere. Both male and female primates have been recorded fashioning masturbatory tools in captivity and in the wild. Female orangutans may bite off just the right size of liana to insert in their vaginas, while one male was seen pushing a hole through a leaf with his finger. He then inserted his erect penis into the hole, rubbing the leaf up and down the shaft.[27] Bagemihl offers similar examples in chimpanzees and macaques. The manufacture and use of tools are regarded as arguments for culture in animals. These examples of masturbatory tools created by primates remind us of how the sexual drive is a significant motivation underlying creative activity.

Dolphins, like bonobos, have the reputation of being—how should I put this—erogenous. Dolphins seem to be even more wide ranging in their sexual behavior than bonobos. Here is Dr. Tatiana, explaining to a mother manatee asking for advice about her son, who kisses other male manatees:

> Or look at dolphins. The bottle-nosed dolphin is catholic in its choice of sex partners. Males are frequently sighted copulating with turtles . . . with sharks and eels. Eels? Yes, when a dolphin's penis is erect, it has a hook on the end—and many a male will use it to hook a writhing, struggling eel.[28]

This gets my vote for the most creative approach to a masturbatory tool I have found, though I cannot imagine that the eel would agree. Spinner dolphins are also the creators, as far as we know, of beak-genital propulsion, a lovely form of same-sexual swimming in which "one dolphin will insert its beak into the other's genitals and gently propel the two of them forward, maintaining penetration while they swim together. The pushee may also turn on its side or rotate belly up during this activity."[29]

Which brings us to same-sex pair bonding, at times a gentler and more affectionate side of animal sexual behavior, signaled by the word "bonding." Bagemihl lists three species of birds about which extensive tracking and documentation exist for same-sex long-term pair bonding. Pair bonds that have lasted up to 15 years in Greylag Geese and six years in Humboldt Penguins have been reported, while Silver Gulls may have several long-term same-sex partnerships during their lives.[30] Records point to fifteen other bird species having lifelong same-sex partnerships, from six years to the lower number of two or three due to the short life of the particular species. Animals often committing to the opposite sex for the long term include wolves, coyotes, black vultures, prairie voles, sandhill cranes, gibbons, bald eagles, albatrosses, barn owls, and beavers.

Coyotes living both in the wild and in urban areas are socially monogamous, pair bonding for many years, and exhibit behavior that speaks to this long-term union: remaining tied for twenty minutes after copulation, defending territories together, and participating in group howls. They produce a yearly litter, usually large, and care for their pups over a long dependency period. Both parents help with pup and den duties. They do not divorce, but only separate when one dies.[31] Janet Kessler, a naturalist and ethologist who has spent 13 years video-documenting the lives of coyotes in and around San Francisco, describes the behavior of a bonded pair in one of her videos of them:

> You'll see affectionate nudges and teasing, fond provocations, tender mouth clasps or little "kisses" and cuddling. This is what goes on between them when they're left alone and not having to constantly watch

over their shoulders for danger—mostly from dogs. The activity occurs throughout the year, not just during the reproductive season.[32]

Sexual choice in animals sometimes involves these long-lasting emotional bonds. The animals involved have made a choice to partner.

Do We Dance and Sing?

What of wooing? Singing, dancing, looking good—these attributes help the admirer to insinuate themselves into the prospective mate's heart, and if not the heart, at least their nether parts. One of the most striking videos I watched in my quest to track down and understand examples of creative mating behavior was of American alligators singing and dancing to impress a mate. Alligators do not have a reputation for being particularly charming. I, too, had a limited knowledge of alligators when canoeing in Florida. My ex-husband, a rather fearless ex-Marine, used to slow the canoe down and let whatever alligator was following us come as close as possible. I was 25 at the time and had spent little time in swamp environments, so this terrified me. I was sure we would be eaten. We were not, luckily, but I still maintain a healthy respect for alligators and their need for space when I see them in person. The mentioned video and back story exposed an entirely different side of alligators. They possess an elegant old-world charm of which I was unaware. For the last 170 million years, alligators have been displaying both vocally and visually to entice mates. American alligators produce very low-pitched rumbling roars, called "bellows," year-round, but most frequently during mating season. While in the water a male alligator raises his head out of the water in preparation for bellowing. He remains still for a moment and then initiates a gulping motion, visibly contracting his larynx, seeming to force air into his body. Then slowly immersing himself lower into the water, he raises his head to a 30- or 40-degree angle and arches his tail out of the water in a sultry curve. In this position, tensing his body, according to researcher Kent Vliet, he "produces an infrasonic signal so powerful that water 'dances' up around the alligator's torso."[33] The male bellows immediately following these sub-audible vibrations. While females may bellow back, only male alligators produce a "water dance." These commanding displays reliably demonstrate to other males and females how large an individual male is. Cognitive biologists at the University of Vienna, Stephan Reber and Tecumseh Fitch, found that the frequency of the bellows correlated with the actual size of the male.[34] Size matters among alligators.

Picture this. You are sitting on the banks of the Upper Klamath Lake in southern Oregon, United States. You are watching the various birds in the water and suddenly two of the ducks rise out of the water. Much to your surprise and incredulity, they appear to be running on the water in unison. Their long, arched necks are perfectly matched as they move through the water until diving headfirst below, only to come up again and start over.

These are not ducks; they are Western Grebes, and this lake is one of the most popular grebe breeding sites in the country. You have witnessed one of the most extraordinary mating dances in the world. Scientists call it "rushing," a dull word for what is a jaw-dropping performance of truly creative form and precision.[35] Western Grebes and Clark's Grebes, two unique species who not only cohabit in large colonies in summer and winter sites but also sometimes mate, are the practitioners of this awe-inspiring ritual. While there are other mating rituals that grebes perform, such as the Weed Dance and the Greeting Ceremony, the Rushing Dance is truly spectacular. This display is often prefaced by Advertising Calls, well-named descriptions of the loud one- or two-noted "creet" or "creet-creet" that lone birds emit while swimming. These calls are so distinctive and consistent that researchers have been able to recognize individual grebes just by hearing these calls. Other single courting birds repeatedly answer unpaired birds in the vicinity. Back-and-forth calling continues until two or more individuals find each other and start display sequences, such as tick-pointing, ratchet-pointing, and dip-shaking.

In a sequence lasting up to several minutes, birds involved in tick-pointing assume a rigid, head-erect alarm posture while smoothing their feathers and crest. They then turn their heads from side to side, expressing a series of sharp tick sounds at regular intervals, maintaining an individual rhythm. Four or five birds may join in, keeping their own rhythms. As the group converges, the ticking grows more rapidly until two birds face each other and may break into a parallel rush.

Ratchet-pointing appears aggressive and often is when it includes two males rather than a male and a female. Eye contact is the central precursor of this display. Holding their head low, with the crest raised forward and the throat bulging, one grebe will point its bill at another. Making a harsh, ratchet-like call (hence the ratchet-pointing categorization), birds may stare at each other while moving forward, at times beginning to dip shake, explained below, only to renew their staring. Sometimes, one bird may inch forward as the other retreats. This behavior also often reaches a climax with a rush. During these intense bouts of paired negotiation, other males try to disrupt the intimacy of staring by either skittering across the water towards the staring grebe or quietly diving beneath the water to attack the male. While facing each other, grebes dip their foreheads into the water and then raise them while wagging their bill from side to side. The dip shake ritual, performed by two males, a male and a female, or several males and a female, almost always ends up in rushing by two unpaired birds.

After these pre-foreplay rituals comes the rush, in which two or more grebes suddenly rise out of the water, turn, and propel themselves across the surface. With wings not extended or flapped, but lifted and held stiffly to the side, head extended in a gradual sine curve on an upright neck, the grebes not so much rush across the water as float above it. The syncopation of the earlier rituals is no match for the precise timing of this aerial water dance. The pull of gravity is replaced with a different force of nature, the need to procreate. Time stops while their dance alone holds the attention of all who witness it.

You Know You Like Psychedelic Smiley Faces.

I would be remiss to leave out the birds of paradise. Watching even a few videos of the over 40 species of these birds is an invitation into a world of intense color, both pigmented and structural, with shifting iridescence, dense black contrasts, unprecedented fine lines of spiral-shaped feathers, swaying oval shapes created with precision, grace, and flair. It is also an invitation to a new addiction, birds of paradise video viewing. Since 2004, Ed Scholes and Tim Laman have been researching and video documenting the entire 40 or so species of birds of paradise who live in New Guinea, the world's largest remaining tropical island, a few surrounding islands, and a small part of adjacent Australia. Scholes finished his PhD in evolutionary biology in 2006 and is now curator of video and a research associate at the Macaulay Library of the Cornell Lab of Ornithology in the United States. Laman is a field biologist and a wildlife photojournalist working with *National Geographic* as a regular contributor. Hosted by the Cornell Lab of Ornithology, the Bird of Paradise Project contains thousands of videos and audio with detailed information about each component of the mating lives of the birds of paradise. Scholes, narrating one of the videos in which the shape-shifting abilities of some birds of paradise species are explained, allows us to see the passion and determination it took to complete the 18 expeditions to document all 39 species known at the time on video:

> You certainly wouldn't, in your wildest imagination, draw a bird that looks like it's wearing a ballerina tutu or some kind of psychedelic smiley face. I mean this is just outrageous and without precedent. And that's just cool. How could you not want to know how birds came to use these kinds of shapes for courtship display?[36]

Scholes is referring to the Parotia Ballerina Dance and the Superb Bird of Paradise Mating Dance. Both hilarious and enthralling, these two dances are gateways to understanding the creative lives of birds of paradise. Both birds employ shape shifting as a pivotal tool used to best reveal hidden features of their extraordinary plumage. The Parotia begins his dance on a stage he has cleared of all forest debris only when a female lands on the low branch he has also cleared of leaves. He first bows down in front of her, almost touching the ground with his beak. Aside from the three long and erect spatula-shaped head wires he sports behind each eye and the v-shaped white mark above his beak, at this point, he is still just a black bird. Suddenly, he rises and spreads what appears to be a perfectly oval-shaped tutu around his torso. He bends and side-steps from one end of the stage to another while shaking his head so that his head wires whip back and forth in front of him. At times, he stands, legs planted apart while revealing his shimmering iridescent blue and yellow breastplate. He ends the dance with a few more bows. To us at least, that is how it looks, but to the female perched above him, he becomes a completely black ovoid shape, punctuated with two waving thin lines topped with small ovoid shapes at one side. A brilliant yellow signal flashes up at her, signaling something only she knows is true.[37]

Since she judges whether this male's dances are worth her time, Scholes and Laman are now documenting the birds of paradise mating dances from the female's perspective. Another species whose shape-shifting dance appears uncanny to us is the Superb Bird of Paradise. Their green crown and opal blue breastplate, while striking, still give little hint of what a radical metamorphosis these male birds are capable of. Initially opening his lime-yellow-lined mouth and calling out to advertise his charms to a passing female, the Superb Bird of Paradise extends his large, iridescent, aqua blue breastplate while unfurling his enormous cape of black feathers once she lands. With mouth closed so that the matching two tufts of iridescent aqua blue crown feathers are more visible, he faces the female, displaying his "Psychedelic Smiley-Face" and hopping from side to side on the narrow branch he has chosen for his stage, all the while making loud snapping sounds with his back feathers. Based on our assumptions about both psychedelia and smiley faces, his assumed shape may seem humorous. To the female Superb Birds of Paradise who choose him, his attractions are impossible to resist.

Scholes identifies a specific component of shape shifting that I would also consider creative. Small muscles attached to the base of each feather allow the birds to control their feathers. Birds of paradise appear to have stronger and more robust control over their feathers through these muscles, which they use with great precision to line up each feather. This kind of control is not genetic but learned, with young birds of paradise practicing for at least three to four years to perfect their style, much like bowerbirds. They do not do this in isolation, but practice on other young males, each taking turns playing the judging females.

Other species' courtships also rely on their evolved coloring and dancing abilities in males, such as peacock spiders, whose teeth are so tiny they cannot break human skin. They wave their colorfully articulated abdomens in time with their third pair of legs. Some have fan-like lateral flaps that are extended from their abdomen as well. All this choreography is from little hairy bodies and legs with front-facing eyes. They hip and hop, flashing their pigmented red and yellow colors, but especially entrancing females with structural blue and green iridescent colors. As part of the jumping spider family, peacocks use the full complement of eight eyes and have exceptional motion and depth perception. Their color vision is much better than ours, with a UV-sensitive photo receptor, and researchers have documented how they learn color. Recently, seven new species of peacock spiders have been found, and their compact size encourages researchers to wonder, "What is the cognitive architecture . . . to produce, perceive, and process complex behavioral displays?"[38]

Much more of this kind of work needs to be done to both record and understand these crucial aspects of animals' lives. Desire is something we can appreciate viscerally. Affection, pair bonding sometimes for life, dance and song mating rituals—all these allow us to see the zest, passion, and meaning individual animals give to their sexual lives.

Creative Desire

Desire is an attribute I neglected to add to my list of qualities conducive to creative behavior, but after reading Richard O. Prum's *Evolution of Beauty: How Darwin's Forgotten Theory of Mate Choice Shapes the Animal World—and Us*, it is a candidate for inclusion. Prum, a Yale ornithologist and evolutionary behaviorist, offers what he considers a revolutionary view of evolution that does not solely rely on "fitness" and the economically based explanations that have colored our understanding of it for decades.

Rather than taking credit for that revolutionary idea, Prum maintains that it is Darwin's original sexual-selection proposal written in terms of aesthetic language, such as the word "beauty," that provides the real revolutionary meaning of Darwin's sexual-selection theory. According to Darwin, the evolution of the prismatic voluptuousness existing in the animal world is the result of females evaluating males on the basis of preferences they themselves have developed over time. Prum asserts that since Darwin was establishing the human lineage from other forms of life, his descriptions of the subjective and cognitive abilities of animals in their choice of mates were not a trivial matter. Prum clarifies, "By using the words 'beauty,' 'taste,' 'charm,' 'appreciate,' 'admire,' and 'love,' Darwin was suggesting that mating preferences could evolve for displays that had no utilitarian value at all to the chooser, only aesthetic value."[39]

In his second book, *The Descent of Man and Selection in Relation to Sex*, Darwin was comparing these abilities in judging mates on the basis of their aesthetic appeal to those found in humans and finding them scientifically similar.[40] Needless to say, the Victorian era's objections to the idea that animals make aesthetic judgments, let alone recognize and prefer differences in their suitors, caused a great deal of resistance. Prum details several critical reactions at the time to Darwin's audacity in even proposing his second evolutionary theory. The zoologist St. George Jackson Mivart huffed in a particularly misogynistic way, "Such is the instability of vicious feminine caprice, that no constancy of coloration could be produced by its selective actions."[41] How could mere females be involved in driving evolution when they are unable to even commit to liking one color? Prum explains that Mivart could not agree with a concept that saw females as anything but harbingers of fickleness, immorality, and sin.[42] Another more consistent critic was Alfred Russel Wallace, the biogeographer and co-creator of the theory of natural selection. Wallace and Darwin were friends, mainly communicating through letters, respecting each other and their unique understanding of natural selection.[43] But, when Darwin unfolded his ideas about sexual selection in *Descent*, Wallace, while initially agreeing, gradually dissented through publications and letters that lasted until Darwin's death in 1882. Wallace's divergence on sexual selection stemmed from two convictions. The first was his belief in human exceptionalism, the idea that humans are special and better than all other species, which collided with the idea of animals being able to make choices in their mates or other matters. The second was his commitment to the idea that adaptation by natural selection is the predominant evolutionary process. Wallace was only able to admit that sexual ornaments themselves, though having nothing to do with female choice, might have evolved to advertise the fitness of particular males.

This view of sexual selection—that the beautiful colors and forms of males, along with the intricate and well-rehearsed dances and songs of many species, are only there to provide purely practical information about a potential mate's adaptive qualities—is still the one that predominates today, according to Prum. It was not until the early 1950s that biologists began to investigate sexual selection again,[44] and as Prum says, now there are reams of data that prove animals can make sensory evaluations leading to mate choice.[45] While appreciating "the focus on beauty and aesthetics," several reviewers of Prum's book take him to task for his characterization of all other evolutionary biologists as only committed to adaptation and survival-based natural selection. According to these reviewers, Prum generalizes the commitment of all other evolutionary biologists to mate choice that is driven only by how the "organism," or the animal, will fit with the environment to survive. This is the complaint of Gail Patricelli and her colleagues, among other items of concern. They also give a useful overview of other theories of both arbitrary and viable reasons for female mate preferences. They disagree with how the book "unfairly caricatures most sexual selection researchers as . . . failing to acknowledge the subjective experiences of nonhuman animals."[46] Other reviewers particularly object to Prum's contention that the null hyphothesis—the hypothesis considered to be true until another hypothesis with statistical evidence indicates otherwise—should be the Lande-Kirkpatrick (LK) version of the English biologist and statistician Ronald Fisher's theory of how Darwin's original idea of sexual selection might work to prioritize traits of "beauty."

Fisher speculated that even if females might prefer what might be considered valueless traits, such as iridescent plumage or Alvin Ailey dance moves, those traits might also correspond with health or survival skills. Over time, this genetic correlation might create a runaway cycle that would greatly exaggerate both preference and trait, perhaps at the expense of the male's survival. In the early 1980s, the US evolutionary biologists Russell Lande and Mark Kirkpatrick demonstrated quantitatively that runaway sexual selection could happen in nature, and "if a mutant showing a mating preference for a male trait with reduced viability reaches high frequency, the trait can be taken to high frequency and consequently cause average male survivorship to deteriorate severely."[47] These other reviews, written by biologists who also study male display ornaments, focus on Prum's use of the LK to support his theories and point to other models to explain the evolution of elaborate (what Prum calls "beautiful" or "arbitrary") male display traits.[48]

The crucial point Prum is making is this: in addition to using the language of aesthetics to describe the sensory and cognitive abilities used by animals in their mate choices, Darwin wished to emphasize the nonfunctional and coevolutionary nature of these choices. Prum makes clear,

Darwin hypothesized that the aesthetic capacities of different species evolved differences in mating preference that could be merely pleasing for their own sake and without any other value, meaning or utility. . . . Darwin hypothesized that species have evolved to their own "standards of beauty."[49]

While recognizing that sexual selection is an evolutionary driver, he calls the arbitrariness of these choices "Beauty Happens." He insists that the pleasure animals take in their choices of what is beautiful to them is a driver not only in their own evolution as a species *but in biodiversity itself.* Darwin viewed sexual selection and natural selection as two distinct, frequently independent evolutionary mechanisms. For instance, Darwin's example of the difference in beak size and shape of the 15 different species of Galápagos finches is a well-known explanation of adaptive evolution driven by natural selection. Seeds eaten by the finches vary in size and hardiness depending on where and when those seeds are available in their environments. Over time, because beak size and shape are heritable traits, the finches in the Galápagos have evolved beak shapes able to assist in handling and opening seeds matching the particular kinds of seeds in the specific Galápagos environment in which they live.

In contrast, sexual attractants such as the bowers of male bowerbirds, the song of the male thrasher, and the colors and patterns of the male Argus pheasant feathers are the result of subjective evaluations by females. These evaluations are "arbitrary," by which Prum means that these choices have evolved through the individual sexual proclivities of each species' "standards of beauty," a phrase originally used by Darwin. Prum outlines at length what Darwin did *not* mean by this phrase. He did not mean that those standards were signals, what is called "honest signaling" in biology, of the fitness of the male being evaluated. What he argues, and I am in full agreement with Prum, is that those standards of beauty were the "consequence of the fact that animals had evolved to be beautiful to themselves. What was so radical about this idea was that it positioned organisms—especially female organisms—as active agents in the evolution of their own species."[50]

While the result of all this open-ended, flexible, and self-directed choice is the overwhelmingly vast array of beautiful beings on this planet, Prum admits that in some cases these choices are maladaptive. In other words, they result in a bad match between the organism and its environment. The peacocks' inability to hide easily comes to mind. For Prum, natural selection alone cannot account for all of evolutionary processes and history. As he so eloquently summarizes, "Evolution is frequently far quirkier, stranger, more historically contingent, individualized, and less predictable and generalizable than adaptation can explain."[51] He then reiterates something that also drew me to his book and theory:

By recognizing signals as beautiful to those organisms that prefer them— whether they are Wood Thrushes, bowerbirds, butterflies, or humans—we are forced to engage with the full implications of what it means to be a sentient animal making social and sexual choices. . . . Beauty and desire in nature can be as irrational, unpredictable, and dynamic as our own personal experiences of them.[52]

Reading Prum's books and articles left me with lots of questions, so I decided to interview him. Early in Prum's book, he says,

I will argue that we need an evolutionary theory that encompasses the subjective experiences of animals in order to develop an accurate scientific account of the natural world. We ignore them at our intellectual peril because the subjective experiences of animals have critical and decisive consequence for their evolution.[53]

My first questions to him were these: Do you see the peril of ignoring the subjective experiences of animals as only intellectual, or do you think we risk other kinds of peril? How does this affect our understanding of species extinction or climate change, for instance?

Prum is a brilliant thinker, and my conversation with him was wonderfully complex. Some people, especially academics, learn to answer questions with questions (I admit I have done this myself) or to adapt the question asked to a topic more amenable to them, but Prum's leaps of thought have nothing to do with evasion. As he does here, his mind jumps with agility down to more fundamental levels of a topic and then back up to examples. He answered that question by speaking to the impossibility of detaching science from values:

> I think that keys into another big aspect of the book which is that aesthetic co-evolution creates aesthetic value within the communities, the species where it arises, and that is a scientific statement about the origin of value. There is a huge belief and I would call it a faith, that the sciences are definable as those inquiries that are not about value. . . . What I am saying is that it is impossible for scientists to stay out of the business of value. The desire to keep science out of that world has in some ways driven the application of adaptation notions of mate choice, and these contortions we have had to do to avoid the obvious are because of the fear of the subjective and the implications of that. You cannot construct a complete science that is devoid of value. Now, where do we go with that? I think we need to have science and disciplines that consider themselves not to be sciences in conversation with each other.[54]

Although I had not asked about how focusing on the birds he studies as individual sentient beings affected him, he then broached a corollary to the discussion by offering that he was just at the beginning of this, "this" meaning the subjectivity of animals. Once a vegetarian, now a "fishitarian," he explained that in his work as a scientist, he collects bird specimens and, for that reason, he felt he "had not fully explored the moral implications of animals as subjective agents."[55]

Prum has thought a great deal about aesthetics, and along with his discussions of aesthetics in the book, he has written a paper entitled "Coevolutionary Aesthetics in Human and Biotic Artworlds." He concludes the paper with this: "This coevolutionary aesthetic theory is based on the understanding that the subjective, individual, sensory and cognitive experiences of humans and non-human animals can have (genetic or cultural) evolutionary consequences that are independent of, and not reducible to, natural selection."[56]

Prum explains that he is very much interested in the aesthetics of artworlds we don't appreciate, and here he refers to both water current and electrical flow and navigation in habitats with electrical fields. Very excitedly, he tells me, "They also sing songs to each other."[57] He then describes what you might hear if you put a microphone into an Amazonian artworld, as he calls them, of animals. A perfect example, he says, are momyrid fishes that live in two independent lineages in dark and obscure water: South American Gymnotiformes and the African Mormyridae. He explains that it is so dark that vision is almost impossible:

> The fish sense the flow of the water with neurons that discern the river at night, it is lit up like Las Vegas, man, wramp, wramp, they are singing to each other. They are territorial, they are involved with seduction, it is the whole gamut of communication functions, it explores frequency and tempo in the same sense that sound does. So, the physics of waves is going to have a role in trying to understand how do these modalities give rise to aesthetic communications. There is something about frequency that is at play in both cases. So that is a world, not only can we not sense it, but we can't even begin to comprehend it as of yet.[58]

For him, this indicates another parallel with humans hearing and singing songs, but in an entirely different way. "But what they are doing is creating a subjective experience and evaluations of 'do I like that or not' in the same way that we do with art and making mating decisions but based on the right frequency."[59]

I ask him, since aesthetics and creativity are seen as different aspects of a very broad area, if he thinks individual animals are creative. He answers with another left turn, but one that inevitably leads back to an answer to the question. For him, evolution is creative in that it gives rise to forms that have not existed before. Prum's research outside of behavior has to do with how evolution creates innovation. His work on the evolution of feathers was groundbreaking. He proposed that feathers evolved in stages, and before the advent of birds or flight. Paleontologists' finds of feathered dinosaurs substantiated his proposal. This led him to his present work, which is at odds with the idea that all selection is due to adaptation, to function. He does agree that, yes, there are examples of creativity in the animal world, citing Don Kroodsma's work and Robert Payne's on Indigo Buntings, which was done over many years and made the case for song learning and how it spreads through culture.

Autonomy plays a crucial role in Prum's thoughts about sexual conflict. Prum worked on a project about female selection with his colleague Patricia Brennan. Their goal was to understand the intricacies of how female autonomy in ducks has evolved to allow for female freedom of choice. Male ducks are often violent suitors and attempt to rape females, evolving convoluted penises for accomplishing the task even when they are rebuffed. Females, however, have evolved vaginas that make that very difficult. This is called sexual antagonistic evolution, and Prum points to this as an example of natural autonomy:

> Sexual autonomy is not merely a political idea, a legal concept, or a philosophical theory; rather, it is a natural consequence of the evolutionary interactions of sexual reproduction, mating preferences, and sexual coercion and violence in social species. And the evolutionary engine of sexual autonomy is aesthetic mate choice.[60]

Prum remarks that the emphasis on only one aspect of Darwin's theories on evolution, that of adaptation, has caused scientists to miss other aspects that are just as important to understanding what nature has to

offer. While Prum also is interested in how this has affected our understanding of our sexuality, among other mysteries, I want to end with a
quotation from his book about how the impact of a constrained and
limited view of animals also has barred scientists from discoveries of
animals' agency in choosing for themselves in many areas of their lives.

> Unfortunately, the anxious remove of sexual science from sexual pleasure
> was built into the structure of scientific objectivity—into the discipline
> of science itself. To imagine animals as aesthetic agents with their own
> subjective preferences was considered anthropomorphic. Scientific "ob-
> jectivity" came to require us to discount or ignore the subjective experi-
> ences of animals.[61]

That is changing, but what else are we missing, when we discount individual animals and the creative agency of their choices, their needs, and
their desires? If the scientists who have peopled this chapter are correct,
and I think they are, we will have lost more than we can imagine.

6

Emotional Agency

The Empathy of Chickens

Emotions are the gifts of our ancestors. We have them and
so do other animals. We must never forget this.
—Marc Bekoff, *The Emotional Lives of Animals*

In the fall of my senior year at university, a group of my friends had a
surprise party for my 21st birthday. I was even more surprised when in
the morning—a number of us had slept over at the party house—they
told me we were all going to the zoo. My love of animals was common
knowledge, but this was an unanticipated gift. (At the time, although I
was unhappy about the living conditions for animals in zoos, I was not
at the point of declining to go to zoos. I never go now, nor do I support
them.) I remember vividly two moments from that trip. Both opened
my eyes to the lives of animals in ways I had not experienced until then.
The first was seeing tropical fish for the first time. I realize it may sound
astounding to say this today, but at that time, at least in my rather shel-
tered experience, I did not even know such fish existed. Though I was a
performance major, I had started to paint and print as well. The intense
coloring of the fish I saw completely changed how I visually perceived
the natural world.

The second moment was when I stood in front of the large male
orangutan. He was sitting close to the front of his cage, gazing out at
the onlookers, his hands wrapped loosely around the bars. Even though
I had never seen a real orangutan before, his posture and facial expression of silently considering the world were familiar to me. Our eyes met
and my whole world changed. I don't remember how long I stood there

or how I managed to leave, but for the time he and I stared into each other's eyes, I sensed an intelligence older and wiser than mine. While his expression indicated he was resigned to his fate, in his eyes I saw great sorrow. For those moments, we recognized each other in a way that surpassed any boundaries made of steel or species.

All three species of wild orangutans, Sumatran, Bornean, and Tapanuli, are considered critically endangered, but the Tapanuli, only discovered in 1997, number less than 800. They are the oldest orangutan species as well. Orangutans are known to be intelligent, passing researchers' intelligence tests with flying colors. In a study of captive orangutans by psychologists, six adult female orangutans modified their communication gestures according to how well their audience understood what they were trying to communicate. If the experimenter appeared to partially understand their meaning, the orangutans narrowed their range of signals, focusing on and repeating more frequently gestures already made. But when they were completely misunderstood, they expanded their range of gestures and avoided gestures that had failed previously. As in a game of charades, these differences in gestures allowed an orangutan's intended goal—in this case, an item of food—to be understood by their audience, the bearer of the food. The researchers concluded, "In the absence of conventional labels, communicating the fact that an intention has been somewhat misunderstood is an important way to establish shared meaning."[1] Reading this study gave me vindication about my perceptions of a shared emotional state between that captive orangutan and me so long ago. My overall emotion, however, continues to be one of profound sadness mixed with not a small amount of anger that such complex beings are either kept behind bars, exiled from their homes due to human destruction, killed, or captured in the wildlife trade as pets.

While I was already immersed in creative pursuits—acting, drawing, painting—my emotional connection experience (also called empathy) with that captive orangutan led to a lifelong commitment to understanding and contributing to better lives for animals of all kinds. It took two more years to shift the focus of my work, but since then all of my work, both in the visual arts and in writing, has been about the lives of animals. Emotion is a prominent driver of human creativity in many instances, and given what we know about the emotions of animals, it informs their creative process as well. Empathy is often a crucial forerunner of the creative process. Experiences in the past contribute to imagining what the present or future experience might be like for ourselves or another. If animals can be empathic, imagination is possible as well.[2] It takes imagination to create something that was not there before.

The eyes have often been deemed the gateways to our souls and, along with our facial and bodily expressions, they play enormous roles in revealing our emotions. Darwin's third book, *The Expression of the Emotions in Man and Animals*, was one of the first serious studies of the communication of emotions.[3] In it, he amasses a great deal of material supporting how the expressions of the emotions in humans are comparable to those in animals. Up until recently, scientific research on emotions in animals, as well as any behaviors that indicated animal awareness, was stunted by a taboo on anthropomorphism, the sin of suggesting that animals think and feel in ways similar to ours. Over the last two and a half decades, the research and publications of prominent animal behavioral scientists have shifted the cloud under which anthropomorphism about animal emotions has existed, making it once again usable for science. Jeffrey Moussaieff Masson's 1996 book, *Why Elephants Weep*,[4] spoke to many laypeople who had no compunctions about using their own emotional abilities to understand the animals they lived with. Jane Goodall's and Marc Bekoff's scientific and popular writings, however, have been a constant in both pioneering and encouraging the scientific and ethical understanding that animals share the gift of emotion with us. Bekoff, in an early article published in *Bioscience*, says,

> The way human beings describe and explain the behavior of other animals is limited by the language they use to talk about things in general. By engaging in anthropomorphism—using human terms to explain animals'

emotions or feelings—humans make other animals' worlds accessible to themselves.[5]

Bekoff insists, however, that animals do feel emotions in unique ways that are particular to their species and that we should continue to work at understanding animals from their point of view. We more than likely feel some common emotions, he adds, "including fear, joy, happiness, shame, embarrassment, resentment, jealousy, rage, anger, love, pleasure, compassion, respect, relief, disgust, sadness, despair, and grief."[6] It is by no means a short list.

I would emphasize the possible uniqueness of some animals' demonstrations of emotions. Even if we tend to rely on visual and aural demonstrations of emotion, nonmammals may use other senses we may not have or even be aware of. Consider the male veiled chameleon communicating his motivation (rage, perhaps) to win in a fight with another chameleon. Researchers from Arizona State University found that rather than changing color to camouflage himself, he changed the color of his stripes to indicate how much he wanted to win. Being open to perceiving changes in color, pattern, and body region, the researchers discovered how complex chameleon communication can be.[7] I include this example because while we now are more open to the emotional lives of mammals, there is considerable work being done to understand the emotions of birds, fish, amphibians, reptiles, and insects. The assumption that those groups of animals do not feel emotion is being disproved as you read this sentence.[8]

Books such as primatologist Frans de Waal's *Good Natured: The Origins of Right and Wrong in Humans and Other Animals*,[9] Marc Bekoff's *Emotional Lives of Animals*,[10] Virginia Morell's *Animalwise: How We Know Animals Think and Feel*,[11] Jonathan Balcombe's *What a Fish Knows*,[12] and biologist Carl Safina's more recent *Beyond Words: What Animals Think and Feel*[13] have helped to encourage what evolutionary biologist George Burghardt calls "critical anthropomorphism"[14] as a useful and necessary method for studying our fellow animals. Gathering data from many sources, such as natural history, individuals' perceptions, intuitions, feelings, careful descriptions of behavior, identification with a particular animal, optimization models, and previous studies would help further understanding of the emotional lives of animals. Recent books by biologists and others concerning animal emotions support and validate my pursuit of determining what roles emotions play in animal creativity, working with the knowledge that animals are emotional creatures, in ways similar to us and also in ways unique to their species and cultural needs.

Some of the foregoing chapters have described fundamental contributors to creative behavior, such as intelligence and communication. Other chapters have offered examples of other domains in which creative behavior appears: play, sex, building, and tool use. Emotion also is an important driver in—and sometimes the form of—creative behavior in animals, as it often is in human creativity. It may be that the outcome of that emotional drive is a tangible product, as we saw in previous examples, such as the bower for bowerbirds, the lodge for beavers, singing for birds and whales. Sometimes the response to emotion is a particularly creative *social* behavior.

Empathic Chickens

While chickens have not been mentioned so far, I would like to start with them. Seriously, you say, chickens? Yes, very seriously. Remember that chickens are a member of the bird family. We have heard from several biologists, animal behaviorists, and psychologists just how intelligent and creative birds are. The abstract mathematical abilities of pigeons, the keen intelligence for creative tool use of corvids, the playful and resourceful capabilities of keas, the aesthetic decisions generated by female birds who then use these decisions to choose mates are all offered as examples in the emerging science of bird intelligence and awareness. I have relied on these findings for considering the creativity of chickens as well.

Until very recently these designations have not been used to describe chickens. As it turns out, they have all the capabilities that other birds have, capabilities that neuroscientists are comparing to those of primates.[15] Not only do they see extremely well, but they perceive a broader range of colors than humans do. They can detect both high- and low-frequency sounds, including perhaps infrasound, possess an evolved sense of smell and taste, and have something called the "bill tip organ," "a specialized cluster of highly sensitive mechanoreceptors" allowing for extremely fine touch discrimination.[16]

Like pigeons, they possess an understanding of counting as well as basic arithmetic. Like the great apes (and prairie dogs), they communicate in complex ways that rely on syntax, semantics, and references to others. This kind of communication depends on self-awareness and the ability to take the perspective of another animal. They respond appropriately to varying alarm calls as well as responding to novel food calls, but not to repeated messages about known food.[17] (Yes, I know dinner is on the table, but I am busy.) These examples also demonstrate self-control and self-awareness. Able to reason and make logical inferences, chickens show sophisticated social behavior in many ways, such as discriminating among individuals, using deceit to manipulate circumstances, and learning observationally in social situations.[18]

Chickens are exceptionally adept at recognizing individuals in their social groups, keeping track of who is who in their social hierarchy, and identifying other chickens who may be in or out of these groups. Able to perceive the passing of time, they can anticipate future events. All these characteristics taken together present a picture of a very smart and self-aware being. Neuroscientist Lori Marino is also an expert in animal behavior and intelligence, and she adds two important points to the list above. The first describes chickens' emotions as complex because their psychology is shared with humans and other animals that have shown equally "accessible" sophisticated behavior. I use the word "accessible" here to note the likelihood that emotion does exist across all species, just not in ways that are easily recognized or verifiable by humans, though that is beginning to change to include insects, for instance.[19] The second point usually shocks people who have not spent time with chickens. They have "distinct personalities, just like all animals who are cognitively, emotionally, and behaviorally complex individuals."[20]

It is difficult to find, even today, books dedicated to the emotions and intelligence of chickens. Almost all the books I found concerned raising chickens for the back yard or, unfortunately, for the stove. There are exceptions. One is Annie Potts's *Chicken*, one of the Reaktion Books Animal series. Potts not only does an outstanding job at boosting ethical awareness of this "intelligent and passionate species" but, as a distinguished cultural scholar, she also draws together evolutionary, historical, biological, and cultural perspectives on how humans have interacted with this bird, who is so revered and exploited.

As Potts surmises, "Chickens are quite easily dismissed as impassive because relatively few people have experience of living alongside them; but those who do need no convincing of their individual responses, their likes and dislikes, and their distinctive personalities."[21] One of the things that chickens find particular pleasure in is dust baths. Like elephants, who also love a good dirt bath, chickens find sheer pleasure in locating just the right patch of ground to shape into a bowl in which the surrounding dirt is then scooped up onto the feathers with their wings. After a 30-minute soak, as it were, the birds rise to shake off parasites and oil. Potts notes that the pests-and-parasites-removal function of dust bathing plays a partial role in chickens' devotion to the activity. They also will repeat a bath even if they have just had one. The pleasure of bathing is sought for its own sake.

Potts also describes the importance of friendship for many chickens, whether that be another chicken, a human, or, as I learned elsewhere, a representative of another species, a horse for instance. There seems to be a history of long-term friendships between horses and chickens, perhaps based on chickens' fancy for eating the insects and flies that bother horses, and the ability of horses to protect them from predators.

The stories, however, all seem to include both species' real fondness for spending time with each other, including bedtime. Pat Rothschild is a psychotherapist who keeps both horses and chickens. While the horses were deliberate additions to her animal family, the chickens were "spent hens" (hens whose egg production had dropped) someone had abandoned on her property hoping predators would dispatch them. But, according to Rothschild, the hens found the horses and began their custodial horse duties immediately. Having seen the relationship between horses and chickens when she was a child, she understood the benefit for both: "Chickens and horses bring one another important psychological and social support, as well as physical protection. The chickens protect the horses from insects. The horses help protect the chickens from their many predators."[22]

As for Rothschild's feelings toward the chickens, "There are few things in this world sweeter than the sounds of hens saying hello. They're cooperative, friendly and peaceable as they go about their business of eating varmints and greens."[23]

Potts, who homes 21 chickens, tells of the gregarious nature of chickens and their inclination to form close relationships with others in their group. Often foraging, sharing tidbits, and nesting together, chickens sometimes have a best friend. If one hen becomes separated from her friend, she will call out and both hens will progress toward each other until they are reunited. Potts suggests that it is entirely reasonable "to understand this as a fondness and concern for the well-being of a particular friend."[24]

It's obvious to me that chickens develop close friendships, and also sometimes lifelong enemies! With special companions, they also develop their own unique ways of getting around together, calling each other and showing each other things, and living with the seasons and times of the day. For example, each spring Hinemoa and Chica would find their own special place to scratch, make dust bowls, and then sun-bathe in their bowls. They decided these places together . . . and sometimes other chooks would sit with them, but if not, this duo went just by themselves, having established "their" special place.[25]

Potts divulged a moving example of this kind of friendship when one of the pair of friends, Chica, became gravely ill with egg peritonitis, the disease bred into commercial layer hens. Chickens naturally produce a couple of clutches of eggs each spring. However, Potts explained, "Commercial layer hen breeds develop reproductive system diseases as they grow older and they can no longer push out eggs due to physical changes. Eggs can break inside hens and then the hens acquire infections and end up with congested reproductive organs. This happened to Chica."[26] The vet was able to treat her and during this time, Annie moved Chica into the house to keep her warm and keep her away from the other hens. "Her friend Hinemoa happily came inside too to stay with her. Chica was lucky to have two months of a sunny room and a caring friend with her before she died, which was devastating for all of us as she was so loved and had always been around."[27]

Potts also noted how Hinemoa reacted uniquely when it became obvious that Chica was near death.

While Hinemoa and Chica had been good friends, they had never huddled together at night, whether in the house or on the perches in the henhouse outside. This evening Hinemoa slept in the corner with Chica, with her head strangely positioned on Chica's body, almost like she was spooning her friend. She didn't leave her side until we took Chica away the next day. Hinemoa was very subdued for the next few days—she wasn't interested in food or in returning to the flock. How else can anyone interpret this other than grief for the loss of a close friend? She stayed inside for a while but she wasn't as curious about the activities in the house as she used to be. . . . I've witnessed this kind of grief before with chickens. It's not unusual. We've seen so many hens become subdued, lose their appetites, and take to dark places when their close friends die.[28]

Karen Davis, a pioneering activist for chickens, founded United Poultry Concerns in 1990, now the best-known nonprofit organization dedicated to promoting the respectful treatment of chickens, turkeys, ducks, and other domestic fowl. Davis has published countless papers in popular and scientific journals and is a tireless advocate for these birds. Possessing intimate knowledge of chickens, she describes their general behavior when free to be exactly who they are:

> Chickens have singing sounds of contentment that resonate through the flock intermittently during the day and often as they are settling down on their perches for the night. They use their voices not only to exchange information intimately and across distances, but to express joy and enthusiasm as well as boredom, weariness, and woe. Having lived with chickens since 1985, I know that chickens are vibrant individuals, cheerful in all kinds of weather from sunshine to snow.[29]

So how do chickens' emotions drive creative behavior in their world? Reviewing the list of cognitive abilities that chickens possess, including the last two abilities, complex emotions and "distinct personalities," it seems reasonable to hunt for evidence of creativity that might make use of those cognitive, emotional, and personality attributes. The list of personality traits utilized in human creative research is long. It contains any number of descriptions of qualities. Most include love or enthusiasm for what is new or novel, tolerance of ambiguity, openness to experience, independence of judgment, curiosity, preference for challenge and complexity, self-confidence, propensity for risk taking, and intrinsic motivation. Psychologist Sandra Russ, when discussing the role of affect (a more restrained word describing emotion) in human creativity, argues for a strong connection between the two: "Access to affect-laden thoughts and openness to affect states are both related to an openness to experience and a tolerance of ambiguity."[30] Here, Russ is solidifying the intersection of emotion and creativity.

The late Russell Greenberg, pioneering ornithologist, insists that an animal's emotional response to a situation surrounding a problem (a lab; among family and friends; a dark barn filled with thousands of other chickens) is a critical component in their problem-solving ability: "In particular, ethologists have long recognized that emotional responses to novel situations may greatly influence an animal's apparent cognitive abilities."[31] Sometimes the problem being solved is an emotional one. Certain animals seem to have the more common ability to be aware of another's emotion (empathy) and also to be able to tolerate ambiguity, to be open to new experiences, such as difficult or conflicting emotions, and to possess cognitive sensitivity to that perceived emotional problem. The result is often a creative emotional response. In recounting her response to a fox killing Pola, one of the chickens in her care, Karen Davis talks about the empathy a chicken, Sonja, offered to her during her reaction:

> It was too much. I sat on the kitchen floor crying and screaming. At the time, I was caring for Sonja, a big white warm-natured, bouncy hen I was treating for wounds she'd received before I rescued her. As I sat on the floor exploding with grief and guilt, Sonja walked over to where I sat weeping. She nestled her face next to mine and began purring with the ineffable soft purr that is also a trill in chickens. She comforted me even as her gesture deepened the heartache I was feeling in that moment about the painful mystery of Pola and the mystery of all chickens. Did Sonja know why I was crying? I doubt it, but maybe she did. Did she know that I was terribly sad and distressed? There is no question in my mind about that. She responded to my grief with an expression of empathy that I have carried emotionally in my life ever since.[32]

Research published in 2011 by applied ethologist Joanne Edgar and her colleagues supports Davis's description of Sonja's response by revealing that chickens, like many other animals, are capable of feeling empathy. Mother hens, when watching their chicks become distressed when a harmless puff of air ruffled their feathers, also showed signs of stress and made clucking noises even though they had not received a puff of air.[33]

"Empathy," as philosopher Jessica Pierce says, "is the ability to perceive and feel the emotion of another."[34] The history of the word itself offers some insight into why its inclusion in a study of emotional creativity is necessary. In 1909, the psychologist Edward Titchener introduced the term "empathy" into the English language from the German term "*Einfühlung*" (or "feeling into"). Since the end of the nineteenth century, it was understood in German philosophical circles as an important category in philosophical aesthetics. There it was used to describe our ability to "feel into" art and nature. But Titchener, as a psychologist, had gleaned his knowledge of what the term implied from Theodor Lipps, a German philosopher, who unlike his predecessors used the notion of *Einfühlung* to explain not only how people experience objects of art or nature but also how they understand the mental states of other people. While the English term was quickly taken up by psychologists to mean having the capacity to understand the emotions of others, disagreements still concern whether acting positively on those emotions is part of the package. The meaning of the term shifts depending on what field or discipline it is used in.[35]

The appearance of "empathy" in the scientific and philosophical literature on animals emerged only in the 1960s or '70s, but today it is used in both areas, as Pierce describes it, "with convergence if not equivalence."[36] Research on empathy in animals has grown not only in terms of the number of scientists focusing their research on this topic but also in terms of what species are included. Psychologist Stephanie Preston and renowned primatologist and ethologist Frans de Waal build on previous work from the last two decades in a recent review of the subject. Their definition of empathy goes like this:

> Any process that emerges from the fact that observers understand others' states by activating personal neural and mental representations of that state, including the capacity to be affected by and share the emotional

state of another; assess the reasons for the other's state; and identify with the other adopting his or her perspective.[37]

When we talk of empathy, we usually refer to individuals sharing emotions as well as adopting another's point of view. There are more cognitively based definitions that rely on imagining or simulating what another is feeling or thinking. But, as Preston and de Waal contend, these overestimate the distinction between cognitive and emotional empathy. They conclude, "Despite each having unique features, affective and cognitive empathy both require access to the shared presentations of emotion that provide simulations with content and embodied meaning."[38] Emotionally understanding another's emotion or point of view and thinking about their emotions and perspective are intertwined. Both add to any understanding of the matter at hand or, perhaps, shape a creative response.

With this particular conclusion in hand, let us look again at Sonja's response to Davis's anger and grief. In Davis's description, Sonja seems to have recognized the extreme emotion that produces not only tears but rage, by connecting it with "content and meaning" from her own experience. She then went further and offered consolation. It is important to note that Sonja did not run screaming from the kitchen as if she was only "state matching," a more basic form of empathy. While this more basic form is one to which more complex states of empathy are connected, Sonja cognitively accessed or, in lay terms, remembered similar experiences and meaning within her emotional past to imagine what kind of consolation was needed. She nestled her face next to Davis's face and "began purring with the ineffable soft purr that is also a trill in chickens." If this explanation sounds too complex for a chicken, it is important to note here that as Preston and de Waal remind us,

For every species, the reach of empathy varies with its social organization, creating differences across solitary, pair-bonded, cooperatively hunting or group-living animals, not because the empathy mechanism works differently but because species and their ecology place different demands on it.[39]

Sonja responded in the same way she might have responded to a chicken friend who was obviously in emotional pain and needed consolation, what de Waal has called "sympathetic concern."[40] She certainly responded in an appropriate way to Davis's distress.

Empathy, Memory, and Imagination

> At 11:10ish Ella gives a "let's go" rumble as she moves further down the swamp. . . . At 11:19 Ella goes into the swamp. All the group are in the swamp except Elspeth and her calf, born 2000, and Eudora (Elspeth's mother). At 11:25 Eudora appears to "lead" Elspeth and the calf to a good place to enter the swamp—the only place where there is no mud.—JP: 3 June 2000.[41]

This research notation by Joyce Poole was written while she watched members of the Amboseli elephant population of Southern Kenya. Studied for over 35 years, elephants in the Amboseli Park have afforded researchers with the Amboseli Elephant Research Project, founded by Cynthia Moss and Harvey Croze in 1972, firsthand and long-term experience with several generations and families of elephants. Due to the protection of the presence of researchers and tourists as well as the support of the local Maasai people, the elephant population in Amboseli National Park is one of the few that has been able to live a relatively undisturbed existence in natural conditions.

Poole's research notes quoted above indicate how cognitive and emotional factors mesh to allow an empathic behavior that attributes intention to another.[42] Eudora has recognized that Elspeth is having trouble finding a mudless place through which her calf will be able to enter the swamp easily and so she guides her daughter and grand-calf to such a place. This may seem to be a quite uncreative act, one lacking any imagination. However, if we shift our assumptions a bit, we can reframe this small act of empathy in terms of emotional creativity. After all, if Eudora had merely left her daughter and calf on the bank of the swamp to fend for themselves, the results for both could have been devastating. Instead, this small act of concern and kindness can be understood as an emotionally creative response of aiding another that "requires self-regulation and perspective-taking."[43] The daily creativity of mothering has always been taken for granted and unfortunately is a neglected area of creativity, though, I would submit, one of the most important. These small, emotionally creative acts have a huge positive impact on kinship, protection of others, communal thriving, and the continuation of a way of life.

Preston and de Waal argue that given the similar neuron systems guiding offspring care across mammals and altruism in humans, all species that have social attachments, including rodents, birds, and reptiles, are more than likely motivated to help distressed and vulnerable others. Indeed, empathy in rats and mice occurring outside the parenting context and shown towards other adults has been demonstrated in numerous experiments. The earliest experiment on these altruistic behaviors in rats that I could find was done in 1959 by Russell Church.[44]

Yet, researchers still feel the need to "prove" that rats are not only sympathetic to other rats but also will risk their own safety or well-being to help another rat. According to Preston and de Waal, rats will choose releasing a trapped cage mate over accessing attractive food. If they have been able to rescue their friend, they share the rewards that they could have had all to themselves. Even if they are blocked from releasing their friend, they respond with attempts to help.[45] One wonders how many more tests like this will be needed to make a dent in the scientific understanding of rat empathy, or the empathy of any species.

Empathy Is Double-Sided

Empathy is not always used for good. The ability to understand the desires or needs of another certainly plays a role in tactical deception. As mentioned previously, scrub jays are very careful to hide the cache they will use weeks later when other birds are not looking. Male cuttlefish mislead other male cuttlefish into thinking they are female by displaying female patterns to a rival male on one side of their body while displaying male courtship patterns to a receptive female on the other side of their body. These subterfuges are examples of just how deceptively creative animals can be when they decide to be Machiavellian.

Think of Santino the chimpanzee, described in the fourth chapter. Lulling his audience into a feeling of security by hiding his projectiles, he waited to throw them at the last minute. This took planning and also an understanding of how the humans might act if he was nonchalant in his advance towards his hiding place. The scrub jay who carefully hides her cache of food when others are not looking is attempting to assure herself that she will find it where she left it. She is capable of perceiving how another might want her food, and she chooses a time to hide it when no one is looking.

The same system of empathic knowledge that allows for deception also allows for empathic clues on how to creatively resolve conflicts and build relationships that sustain cohesive social groups.[46] These goals are equally important drivers of behavioral diversity.[47] Jane Goodall describes how adolescent males often challenge older females, at times using branches to hit the females. Sometimes females will hold onto the branches so the youngster cannot make contact, but as Goodall explains, depending on the age of the male and the older female's ranking in the troop, responses from the females vary. Fear, avoidance, retaliation, or ignoring the offender make for various reactions from the adolescent male as well. One female, whom Goodall calls Winkle, reacted in two different and innovative ways on two different occasions. On one occasion, having anticipated the young male's next move, she removed the branch from his hand before he had a chance to even begin to sway it. On another occasion, Winkle reached out to the youngster who was displaying towards her and tickled him "vigorously" so that he began to laugh and stopped the display altogether. Both of these creative tactics show evidence of a tolerant approach more than likely based on experience. Expertly diffusing the situation before it becomes hurtful either to herself or to the youngster is in this situation, and for Winkle, a socially creative response.[48]

It Is Good to Forgive

De Waal's research on what he terms "reconciliation" has spanned decades. In discussing altruism in animals, he notes that biologists rarely use the term in the way scholars outside the field do: unselfish concern for the welfare of others. He continues,

> I experienced similar taboos when first describing how chimpanzees kiss and embrace their adversaries during reconciliations after a fight. I was urged to speak instead of "post-conflict reunions with mouth-to-mouth contact." That the term reconciliation is now widely accepted in primatology is the product of three decades of systematically countering "simpler" explanations, so that the only one left standing is that primates monitor the state of their social relationships and undertake reparatory actions following conflict.[49]

He offers one of his photos and a description of the following scene as an example. After a fight between two adult daughters, a mother rhesus monkey negotiated reconciliation by sitting in the middle while the trio closely huddled together while loudly "girning" (a friendly vocalization) and also lip-smacking at each other's infants.[50] Similar to scenes from my baby mothering days, eye contact is not initially made, allowing all the attention and any lingering hard feelings to be diffused by making "ohs" and "ahs" over each other's babies. Dolphins, hyenas, and goats, among other social animals, also can diffuse any hostility among their friends and family, otherwise known in humans as a complex emotional process called forgiveness. "Do animals, too, know forgiveness?" asks de Waal.[51]

Jessica Pierce and Marc Bekoff answer yes. Bekoff's extensive research on play and their joint work on morality in animals provide them with numerous examples of how forgiveness works in social situations. Forgiveness itself may be the inner emotional and cognitive process for humans and animals that allows reconciliation to take place. As Pierce and Bekoff report, using Bekoff's dogs as an example,

> Play sequences often involve acts of forgiveness and apology. For example, if Jethro bit Zeke too hard, play stopped for a moment, Jethro would then bow and tell Zeke by bowing that he didn't mean to bite Zeke as vigorously as he did. Jethro is asking for forgiveness by apologizing. For the play to continue, Zeke has to trust that Jethro meant what he said when he bowed, that Jethro was being honest.[52]

Wolves, for instance, are highly social and cooperative within their families. But, as with most members of families, fights and disagreements do happen. One wolf may charge another with hair bristling and ears back, chase another wolf, or jump on them. Even a forceful shove indicates aggression, as does a growl with teeth showing. Being pushed down or a dominant wolf standing over another is a significant message of displeasure. However, as Bekoff explains, the well-known wolf researcher David L. Mech found that the size of wolf packs (the term Mech used) is regulated by social, not food-related, factors. In other words, for wolves, the number of wolves in the pack with whom individual pack members could bond while still being able to deal with competition within the pack regulated the size of the pack.[53]

It behooves social living animals to show some forgiveness for bad behavior. In a study of reconciliation in wolves, primatologist Elisabetta Palagi and evolutionary biologist Giada Cordoni found that wolves found the means to forgive and reconcile with each other by rubbing up against each other for at least ten seconds, sniffing or licking the other's anus or genital region or another part of their body. They also used actions such as biting or chasing in playful ways. Whether the aggressor or the victim of the previous aggressive behavior initiated it, the reconciliation was equally spread through the collection of incidents, as were male- or female-initiated gestures. In general, wolves who already had the most support to reconcile from the other partner were more interested in forgiving and forgetting as well.[54]

For the skeptics, de Waal outlines why a new and more open-minded parsimony test is needed to replace the original parsimony test (a basic tenet of science that demands one must choose the simplest scientific explanation that fits the evidence). He insists that since research has documented that humans and related species respond similarly in comparable circumstances, it is more likely that the emotions behind animals' and humans' responses are similar, too. So, de Waal concludes, "The later view postulates few psychological changes in a relatively brief evolutionary time, hence is more parsimonious than the assumption that unique mechanisms underpin human behavior."[55] More simply, humans are only one part of the natural world at this time in evolution, and share emotions with other animals.

Take This Personality Quiz

Truly one of the most handsomely enigmatic animals in the world, the spotted hyena has been shown to exhibit traits indicative of creativity. With the overall posture of a slim bear, the spotted hyena is the largest of the three hyena species. This species of hyena appears dog-like and is considered part of the Carnivora order, but is part of the feliform suborder of lions, tigers, cheetahs, and other "cat-like carnivores." Hyenas have several dog-like characteristics, such as catching prey with their teeth instead of with their nonretractable claws. Unlike many feliforms, hyenas do not climb trees and share some social traits with dogs:

grooming habits, scent marking, defecating habits, mating, and parental behavior.[56] While they have been maligned throughout history as scavengers, most recently described in the Disney movie *The Lion King* as "slobbering, mangy, stupid poachers," some scientists are discovering how wrong that description and others like it are. Hyenas have been found to exhibit specific characteristics that scientists think foster innovation and creativity, such as exploratory behavior and flexibility.

Biologist Kay E. Holekamp has been studying the behavior of spotted hyenas for the last 30 years in the Maasai Mara National Reserve in Kenya and has probably done more than any other person to try to understand these maligned but fascinating and important beings.[57] Refuting the scavenger-only myth, Holekamp insists, "Unlike the three other extant hyenas, spotted hyenas are adapted for hunting medium- to large-bodied ungulates. They feed primarily on prey they kill themselves, though they will also scavenge opportunistically."[58] Using a diversity of tactics to hunt at least 30 different species, spotted hyenas are widely distributed and the most abundant large carnivore in sub-Saharan Africa. Far from their Disney description, they are cognitively complex social beings who recognize third-party relationships, form coalitions, reconcile after fights, and demonstrate cooperative problem solving. Remember the sneezing hyenas described in the fourth chapter.

Holekamp and her former graduate student, Sarah Benson-Amram, now a zoologist and evolutionary biologist directing her own graduate program in animal cognition, were interested in learning more about what kind of personality traits might exist in individual animals within a species to make them more or less innovative. Considering the list of characteristics that spotted hyenas as a whole exhibit, and their extensive knowledge of the spotted hyenas living in the Maasai Mara, Holekamp and Benson-Amram decided that the gregarious spotted hyena would more than fit the bill.

Benson-Amram and Holekamp devised a hyena-sized steel bar puzzle box with a single door through which a hyena, having smelled the meat placed inside and having successfully slid the bolt latch to swing open the door, would be able to put his head inside the box and grab the meat. The box also had two handles in the center of each short side. For each test, Benson-Amram drove through the reserve until spotting one or more of the approximately 86 hyenas of various ages and genders. These would be members of the Talek West clan of 48 members or the Fig Tree clan of 38 members. She then stopped the research truck carrying the box, deposited it in a visible location with the door pointed towards the hyena and the latch handle left protruding at a ninety-degree angle from the box, parallel to the ground. Moving the truck approximately 50 meters from the box, she started videotaping.

During a year of watching 417 of these trials with 62 individual hyenas, 88 of those trials were conducted with lone hyenas, and 329 trials were considered group trials. All of these hyenas were recognized by their spot patterns and other distinctive characteristics. Benson-Amram videotaped each trial, which included at least five "exploratory" behaviors: investigating, biting, digging, flipping the box over, and pushing or pulling it. Individuals were also scored on how long it took to start exploring the box once they had noticed it, how long they attempted to open it, whether they were able to open it, and how easily the hyenas who had previously opened the box opened it again.

The researchers found that age, gender, or social status did not matter, but the nine spotted hyenas who solved the puzzle box did so because they fearlessly and wholeheartedly investigated this brand-new object. First, it was something they had not seen before. Second, they continued to explore various solutions before they found the one that worked.[59] Neophilia and exploratory behavior are considered two personality traits in humans and now in nonhumans. Neophilia, having an interest in the new, and its opposite, neophobia, as Greenberg says, are important emotions that contribute to or constrain creativity and innovation. But, the researchers found that the addition of trying numerous ways of solving the puzzle was just as important.

In teaching creative arts, one of the most helpful and eye-opening assignments for students is being encouraged to try many different avenues for approaching a creative solution. Some, often just a few, students come to the task with so many ideas they find it difficult to choose a few to try in the time frame they have for the project. Some students, however, tend to land on the first solution and work on that or tend to stick with an approach that worked in another situation (and perhaps received praise), implementing that approach for every project. If a student is persistent with an unsuccessful approach, insisting on using that approach with every project, no matter how obstructive the repeated approach might be to the needs of the present project, the project outcome itself often falters and has to be put aside. Just throwing out that first approach and trying others might have worked wonders.

Benton-Amram and Holekamp found that to be the case in their study. Persistence alone did not help solve the puzzle. They state very clearly, "Our results suggest that the diversity of initial exploratory behaviors, akin to some measures of human creativity, is an important, but largely overlooked, determinant of problem-solving success in non-human animals."[60]

So if boldness and creative thinking are two personality traits of at least nine spotted hyenas in the Maasai Mara nature reserve in Kenya, what are the emotions that underlie those traits? Emotions in humans and animals can be a complex mix. Confidence, certainly an emotion that may materialize in boldness, might be mixed with fear or feelings of uncertainty. The same mix is present in most creative processes. Curiosity may be the emotional driver of creative thinking, but competition, hunger, lust, or pleasure may all play a role as well. What this research does tell us, however, is that the particular combination of emotion and cognition, due to genetics, physiology, and environmental factors, long called "personality" in human parlance, also serves to reveal the nuances of creativity in the lives of individual animals.[61]

That animals have personalities is something many of us have now taken for granted, though it has taken the larger scientific academic community quite a while to catch up. In the last two decades, a sizeable number of animal studies have been published showing that individuals of the same species, independent of sex or age, differ in behavior and underlying physiology. These differences have been documented as consistent across contexts and time.[62] While I was working on this chapter, a new chimpanzee personality study conducted with chimpanzees at Gombe National Park in what is now Tanzania was published.[63] Gombe and its chimpanzees are famous for Jane Goodall's pioneering research, starting in 1960, into the lives of the chimps living there. Goodall's findings and the way she approached her subjects drastically differed from the norms of studying animals in the wild at that time. Goodall herself recalls,

> These people were trying to make ethology a hard science. So they objected—quite unpleasantly—to me naming my subjects and for suggesting that they had personalities, minds, and feelings. . . . I think every single one of those scientists knew it too but because they couldn't prove it, they wouldn't talk about it. But I did talk about it. In a way, my dog Rusty gave me the courage of my convictions.[64]

Goodall has often pointed out that her dog, Rusty, had opened her eyes to the intelligence, emotions, and personalities of animals. In that way, she was like many nonscientists who learned that as well from the animals they live with.

The recent study done on chimpanzee personalities in Gombe updates one done in 1973 by the psychologist Peter Buiski and includes 100 chimpanzees that were also tested a few years ago. Not surprisingly, the most recent study, led by psychologist Andrew Weiss, found that chimpanzees in the wild have personalities similar to those in captivity, and both strongly overlap with traits that are familiar in humans, everything from playfulness or aggressiveness, openness or fearfulness, agreeableness or obstinacy to combativeness or self-control.[65] An article in the *New York Times* allows Goodall to have the last word, as she should: "Today you can get your Ph.D. studying animal personality. I think we've come around full-cycle. It absolutely vindicates all that I've ever believed."[66]

Weiss makes the point that biologists and comparative psychologists use what is called "trait theory" to understand personality in humans and nonhumans. Traits are recurring patterns of thought and behavior, such as anxiousness, trust, and openness to new things. Basing their study on personality traits, anywhere from five for basic tendencies to six hundred for more specificity, researchers can then assign a degree to which a particular trait exists in an individual to determine their personality. Weiss admits that personalities in humans or animals are not so clear cut. Humans and animals both exhibit a blend of personality traits. For instance, a chimpanzee who up to a certain point has been considered very agreeable may surprise everyone by using deceit to obtain the bananas that he was coveting.[67]

Creativity research has come to agree that creative personalities are often a blend of many, sometimes contradictory, personality traits. As Scott Barry Kaufman and Carolyn Gregoire explain,

> Creative people seem to be particularly good at operating within a broad spectrum of personality traits and behaviors. They are both introverted and extraverted, depending on the situation and environment, and learn to harness both mindfulness and mind wandering in their creative process.[68]

One important thing to remember here is that the blend of personality traits in creative people also incorporates how situations and environments affect why and how those traits might surface or display. Evolution has taught us that there is continuity between humans and other species, and so we can assume that a blend of personality traits and the particular state of affairs in which animals find themselves will interact as well. Weiss admits that relying on personality traits may seem to clash with social theories that are founded on the ability of humans to modify their behavior. While wading into academic theoretical battles is not my goal, like Weiss I see the values behind these social theories as crucial for believing in any kind of positive change, either for individuals or societies as wholes, human or animal. Using personality trait theory has helped us see that animals *have* personalities, and that is a big step forward, but the takeaway is not an either-or choice. We need to keep learning to grasp the complexity of personality in human and animal persons and consider how environmental or situational contexts might affect it.[69]

Questions about how social environments, for instance, affect a fish's personality encouraged biologist Maria Filipa Castanheira[70] and her colleagues to construct a study in which fishes were first tested to see whether they were bold or shy and whether this aspect of their personalities was consistent across different social situations. The fishes were then organized into two different schools on the basis of these personality types. A third school, however, was composed of fishes that were neither overly shy nor overly bold, in other words, who had tested to be what the researchers called "intermediate." The fourth school included an equal number of fishes who had one of the three personalities, shy, bold, and intermediate.

One month later, the researchers found, not too surprisingly, that the individual fishes that had been placed in the intermediate or equally mixed personality trait schools tested the same as they did in their original personality test. This finding confirmed that personality is generally consistent. However, and here is where this study gets interesting, some of the fishes in both the only-shy and only-bold schools showed varying results when tested a month later. The researchers found that some of the shyer fishes became bolder when hanging out with other shy fish. Similarly, some of the bold fishes became shyer when surrounded by many other bold fishes. This makes intuitive sense, of course. Surrounded by pushy people, I step back a bit, but if I am surrounded by shy people, I tend to become Miss Congeniality and try to keep the conversation going so no one feels left out.

These changes in personality when in a different social context, surrounded by other fishes who are very like each other in temperament, suggest that different social contexts have varying influences on how an individual fish might behave. The fish adjusting their social behavior based on their knowledge of how surrounding fish were behaving was indicative of a more complex social awareness. For the researchers, there could be many explanations for this, including the need for cooperation when mating, foraging, or exploring; species-specific behavior; past experiences; or social stress. But two things stand out: personalities in fishes do exist, and they can be influenced by how others around them are acting.

At the Fish Wash

As I was writing this chapter, Catarina Vila Pouca and Culum Brown published a review article outlining four major areas in research on fishes' "spatial learning, social cognition, numerical competency and cognition, consciousness and pain."[71] All of these areas have been studied for years in mammals, birds, and insects, but not fishes. As the blurb on the first edition of *Fish Cognition and Behavior*, edited by Culum Brown, Kevin Laland, and Jens Krause in 2008, says diplomatically, this was due to a historical bias leading "to the belief that learning plays little or no part in the development of behavior in fishes and reptiles."[72] The second edition came out in 2011. Brown and other fish researchers are still updating information on fish behavior, including emotion, personality, intelligence, and consciousness.

The "historical bias" against perceiving fishes as individuals still exists, but so much research is being done on differences in individual fish behavior—Google Scholar gave me 348,000 results for studies that were linked to fish personality—that it is difficult to continue to see fishes as mindless schools roaming the oceans as one group. Jonathan Balcombe, in his wonderful book, *What a Fish Knows*, says in a note, "We traditionally refer to anything from two to a trillion fish by the singular term 'fish,' which lumps them together like rows of corn. I have come to favor the plural 'fishes,' in recognition of the fact that these animals are individuals with personalities and relationships."[73]

Aside from the facts concerning how many fishes are in the sea (approximately 33,554 species as of 2017 when I checked FishBase, an online database Balcombe used for his count),[74] Balcombe points out that the number of fish is more than all species of mammals, birds, reptiles, and amphibians combined.[75] Not surprisingly, we know less about the details of the lives of our fish cousins than we do about our land-based relations. Thanks to researchers like behavioral ecologist Redouan Bshary, we are beginning to know more. Bshary's first hint that fishes were worth the respect that he had always had for them was watching a grouper and a giant moray eel team up to hunt together.[76] As these are top predators in the Egyptian Red Sea where he was snorkeling at the time, Bshary was astonished to see the grouper nod his head back and forth while pointing it downward in a handstand position to signal the eel. The eel then swam beside the grouper, poking into cracks and fissures where fish were hiding so that he and the grouper could have lunch together. Here were two different fish species who not only had used a gesture to communicate but then created a way to cooperate for mutual benefit. Fascinated, Bshary and his colleagues spent a total of 406 hours observing and videotaping grouper and eel interactions when hunting together.

Up until the study was published in 2006, communication by gesturing in animals and cooperation were thought to be the province of mostly primates and monkeys, but to have found both in fishes demanded a rethink of just how smart fishes may be, as well as a reconsideration of how intelligence has evolved. Who was the first grouper to figure out that moray eels would make good hunting partners? While Bshary and his study team did not ask this question, it would be fascinating to surmise how exactly this unique and creative cooperation began. How is it continued? Do individual groupers figure this out for themselves, or do the eels wait around for a knowledgeable grouper? Have both the groupers and the eels observed previous partnerships in their kin and then tried the behavior themselves?

Bshary's subsequent work on cooperative fish behavior is just as interesting as eel-grouper cooperation and speaks to differing fish personalities.[77] Cleaner fish (not fish who are cleaner than others but fish who clean other fish for a living) are the central characters in another example of fish cooperation Bshary studied. In the coral reefs of the Red Sea of Egypt, he and his graduate students use this living laboratory to study the cognition, social cooperation, and idiosyncrasies of both the cleaners and the clients. In small coral territories called "cleaner stations," multicolored wrasse cleaner fishes industriously chew parasites, a favorite delicacy of theirs, off the skin of client fishes. Even better is mucous that protects the skin of the fish they are cleaning. Sometimes, when the cleaner fish was just not able to resist taking a bite of that delicious substance as well, the client would jolt from the bite and Bshary and his team would be able to tell when the cleaner fish had cheated on the deal. Using game theory, "the study of mathematical models of conflict and cooperation between intelligent rational decision-makers,"[78] Bshary was able to analyze the behaviors of the cleaner fishes and their clients as a market economy. In the case of cleaner fish and their clients, factors like numerous clients, local or nonlocal clients, or the presence of other clients watching while the cleaning was taking place determined how the cleaner fish treated their clients. Just as some store owners overcharge when there are many other customers, an abundance of clients would tempt the cleaner fish to take bites out of the client's mucous more often. Cleaners would treat travelers, such as groupers who had stopped by for a cleaning, better than the smaller local fish who had to stay in the area. Some cleaner fishes with a known deceptive disposition were being watched by other clients and instead behaved well, stopping themselves from biting the client they were working on. Cleaners also reconciled with clients whom they had bitten by massaging the clients' backs with their pelvic fins. Some clients did not always accept the reconciliation massage tactic, however, especially if they had an ongoing client relationship with the cleaner. In an angry state, these clients chased the cleaner around, resulting in those particular cleaner fish cheating less for a while.[79]

Bshary and primatologist Sarah Bronson, taking game theory to heart, devised several trials in which the cleaner fish, capuchin monkeys, chimpanzees, and orangutans were tested with colored food plates. The game was to see how quickly any of the animals realized that the food on the differently colored temporary plate should be eaten first before it was taken away. The cleaner fishes prevailed in this test and also came out in front when given a more advanced version that switched the function of the colored plates. Primatologists and others who have based intelligence on brain size admitted that they felt challenged.[80]

Whether these findings point to fish who happen to be smarter than primates and humans is not the point. "Redouan [Bshary] has thrown down the gauntlet to us primatologists," says Carel van Schaik, an expert in orangutan culture at the University of Zurich in Switzerland. "He has made us realize that some of the explanations of primate intelligence that we have cherished don't hold water anymore."[81] Frans de Waal points to Bshary's work explicitly when he says, "Primate chauvinism may now be poised to decline, thanks in large part to Bshary's fish work. . . . They now really do have to take on board that most species are going to have a smart intelligence."[82]

Kevin Laland, one of the pioneers in the study of animal innovation, says this about the recent research on fish: "There is now extensive experimental evidence that social learning and tradition play an important role in the behavioral development of many fishes, and frequently underlie differences in the behavioral repertoires of different populations."[83] He points out that like other social animals across species, they constantly and flexibly adjust to information and resources in social and other areas of their lives, often taking creative advantage of opportunities that might be beneficial to them or their groups. Like many other animals, they learn from others what the best mating sites might be, where best to forage, and how best to defend themselves from predators, among other daily life challenges.

I am going to let Jonathan Balcombe have the last word about cleaner fishes because it leads directly to our next topic, creative culture. He says, "Given its complex social nuances, it would not surprise me if the cleaner-client mutualism involves culture. To biologists, culture is non-heritable information transferred across generations."[84] Studies have documented that many fishes maintain traditional breeding sites not according to any intrinsic element of the site itself but because of social convention. Blue wrasses, herrings, groupers, snappers, surgeonfishes, rabbitfishes, parrotfishes, and mullets also return to the same breeding areas, and fishes also follow cultural standards in daily and seasonal migrations.[85]

Emotions play an integral role in the creative process, as a driver, as an incentive, as an integral part of the process itself. If anything has changed in our view of animals over the last few decades, it is the growing acceptance of animals as emotional beings. A large portion of the population—69 percent of US adults surveyed by the Humane Research Council—support "the goal of ending cruelty toward and suffering of animals," and so it would seem this chapter is redundant. Unfortunately, it is not. Even the people who support this goal do not always connect their everyday behavior with how that might affect an emotional being. The idea that reptiles, such as turtles, fish, or insects, might grieve, show courage, seek revenge, or, for that matter, exhibit compassion is a far-fetched idea even among animal lovers. Yet, many scientists are investigating these emotions in all kinds of species.

Crayfish, for example, exhibit complex responses such as anxiety or fear to stressful situations, while honey bees exhibit pessimism. Documented in recent issues of prestigious journals such as *Science*[86] and *Current Biology*,[87] these kinds of studies encourage us to consider the emotional lives of all kinds of animals. Like us, animals' emotional lives are influenced by their innate nature as well as environmental influences. As with us, their creativity may be enhanced or obstructed by positive or negative emotions. Animals have a great deal to tell us about our emotions and how they might affect our creative choices. Just as importantly, the general creativity that fuels this planet relies on the emotional health and creative flow of the millions of animals who individually and collectively practice it in their everyday lives.

7

Culture across Species

Tools, Songs, and Moral Codes of Conduct

Culture is like a flower. It needs to be in the sun to thrive.
—Barry Edgar, in Krista Langlois, "First Nations Fight to
Protect the Rare Spirit Bear from Hunters"

A large, brown, hairy head pops up above the tall, gently rolling sedge grass. It quickly rises further on top of a massive shaggy chest, an enormous nose to the wind, eyes squinting in our direction. I have no time to register the fear I expected but do not feel as just below and to the right of the first head, another slightly smaller head appears, duplicating the rising behavior. The effect is so comical and charming in its artlessness that any anxiety I have had about this moment vanishes. The mother grizzly and one of her cubs have scented and seen us and now ponder whether we will bring them any trouble. Their visible anxiety calms my own. The mother drops onto all fours, camouflaging her from our position on a hollow red cedar log about 100 feet away. There is a pause as Doug, our guide, turns to us and brings his finger to his lips. Then he says, almost inaudibly, "Here she comes."

We are not sure for a moment where she will appear, closer to us through the grass or farther away headed towards the riverbank. When she appears, about 50 feet to our left, lumbering through the sedge grass with her two cubs following close behind, she appears to be taking her time. She glances at us every so often, giving us a very wide berth. When she reaches the closer and shallower arm of the estuary, she stops and takes one long look to make sure we are staying put and then wades knee-deep into the rushing water. The cubs follow close behind. They, too, throw glances our way, but more directly, swiveling their heads as far back as they can while still moving. All three disappear for a second behind the jumbled roots of an enormous rotten and fallen cedar just this side of the bank. And then the mother grizzly is in the water, wading in up to her flanks, crossing the wider arm of the river, still turning her head our way for a few quick looks. The first cub enters the water when her mother is halfway across, but the water is up around her neck and so she paddles strenuously, struggling to get a purchase on the opposite rocky shore. Still lingering near the tree trunk, the second cub, captivated by something he is sniffing on the ground in front of him, suddenly turns directly towards us and stares. Despite the constant whistle of wind, I hear a group intake of breath from everyone but Doug.

Just as suddenly the cub turns and splashes into the water, swimming furiously to catch up with his sibling and mother. The other cub turns to greet him from the shore, but the second cub continues until he emerges from the water further downstream, sniffing his way along the shore and through the brush and sedge until all three of them disappear. The wind still whistles through our hoods and parkas, but we are quiet. As much as the bears must have been taking in our scent, it occurs to me that I only smelled them in one strongly pungent gust as they passed us going to the stream. It is that unforgettable odor, even more than seeing the bears so closely, that allows me to register the truth of them. I saw a grizzly bear and her two cubs less than 50 feet from me. Slowly the four of us turn to each other with gleeful and awed looks, though few words. We all are speechless. I know that an important moment in my life has just occurred, a pivot upon which other experiences will revolve, not so much in comparison but in reverberation. The world as previously perceived will now have to be reconsidered. I had known that wild animals had their own lives and families, but seeing and smelling the mother bear and her cubs in their homeland shift my somewhat intellectual notion of wild animals' lives to a visceral understanding of these specific bears in their home.

We are in Mussel Inlet, in what is now called the Great Bear Rainforest (Great Bear), the largest intact coastal temperate rainforest in the world. With a human population of only one person per 6.75 kilometers, the Great Bear lies within the central and north coast of British Columbia, Canada. This immense, isolated land of ancient coastal forests, mountain ranges mixed with glaciers and ice fields, mazes of islands, and estuaries leading into deep fjord inlets has a biomass (weight of organic matter) four times greater than comparable areas in the Amazon jungle. Stretching from the landfall of Port Hardy across Queen Charlotte Strait on the northern tip of Vancouver Island to the Alaskan border, it is roughly the size of Switzerland.

This is home for a profusion of animal, plant, and sea life—and home as well for six major First Nations groups. Although media labels the Great Bear an unspoiled wilderness, my first visit to the Great Bear left me with the profound but simple understanding that what we refer to as wilderness has always been, for many animals and some humans, not wild at all, but simply their home.

One of the most valuable experiences of my life, and one that opened my eyes to animals as members of families and cultures, was this stay with the Kitasoo/Xai'xais First Nation in the village of Klemtu on the island of Princess Royal in northern British Columbia, home to the Spirit Bear. There was no lodge, as there is now, only a swaying float house to stay on. Getting there took two plane rides, a water taxi, and a tumultuous ferry that only ran twice a week. There are still no roads there. It is the "wildest" place I have ever been to and also the most outrageously gorgeous. When I say "wild," I mean that for most of the Great Bear, the ratio of humans to land is quite low and so, compared to many places on earth, untouched by humans. Klemtu's name is from "Klemdoo-oolk," a Tsimpsean word meaning "impassable."[1]

When I was there in 2006, Klemtu's population was 420, and in 2007 it was 505. The Kitasoo/Xai'xais, along with other First Nations bands and hundreds of species of animals, call this area home. Kitasoo/Xai'xais First Nations assume strong ties to animals in this indigenous community because their culture and heritage are directly connected to their intimacy with the land, sea, and animals surrounding them. Historically, specific animals are clan members, including the Spirit Bear (grizzlies with white fur), brown grizzlies, black bears, wolves, eagles, raven, orca, and salmon.

Invited to watch a dance practice in the Big House, I noticed that of the animal-named clans represented, only the raven, wolf, orca, and eagle appear. Later, our guide and member of the Kitasoo First Nation, Doug Neasloss, explains that the remaining clans, the Grizzly Bear and Black Bear, were killed off by smallpox. Contact with Europeans and the viruses they brought devastated First Nations people across North America. Not once, but twice on the north and south coasts of British Columbia in the 1700s and 1800s, diseases like smallpox decimated the rich and varied cultures of the estimated 200,000 to one million indigenous groups that lived there.[2]

I was lucky to have had Doug as a guide when I visited, as he is a driving energy behind what is now a thriving sustainable wildlife tourism business, Spirit Bear Lodge. Then and now, I have the greatest respect for Doug and the people I met in Klemtu. Doug became the elected chief of the Kitasoo band for a time until 2020. Where once unemployment was 80 percent, it is down to 10 percent, thanks to the new lodge and its place as the second-largest employer in Klemtu. All the money goes to meet the needs of the people of Klemtu in sustaining families and communities. This includes the Coastal Guardian Watchmen, who protect the bears, wolves, raptors, and other animals from trophy hunting. I traveled with a watchman on his rounds on the inlets and channels and spent many hours with Doug and others talking about the relationship of his band and the animals who also inhabit their tribal lands.

Protection of predators in their environment comes from a deeply held culture of kinship with the animals they live with every day, often seen elsewhere as ferocious, as evil, or as hunting trophies. I experienced firsthand how intimately knowledgeable Doug and his fellow bandmates are about bears they recognize and know year after year. Doug disclosed how he often attempted to understand the bears' reactions to color by wearing different-colored clothes on different days. Images of that stayed with me and eventually filtered into my thoughts on creativity in animals. That day at Mussel Inlet there were five of us, including Doug and myself. After our journey there by tugboat through glacier-carved fjords, past sparkling inlets and dense green islands, one visitor with us finally asked Doug what was in the case he was carrying. It was obvious she was hoping he would say it was a gun. "A camera," chuckled Doug. He explained that there was no need for a gun. He had been coming here, often alone, for years and knew these bears. Bringing a gun only made things tense, fostering a feeling of distrust, he said. He did not actually say that bringing a gun fostered a feeling of mistrust in the bears and in the onlookers, but having spent time with him, I assume that was what he meant. The cultures of the Kitasoo/Xai'Xais and the cultures of the animals who live in the Great Bear Rainforest are entwined, recognized on both sides, and respected. Something we all could learn from.

In Culture, We Trust

Animals of all kinds across the globe have myriad types of social arrangements. Social animals rely on staying close to the family members where help is abundant. This has long solved a problem that all parents face. Meerkats of southern Africa, like the prairie dogs of the third chapter, are one of the various groups (in this case, a clan) of animals that stay in collaborative formations, sharing food gathering, protection duties, and "babysitting." Mammals, such as elephants, wolves, and vampire bats, and invertebrates, such as bees, termites, ants, and spiders, live in communities of diverse social structures. African wild dogs, chimpanzees, naked mole rats, lions, bee eaters, kookaburras, pied kingfishers, and Seychelles warblers are part of a long list—220 birds and 120 mammals—found to help rear others' young.[3] "*Alloparenting*," or babysitting another's offspring, is referred to as "reciprocal altruism" in animal behavior research. Researchers have also noted that empathy may play an important role in these kinds of behaviors in animals, especially if the offspring is an orphan.[4] We know that empathy is often a tool of creative activity and, as I mentioned earlier, the ways parents devise means to take care of the young are possible examples of creative behavior. These instances are useful for researchers who are approaching the cultural lives of animals through what biologists call "social learning."[5] It is one way in which the young of the species learn both traditional and newer, innovative behaviors or artifacts that may spread through the population.[6] Definitions of culture are expanding to include animals. One major way of recognizing culture is to look for creative behaviors or products developed and passed on in their communities. Let's return to my definition of creativity, given in the introduction: *"a dynamic process in which novel and meaningful behaviors are generated by an individual with the possibility of affecting others at cultural, species, and evolutionary levels."* Individual creative behavior may lead to new information, novel behavior, or new artifacts and have the possibility of being passed along to others and installed as a cultural way of doing things. Hal Whitehead and Luke Rendell, authors of the book *The Cultural Lives of Whales and Dolphins*, define "culture" as "information or behavior—shared within a community—which is acquired from conspecifics through some form of social learning."[7] They argue that it also can cross species, as it does in the vast community of the Great Bear Rain Forest.

Contentious Culture

When first collecting research for the book, I found animal culture still being handled as a contentious topic in fields such as psychology, biology, anthropology, evolutionary biology and ecology, and philosophy. Over time, what constitutes an acceptable, even important, topic may alter if enough brain power and political will support its study. In 2009, the book *The Question of Animal Culture*, edited by biologist Kevin Laland and psychologist Bennet G. Galef, included writers from a wide selection of these fields.[8] Opinions in the book were divided, with skepticism coming from one psychologist, three anthropologists, and one philosopher out of 15 chapters. Six years later, a Sackler National Academy of Sciences Colloquium about "The Extension of Biology through Culture" hosted researchers studying both human and animal culture. The "culture wars" in which proponents of animal culture and naysayers on the topic published effusively to support their side of the argument have ended. An increasing number of new studies demand that we recognize that many animal species not only creatively innovate but often change their cultural traditions by doing so. Andrew Whiten and his colleagues who led the Sackler colloquium recall that it was not until the mid-twentieth century that the idea of other species besides the human transmitting cultural information through their behavior became a topic worthy of scientific investigation.[9]

During that time, reports of animal culture recognized innovations by animals and acknowledged their widespread use. Three of the most famous were titmice tearing the foil from the tops of bottles to drink the milk inside, primates crafting and using tools, and Japanese macaques washing wheat and potatoes before eating them.[10] These were early indicators of innovations by animals that were then spread widely enough to become a cultural tradition in each case. As well, within this window of time, researchers found that many birds culturally transmitted their songs through social learning. For some birds, songs are not genetically inherited but passed from individual to individual with songs differing in local dialects.[11]

But the acceptance of culture in animals had to leap over the cultural barrier of human exceptionalism—the belief that human beings have special status based on our unique capacities—and the scientific barriers to accepting definitions of concepts from other scientific disciplines. The way a cultural anthropologist defines culture substantially differs from the way a sociologist does so, and an art historian's definition is different still.

As Whitehead and Rendell explain, culture is important to many fields: "Culture is central to anthropology, art history, and some areas of psychology and archaeology. But it is also studied by sociologists, biologists, economists, and historians. A scholar's definition of culture often highlights what he or she studies."[12] Those studying human culture, and basing their definitions on peculiarities of that species and that species alone, might miss the cultural and behavioral nuances belonging to other species. Whitehead and Rendell's definition is like those of other researchers in how they prioritize the words "information" and "behavior." They agree with others who see culture as a way that behavior moves from animal to animal, in contrast to genetic inheritance. Culture may interact with genetic evolution on a large scale. One individual's creativity may spread in small groups, then neighbors, and mushroom within a wide range over time, shifting the behavior of a species. Might that change affect the biodiversity of an ecosystem? Well, yes, we would have to say that it is not only possible but also probable. Think of Patrick Bateson's suggestion that humpbacks' using bubble screens to catch fish was originally a creative behavior that emerged from play. The scientists who documented the first known instance of bubble netting used for catching fish theorized that to be the case.[13] Look around for the nearest piece of plastic and you will have another excellent example of a novel product generated through a creative process that spread throughout many populations and cultures, even though this example is from the human species, and it has turned out to be an environmentally destructive one.

Philosopher of biology Grant Ramsey has constructed another definition, hoping human cultural researchers and those who study culture in animals might use it: "information transmitted between individuals or groups, where this information flows through and brings about the reproduction of, and a lasting change in, the behavioral trait."[14] This definition omits what he perceives as the "somewhat vague and controversial concept of social learning" and does not predetermine who exhibits culture.

He says, "If guppies, lizards, or octopuses transfer information amongst themselves in such a way that it flows through and brings about the reproduction of, and a lasting change in, a behavioral trait, then it is a cultural species."[15] I like the content of this change, as it encourages research on cultures across species that do not fit the assumption that only social learning can transfer cultural information and adds the possibility of change being inherent in its spread. He also clearly links innovation (the product of creative behavior, exploratory behavior, or an environmental response) in this way: "It may not be wrong to use innovation as an indicator of culture since they are empirically highly correlated."[16] As I was completing the final edits on this book, I came across a more recent review of the diffusion of traditions or innovations in communities of both animals and humans. Andrew Whiten and his colleagues reviewed field studies with evidence of culture in species as diverse as insects and primates. More to the point, he acknowledges,

> Whilst as in 2008 most of the animal social diffusion experiments were addressing only the (fundamental) question of the capacity for cultural diffusion in the species and context studied, these newer studies analyzing social networks illustrate a shift to tackling the underlying decision rules.[17]

In simpler language, in 2008 research focused on *whether* a particular species had culture, whereas now the focus is on *how* culture spreads in many species.

What I appreciate most in Whitehead and Rendell's work with whales and dolphins is their firsthand knowledge of the animals they study. They could not have chosen an order of animal whose behavior is more difficult to investigate since much of it takes place underwater and over immense ranges of the ocean. Whitehead and Rendell have spent a combined total of 50 years observing and documenting the behavior of wild whales and dolphins. Several well-known culture researchers insist on experimental work in captivity as a necessary legitimizing seal of approval for whether culture exists in animals.[18] But the observations and data analyses made by the combined knowledge, experience, and tenacity of Whitehead and Rendell prove the case that field research yields knowledge of behavior missed or not available in a captive environment. Studies on captive animals are carried out under human constraints that often hinder any actual social behavior, let alone innovative or cultural behavior. As Lori Marino and Tony Frohoff argue, "Captivity for both wild-caught and captive-born cetaceans is devastating on several levels ranging from harm to the captive individuals to negative effects on entire populations in the wild, even when a small number of individuals are removed from their social groups."[19]

Whitehead and Rendell describe their lifetime of work on cetaceans in this way: "We whale scientists only stumbled into whale culture in the first place, and our discoveries are still largely the result of long-term, large-scale observation together with happenstance—lots of happenstance."[20]

Culture across Species

Hoping to clarify just how much work has been accomplished by researchers on social learning and animal culture, a 2017 review reported that 100 research groups published work covering 66 species, with two-thirds involving field research with wild animals.[21] These included mammals, primates, fishes, birds, and insects. Science changes constantly, and reptiles now have a place in this group of social learners. Bearded dragons were tested in cognition experiments, one of which showed that they were capable of imitation. As discussed earlier, imitation has become a lynchpin to understanding animals' cognitive faculties, and for some psychologists, it has been a necessary indicator of whether a species has culture or not.[22] For other researchers, it is a helpful but not an essential sign of culture in a particular species. In this study, one bearded dragon was trained, using a mealworm treat, to open a wire door covering a hole in a wooden board. With his head or foot, he moved the door along sliding horizontal rails. He became the "demonstrator" for the experimental group who all successfully imitated him to open the door and get a mealworm treat. The "demonstrator," however, did not show the control group how to open the door, and so no dragons in that group could open the door. Lead researcher Anna Wilkinson asserted, "The finding is not compatible with the claim that only humans, and to a lesser extent great apes, are able to imitate."[23] She suggests that learning by imitation is likely based on ancient mechanisms. The next question is, Why have we never thought of discovering whether these reptiles could imitate before this? Imagine what studying bearded dragons outside captivity would teach us about their lives.

If imitation shows how behavior transfers from animal to animal, what does one do with octopuses, notoriously nonsocial beings? I became fascinated with octopus mimicry when Leesa Fawcett, a marine biologist in the Environmental Studies Department at York University in Canada, presented a paper entitled "The Case of the Mimic Octopus: Agency and World-Making" at a conference I was cohosting.[24] The confounding images of mimic octopuses imitating the exact form, colors, and behaviors of sea snakes, lionfish, and flatfish were one of the many high points of the conference. A recent study on how octopuses use mimicry to camouflage themselves found that while many animals' colors blend in with their environment, octopuses match the texture of part of the environment—say a coral reef—by not only changing shape but also changing their color to blend in. They can do that so completely that predators at any angle cannot see them. And they accomplish this while being color-blind.[25]

Sadly, octopuses have brief lives, and until now have been thought to be solitary. However, a small underwater city where octopuses congregate exists in Jervis Bay off the East Coast of Australia. The team of researchers led by David Scheel named it Octlantis.[26] A similar site named Octopolis by its discoverer Matthew Lawrence in 2009 revealed a stable, if somewhat combative, social life in octopuses. It exists not too far from the preceding site in the same bay. Peter Godfrey Smith highlights this site in his fascinating book *Other Minds: The Octopus, the Sea, and the Deep Origins of Consciousness*.[27] With this example of heretofore unknown behavior of beings that have lived on earth for the last 500 million years, my suggestion is that we trash any belief that we have learned all there is to know about *any* animal. Assumptions that only humans are intelligent, social, and creative enough to have developed cultures are not only being questioned but also are being proved wrong.

The Way We Do Things

Animals unlike us in physical form or behavior have cultures of their own making. While the research literature on primates outnumbers that on any other group, I want to focus on two bodies of culture research opening up extremely valuable questions about how the creative abilities of animals might lead to important answers about their cultures. Whitehead and Rendell have simplified their definition of culture by using the more memorable phrase "the way we do things." Their research, along with that of others studying cetacean culture, has had an enormous impact on the opening of scientific minds to the idea that all kinds of animals have culture.[28] The matrilineal units of enormous sperm whales have dialects that match those of other clans who speak with the same codas of a click language. These social groups of mothers and calves are the basic unit of community for sperm whales. Sperm clicks are like a South African Xhosa speaker but oh, so much louder, since sperm whales are the owners of the "world's most powerful sonar system." Clicks function for sperm whales as both language and echolocation. Differences in codas—culturally transmitted dialects made up of different numbers of clicks—have helped researchers distinguish five vocal clans in the South Pacific not by genetics but by differences in the clans' language and behavior, two components of sperm whales' cultures. Female sperm whales are nomadic, and as killer whales are among their predators, Whitehead and Rendell conjecture,

> Their stable points of reference are each other, the members of the social unit with whom they travel. Female sperm whales are intensely commu-

nal. . . . "We" and "us" may be more important than "I" and "me" for female sperm whales. And "we" have a characteristic set of behavior, "our"
culture, the way we do things.[29]

Vocal dialects are key to understanding orcas' cultural heritage, since
their group's dialect, learned from their mothers and other members of
their matrilineal group, is one way they identify with their social conditions, the calls changing subtly over time. Other aspects of orca culture
are even more differentiated by "ecotypes," distinct ways of life defined
primarily by food. Since I am of Italian descent on both sides and was
brought up in the United States, where assimilation was alluded to but
not entirely practiced, the thought of cultures built on food makes a
great deal of sense to me.

Even in the same waters, some orca ecotypes eat fish, some eat
mammals. The Pacific Northwest, where I live now, has three distinct
ecotypes, Antarctica has four. Whitehead and Rendell describe what
happened when three mammal-eating orcas were captured off the coast
of British Columbia and housed with fish-eating orcas. After refusing to
eat the salmon they were given for 75 days, one of the three died rather
than eat it. The other two took four more days to decide to eat the of-
fending fishes but immediately returned to eating mammals after being
returned to the ocean after a few months. If one had any doubt that
orcas were cultural animals, this example ought to remove any hesita-
tion. Certain types of food have always played important roles in how
a culture identifies itself and how its members enjoy each other's com-
pany. Being "picky eaters" is just one of many aspects of orca cultures.
For our use, one of the most interesting insights from these findings
in orcas is that the researchers who have worked for long periods with
orcas believe, along with Whitehead and Rendell, that the differences
between ecotypes are established for many generations and the importance of culture in the lives of orcas has over time driven the evolution
of genetic patterns. As Whitehead explained at the Sackler conference,
"Evolution is dependent on inheritance. Although the transmission of

genes is primary, it is not the only mode of inheritance. . . . Culture, as an inheritance system, can be defined as behavior or information shared within a community that is acquired from conspecifics through some form of social learning."[30] Whitehead's inclusion of social learning in this definition, while working for whales and dolphins, might eject some species from the cultural circle. Whitehead's is an example of how most researchers learn from their primary research animal and gives us a picture of how definitions limit experience with other species. The research by Whitehead and Rendell, however, affirmed by the long years of firsthand experience with whales and dolphins, proves the existence of culture in these animals.

Whitehead and Rendell's work on culture in whales and dolphins is affecting other researchers' interest in how culture not only may form animals' lives but also may affect animal evolution. In the 1990s, Whitehead coined the term "cultural hitchhiking." Part of his argument for gene-culture coevolution in cetaceans began with noting that the matrilineal whales—the killer whale, the sperm whale, and the blackfish species—have a genetic anomaly. Compared to other whale and dolphin species' diversity of mitochondrial genomes, theirs is approximately a tenth of that for other whales and dolphin species, even though mitochondrial DNA is handed down from the mother in all cases. Aside from the DNA inside the nucleus of the cell, mitochondria also have DNA. One of their functions is to convert the sugars from food into energy, among other jobs. Since daughters stay with their mothers for life and matrilineal whale species have low genetic diversity of mitochondrial DNA, he used the term to explain how this might occur. He insisted, "In cultural hitchhiking, smart, as well as stupid, cultural behavior passing through the matrilineal societies drags neutral mitochondrial genes with it."[31]

If staying with their mothers would act to increase their chances of surviving and reproducing, the behavior would become more common throughout this population. Another example might be a communal defense. Sperm whales sometimes use a head-out defense, with all members facing out towards the attackers, and sometimes they turn inward with their heads together and protect themselves with their flukes. The researchers have not documented which method is better, but Whitehead argues, "The mitochondrial genes have hitchhiked on the good idea because the genes and the ideas travel in the same vehicles—individuals—along the same road—through the maternal lineage, with the cultural variants driving."[32] Bad ideas, however, will reduce the frequency of the mitochondrial genes being passed along in parallel with them. A bad idea or a good idea—heads out or heads in—may drive down the genetic diversity of the matrilineal whales.

One of the many examples of cetacean culture is the creative use of sponges as tools by dolphins. Sponging dolphins who live in Shark Bay, Australia, have long captured their corner of the media since they were first documented in 1997. Some dolphins carry sponges on their rostrums (noses), and they probe along and into the crannies of the sea floor. Of course, there has been debate over what the definitive reason might be for their use of sponges. A recent book, *Deep Thinkers*, edited by Janet Mann, a member of the team that first documented this behavior, thinks they have pinned down what the dolphins are doing with this tool.[33] She and her team tested various scenarios and found that the sponges allow the dolphins, who usually use echolocation to detect their prey, to find prey that is difficult to detect even with echolocation. Most fishes have a swim bladder, a gas-filled organ that controls buoyancy and allows dolphins to detect these fish with echolocation. Bottom-dwelling fishes, however, have lost their need for swim bladders since they don't move up and down in the water column but stay at the bottom of the ocean. The dolphins have discovered that using a sponge helps to disturb and catch the fish living there, often the bladderless barred sand perch, and it also protects their noses from harm while doing so.[34] Not all dolphins in Shark Bay sponge, but the dolphins who do come from one matriline. Mostly females practice sponging, only a few males do it, and while no one has documented the mothers teaching their calves this technique, the calves who sponge have mothers who sponge.[35] Like the humpback whales who bubble net, the dolphins who sponge have created a unique tool to help them forage in their particular environments. Whitehead and Rendell and others see this as an example of cultural hitchhiking and an example of how creative tool use by "the Eve of Sponging" radiated through a particular community of dolphins.[36] It has not become a trait but has changed the culture of a large community of dolphins.

Mann specifies that there are some differences between tool use in terrestrial animals and tool use in those whose home is the ocean. Chimpanzees and capuchins crack nuts with stone tools at sites that are revisited by many others. Communal use of tools at these sites allows the young to learn from others and their mothers. Tools used in the sea are not stable and eventually are buried by sediment.[37] Nonetheless, all the attributes that indicate culture in chimpanzee and capuchin tool use are recognizable in dolphin sponging behavior, including another social aspect of sponging. Spongers prefer hanging out with other spongers. "This is the way *we* do things."

Whitehead and Rendell pinpoint the mother-calf bond as a constant in their understanding of cetacean culture. For the calf, the constant of a potent source of information, learning, milk, and mother love for many months sometimes, and for a lifetime in others, is the foundation of a stable island in a vast sea. The effect over time of this bond and sense of "we-ness" on the mitochondrial DNA may result in limits to mating with others, which could allow for gene-culture evolution. Whitehead admits that the cultural hitchhiking on the mitochondrial DNA producing low genetic diversity (as in conservative matrilineal units such as orcas) may be rare, but he suggests that there may be other cetacean species in which either physical or social barriers to mating between cultures could involve nuclear genes on gene-culture coevolution.[38] I want to describe two examples of cultural importance in cetaceans revealing the comparable and yet unique aspects of their ways of life, and how creative behavior is the foundation of these cultural phenomena.

Creating Songs

The haunting songs of humpback whales have been heard around the human world because of Roger and Katy Payne's recording and subsequent distribution of the vinyl album, *Songs of the Humpback Whale.*[39] Ten million copies were inserted into the January 1979 issue of *National Geographic* and distributed around the world in 25 languages.

For humans, listening to humpback whales' slow and purposeful communication from a world so foreign to the terrestrial life of cities evokes a powerful response. The slow spirals shape a vortex of wonder even the most cynical of us rest in while listening. I want to revisit these songs because, like bird songs and other nonhuman sounds, they reveal the enormous gaps in knowing other species for themselves. Understanding where these gaps in our knowledge are is important because they might tell us something more about ourselves, but they are crucial in learning more about the lives happening all around us, something we desperately need to do.

The songs of humpback whales change through both cultural evolution and revolution. Those listening to them have heard large-scale changes in these songs over decades. Previously it was thought that adult male humpbacks sang these songs to attract and seduce females. Research published recently found that overwintering males in the subarctic feeding grounds sang changing song cycles throughout the dark winter even though these males were not actively pursuing females.[40]

The songs themselves are complex and organized in a nested hierarchy of what researchers call units (single sounds), phrases (a sequence of units), and themes (repeated phrases). Different themes are sung in a set order to produce a song. Different versions of these songs contain different themes, and singers within each population usually conform to a song type at any given time. However, songs constantly change, and males must learn and incorporate these changes to continue this conformity pattern. This is a cultural evolution in which extremely subtle changes from one song type to the next occur over long periods, sometimes several years. It is kind of like those categories of music on radio stations: all '70s radio, all '80s radio—you get the picture. Researchers who study humpbacks in the western and central-western Pacific region have found that cultural revolutions in a song also take place. All the males in a neighboring population of whales rapidly adopt a song type from a nearby group. While song revolutions seem to be rare in humpbacks, they allow researchers an opportunity to understand how singers such as humpbacks learn those songs.[41]

Looking specifically at hybrid songs, those that whales have spliced together from new and old songs, researchers found that the whales were accomplishing this even before the new song was adopted. Like other students everywhere, including humans and songbirds, whales split songs into theme segments that are more easily learned separately. As an individual whale learns a new song, he combines these new segments with the old one. A male would need to hear the new song from multiple singers, giving him a general overview from which he would be able to know what to learn. As in bird song and, let's say, human poetry or prose, pauses and repetition may help with memorization. The researchers in this study also looked at transitional phrases, often excluded in analysis, that helped to mediate the change from an old song to a new song. Including these phrases suggested that whales recognized similar anchor points that show at what position in the old song switching to the new song musically makes sense. These transitions might help the whales learn these complex and lengthy songs. Once a population of whales learns a new song, all males switch to it.[42]

Does this mean whale song is music? Where do the new songs come from? Are there specific individual whale composers who send out sheet music to whales around the world? If the humpback males conform religiously to the dictates of these songs in their population, even when learning a new song, does this mean that these songs are not creative but just copies? It is very difficult to hear humpbacks sing and not find that the singing itself is an appreciable part of their songs' profound musical power. The copying, combining, and remixing described above is an indispensable part of the creative process. We know human creatives make use of this process in disciplines from poetry to design to music to science. Remixing ideas, words, images, phrases, sounds, structures, and data is how the arts and the sciences build upon some older ideas while jettisoning others.

A recent book by Hollis Taylor, *Is Birdsong Music? Outback Encounters with an Australian Songbird*, also may help answer those questions.[43] An accomplished violinist and composer with a doctorate in musicology, ornithology, and composition, Taylor is now a research fellow at Macquarie University. Her book offers an in-depth and long-term exploration of the vocalizations of the pied butcherbird set against her firsthand recordings and knowledge of these birds in the outback of Australia.

For Taylor, pied butcherbirds share with human musicians, among many musical sounds and behaviors, the use of repetition and variation in creating their songs. She confirms for me that although they are masters (and mistresses, since both genders sing) of solos, duets, and choruses, pied butcherbirds are not unique, since other species like nightingales, European blackbirds, humpback whales, and, oh yes, humans, use these same techniques.[44]

In great detail and with the rigor and expertise of musicology, Taylor has spent 12 years attempting to understand their potent and abundant use of combining, or what she calls "combinatoriality." What she has found is that this widespread technique is an excellent way to "generate new ideas and achieve complexity."[45] "We developed a statistical estimate to quantify phrase order. We found that while birds of high repertoire complexity keep interest going by having different phrase types, they avoid confusing their avian audience by placing familiar motifs into their phrases."[46]

When discussing originality and creativity, Taylor insists that borrowing and copying play a significant role at every level of music, including that of songbirds. Our reactions to the songs of the humpback and this research on their songs encourage us to include humpbacks as well. Copying and borrowing in the symmetry of dolphin swimming also may be included. The meanings it has for the dolphins themselves seem to revolve around safety and alliance. I wonder, however, if like dancing or sex, the synchronization of swimming has a choreographed aspect. We have looked at choreographed or communicative movements in birds, insects, and fish. Why not in cetaceans? If there is a kinesthetic intelligence, there is certainly kinesthetic creativity, and investigating that is more than likely a rich source of knowledge about how animals might use this form of creativity in their lives. Let's look at another topic not always associated with creativity, morality.

Culture and Creative Morality

What Whitehead and Rendell call "how we do things" includes moral codes of conduct that involve how animals behave towards others. It only makes sense to ask, Do animals have moral codes as part of their cultures? Although morality is always a tricky topic, I would be remiss not to include the many discussions in the research of morality as a component of animal culture. A timely paper in the journal *Current Anthropology* explained the outcomes of testing 60 unique human cultures across the globe on seven cooperative behaviors: helping kin, helping one's group, reciprocating, being brave, deferring to superiors, dividing disputed resources, and respecting prior possession. Those seven behaviors were considered positive except in one culture where respecting prior possessions was seen as a weakness. The authors propose that since cooperative morals are observed in the majority of cultures, with equal frequency across all regions of the world, the morality-as-cooperation theory could stand as the unified theory of morality for anthropology, at least.[47] That a universal morality might be encapsulated in other-regarding behaviors is something I would like you to entertain. Does a behavior help the good of others or work against it? Since we have not yet dried off from being in the ocean for most of the chapter, let's see what Whitehead and Rendell might contribute to this conversation.

Paraphrasing the arguments they have heard from those who deny that animals are capable of morality, they cite rationality and culture as two strong obstacles against the idea of morality in animals: "So only humans can be moral because only they can rationally consider their own actions and only they develop in a cultural context that imbues a moral sense."[48] Whitehead and Rendell proffer several examples that certainly disprove the first requirement, rational consideration in human situations. They quote from interviews with people who have rushed to save someone, despite the obvious danger to themselves, who say rationally considering their actions did not occur to them until perhaps after the event. (A personal aside: those who would consider in a rational way whether they might be hurt and therefore not save the baby from the fire are probably not the people you want in your moral camp.) Whether or not animals think rationally at other times has come up in discussion elsewhere in this book. We have made the case that some animals do think in ways that pass the rationality test, but like humans, not all the time. That rationality is the only order of "good" thinking is false. It certainly does not help if one has only ten seconds to save that baby from a fire that may kill or maim you.[49] In their book, Whitehead and Rendell offer several anecdotes that frame how individual whales and dolphins have acted in a kind and moral way. One example, however, demonstrates that animals are able to consider their actions rationally and place those actions in the context of their cultural mores. I will start with that since it offers a good rebuttal to the argument that animals cannot be moral on terms set out by those who say they cannot because they are not rational.

Morality includes both right and wrong. Among the most compelling anecdotes suggesting that dolphins have concepts of "wrong" behavior is Thomas White's description of how a human snorkeler observing Atlantic spotted dolphins off the Bahamas went outside the bounds of behavior norms expected by the dolphins of human observers at that site. The swimmer approached a calf engaged in learning to fish with its mother, a no-no in the rules of engagement between swimmers and these dolphins built up over years. When this happened, the mother then swam not to the hapless trespasser but to the leader of the group of swimmers, whom she could identify and tail-slapped, her displeasure apparently directed at the leader who had not controlled the behavior of those being led.[50]

The mother dolphin showed that she not only knew the rules of behavior for her own species but was knowledgeable about how the humans in her waters were expected to act as well. She knew exactly whose authority she should consult to complain about this egregious transgression of the terms of engagement already in place. The fact that she complained to the leader of the group of swimmers is, in my estimation as a mother, a much more rational behavior than one that might have included ramming the snorkeler for his impropriety.

I also point you to Whitehead and Rendell's book for examples of a humpback whale saving a hapless seal from the orcas who were about to eat him; a bottlenose dolphin guiding a set of pygmy sperm whales off a sandbar and out to the ocean; a group of dolphins who sought out and stayed with a lost swimmer until the Coast Guard came to pick him up.[51] One other example from the book bears mentioning, and that one comes from the pioneering and influential biologist and marine researcher, the late Ken Norris. Norris recognized what he called "echolocation manners" in dolphins. Being zapped by an echolocating dolphin is an unpleasant experience. Norris found that dolphins did not turn their echolocation on each other, always angling it down and away. He thought this corresponded to the staggered and layered swimming formations of larger groups of dolphins.[52] Whitehead and Rendell, when explaining these examples and their position on cetacean morality, assert, "If a human did what the cetaceans did in the episodes we just described, there would be no debate as to whether they were moral."[53]

Whitehead and Rendell also note how damaging the enormously loud sonar of sperm whales might be to other sperm whales. These whales also seem to have values that preclude them from using their echolocation on each other. We, however, do not seem to have those values completely handled since the use of sonar by humans damages and sometimes contributes to the death of whales, dolphins, and other sea life. Human-generated sonar is still being used across the globe.[54]

That animals have morality is not entirely new. Darwin had an opinion on the topic, as did the philosopher Hume, though both felt the need to qualify their belief by limiting its reach. Both Darwin and Hume felt that animals possessed the essentials of moral behavior in the emotions they possess, but their moral behavior had not been developed into the moral agency practiced by humans. In other words, Hume and Darwin and, more recently, de Waal, according to philosopher Mark Rowlands, acknowledge that animals have both the emotional and the cognitive equipment to act morally, but not the extra something humans have that allows them to reflect on their motives and formulate or understand the principles on which they have acted, nor do they have an impartial sense of justice. Rowlands argues that animals are able to act morally, but should be considered not moral agents but moral subjects. He argues that *animals as moral subjects are capable of being motivated by morally laden emotions involving a moral evaluation or judgment.*[55] My goal here is not to argue those points.

Rowland's argument will assist me, however, in making the case for the role of morality in the creative lives of animals. The subject of animal morality has been gaining momentum since 1996 with the publication of de Waal's *Good Natured: The Origins of Right and Wrong among Humans and Other Animals,*[56] followed by Bekoff's and Jessica Pierce's *Wild Justice,*[57] Dale Peterson's *Moral Lives of Animals,*[58] Rowland's *Can Animals Be Moral?,*[59] the edited book by bioethicist Jonathan K. Crane, *Beastly Virtues: Animals as Ethical Agents,*[60] and a recent essay in the *Journal of Ethics* entitled "Animal Morality: What It Is and Why It Matters."[61]

Morality and Creativity

The larger topic of morality in animals is truly important. The books listed above have added a richer layer of meaning to the more universal definition of creativity I am arguing for in this book, and I am in debt to those who have written them. How the morality of animals gives us further insight into their creativity is another topic one needs to keep an open mind about. I hope my examples throughout the book about creativity in animals and the research supporting them have given you a picture of a different creativity, a larger, more inclusive creativity existing throughout the animal world. I have drawn out similarities and differences between our notions of creativity, including the creative process, and the creativity found in the individual daily lives of other species. Judgment or, more simply, choice, is a crucial step in the creative process. At some point, an animal or a human animal has to decide to commit to one action at a time. "The idea of judgment in ethics is all-encompassing. It involves one's entire being, for it is the way we choose among many possibilities. Those choices commit us to paths which are more or less consistent with our nature and the rest of our lives."[62] Both creativity and morality rely fundamentally on the ability to make judgments. With that in mind, let's look at why several scientists and philosophers think animals have morality, including a sense of justice, as part of their cultural repertoire.

Marc Bekoff and Jessica Pierce say this in *Wild Justice*: "We argue that animals have a broad repertoire of moral behavior, and that their lives together are shaped by these behavior patterns. Ought and should regarding what's right and what's wrong play an important role in their social interactions, just as they do in ours."[63] Their book collects research on this topic across species. Bekoff accomplished a great deal of pioneering research on play in wolves, coyotes, and foxes, and this informed his ideas about animal morality. I have a personal example I would like to share.

Quite a while ago, I had the pleasure of living with a wolf. The details of how that came about are not as important as what I learned from my time with him. From that experience, I wish to share one instance that has influenced my belief that animals can be creative and sometimes in a moral way. At the time, two dogs also shared my home, a gentle and playful male golden retriever, Radicchio, and a female mixed golden, Sophia. Thunder, the name given to the wolf, was about three times larger than either dog. Radicchio and Thunder often played together, and as was usual with Radicchio, he was fine with Thunder always getting the best of him. Sophia was another matter entirely. Sophia had often given Radicchio a hard time in their life together. As she was three years older than he was, she had always treated him like her errant child. Lately, she had suffered from both internal and external ill health, and she had grown less patient with all of us. She was not happy about this new and much larger member of the family, but I noticed that Thunder went out of his way either not to interact with her or, when interaction was necessary, to carefully show her polite deference. One day, after I had just put food out for everyone, Sophia marched over to where Thunder was just tucking into his meal. Before I knew what was happening, she had bitten his haunch. For the first and only time in my experience with him, he morphed into the snarling wolf of fable. It lasted only a second, but Sophia backed off, and I realized Thunder was bleeding. As I was trying to discern how serious the wound was, Sophia, seemingly fearless, returned to challenge Thunder. If a wolf could roll his eyes, Thunder did. He looked at me as if to say, "You have to be kidding me!" Instead of lunging at her again or worse, he spread himself over the food so that she would have to pry him off to get at it. At this point, I grabbed her collar and escorted her and her food bowl to another room and shut the door, wanting no more conflict between them. The creative solution Thunder performed of protecting his bowl with his body and the fact that he had not followed up with an all-out attack on her told me two things. First, he was aware of the fact that she was old, sick, and part of the family, and attacking her was out of the question, and two, another solution had to be found quickly that would still protect his food. If anything in our time together allowed me to perceive Thunder's mind and morals, this experience said volumes about who he was as an individual.

Jim and Jamie Dutcher studied wolf culture firsthand over six years: "Wolves are complex, highly intelligent animals who are caring, playful, and above all devoted to family. Wolves educate their young, take care of their injured, and live in family groups."[64] As we have seen in other species, close friendships run deep with caring and attention. Yes, the alpha mating pair play a significant role in leading the pack, but individuals in the pack also have their own personalities and roles—even the omegas, the lowest-ranking member of the pack. Researchers and advocates Jim and Jamie Dutcher describe the intense friendship between the beta wolf Matsi and the omega wolf Lakota in the Sawtooth pack that they observed and documented from 1991 to 1996. Lakota was the brother of the alpha male and the largest wolf in the pack, but still the lowest-ranking wolf. Matsi often protected Lakota and didn't seem to mind if Lakota got the better of him in play. Omegas are often the instigators of play to diffuse tension in the pack.

Another example of wolves caring for individual family members involves a female omega, Motaki, who also was very good at initiating play with her packmates. Because of her omega status, she often spent time alone far from the pack, and alone she was killed by a mountain lion. The Dutchers describe how the pack mourned after her death:

> For the remainder of that spring and well into the following summer, their behavior changed and they appeared depressed[;] hanging their heads they drifted about their home in a listless manner. . . . After Motaki's death, their howling changed for a time. No longer gathering together, they would howl separately with very little energy. Their vocalizations had a mournful searching quality, as if they expected her to come back. These behavior changes continued for over six weeks.[65]

Françoise Wemelsfelder's work on the accuracy of untrained observers of animals' behavior shows the human animal's ability to judge how other animals also react to situations and sometimes make judgments that can be called moral. Bekoff and Pierce agree and argue a strong case for animals having "the cognitive and emotional capacities for moral behavior."[66] They assemble research and data from Bekoff's and others' long-term studies, all substantiating play, but also other behaviors, as evidence for moral emotions in animals. Fairness and cooperation are important to animals that live in extended families, such as wolves. Wolves rely on those qualities when hunting cooperatively, both to hunt safely and effectively and also to ensure that everyone gets to eat. Although lower-ranking members of the pack have to wait longer, they do eat. Learning how to be fair and the pleasures of cooperation are experienced in play. Empathy, say Bekoff and Pierce, is a building block of morality. Neural and behavioral examples in varying species appear throughout their book and help us place similar behavior in wolves into this context. The flexibility needed to engage in play, to recognize both when a partner is apologizing for being too rough and when a partner fleeing is a playful suggestion to chase is great practice for the everyday creativity needed to live cooperatively and fairly among kin. Bekoff and Pierce specifically assert, "Moral agency is species specific and context specific. Furthermore, animals are moral agents *within the context of their own communities.* . . . Wolf morality reflects a code of conduct that guides the behavior of wolves within a given community of wolves."[67]

Within their pack and sometimes outside of it, wolves are emotionally moral beings. Ethologist and conservation biologist Jane A. Packard agrees with famed wolf researcher David L. Mech in thinking that the terms of the dominance hierarchy, such as "alpha," "beta," and "omega," do not fit the typical wolf pack social organization. She argues that the model, defined by some researchers and perpetuated by popular education materials, is "inappropriate for typical packs consisting of parents and offspring."[68] She insists that in most packs, family dynamics are typically more complex. Packard prefers to consider the alpha behavioral profile as something that a wolf feels internally, a "mood."[69] As she explains, moods change with the health and environment of the individual and are affected by both temperament (inherited tendencies) and character (learned styles of coping). This description fits with the personality research we have discussed and shows how some wolves end up as leaders and others do not. She says, however, that situations and outcomes of family dynamics may change the overall personality of an individual. Remember the fish personality studies described in the last chapter. Some shy fish morphed into brave fish when surrounded by shy fish. Individuals sometimes change their behavior to fit circumstances.

Individual animals play essential roles in the flourishing of species. As individuals, their individual qualities contribute to how and whether their social group, even if their group experience is only during mating or gestation, will contribute to the continuation of their species. Packard, in a more recent article on wolves' social intelligence, connects the intricacies of the changing social environment to how "littermates, care-givers, mates, rivals for mates, hostile neighboring groups, and permeability of group barriers to immigration" affect and are affected by behavioral resilience.[70] How does an intact family structure of wolves, with one breeding pair, compare to the fragmented nature of wolf packs that have been hunted? Reviewing the major stages in the lifetime trajectory of individual wolves—dependent pups, pre-reproductive adults, reproductive adults, and post-reproductive adults—she finds the idea that wolves are social due to group hunting a simplistic notion and one that comes from those unable to examine "the more complex, and fascinating, evolutionary processes at these nested levels in wolves." The intact family structure of wolves, and other social animals, contributes to the behavioral flexibility of individuals within these nested structures. Individuals are more able to generalize from one situation to another because of their initial and ongoing interactions with their family members.

Generalizing and flexibility are indispensable in creating novel solutions to situations not experienced before, and, for wolves, situations of many kinds. The kind of learning that happens in play is a good example. Wolves do more than hunt together; they live together as a tightly integrated unit. This includes sharing food, raising or helping to raise pups, protecting kin, and reconciling after spats. They bring the full force of their intelligent, emotional, empathic, and creative personalities to bear on those interactions. They are aware of themselves as individuals but also as part of a family with whom they share their lives.

Packard, who has studied wolves and other animals for over 35 years, offers an event she documented in 1988 of an intact wolf family as evidence of the awareness and empathy of wolves in interactions between pups and their caretakers, in this case, their mother, Nipples (NI), their father, Grayback (GB), their older sister (WH), their brother (GN), and their uncle:

> NI started across the slope and the movement of the other 3 adults compelled the pups to follow, walking amongst them. However, a couple of pups balked at climbing a small drop and started to wander back the way they came. First, one adult then another turned back to watch the pups. . . . WH returned, sniffed the ground, stood near where GN had laid and howled. Puppy voices answer from a pile [of pups lying together] that looked like a nearby rock. GB returned to WH and GN stood and howled. GB laid near the pups and WH trotted toward GN, followed by GB. NI returns across the skyline with WH nose-touching eagerly (did WH get NI?). As WH and NI return to the pups, GB lies at the ridgeline watching the outcome. NI walks right past the pups who start to follow, pause, then follow as they are joined by the 3 adults.[71]

She summarizes and evaluates her notes in this way:

> In this episode from my experience, I see elements of communication, learning, problem-solving, and awareness. Although the mother, Nipples, was unaware that the pups stopped following her, all the other adults were very aware and adjusted their travel to the change in behavior of the pups. . . . When GB laid near the pups, my impression was that the behavior of the pups was the deciding factor coordinating the travel of the adults.[72]

The creativity of individual animals is bound up in their everyday lives. Packard wonders whether the female yearling (WH) perhaps brought Nipples (NI), the mother, back to her pups. The males were just as concerned. They were patient and mindful of the needs of their young. Losing one of these individuals would rip apart the fabric of that familiar care and, I insist, love. Life for all animals, including humans, is difficult and full of loss and grief as much as it is full of joy and happiness. And yet, as we open our eyes to the varied gifts of animals and nuances of their creative lives, we are simultaneously aware of the large proportion of loss they are suffering, not only individually but as entire species. If we turn our thoughts to our own cultures and their varied recognition of moral compassion and moral justice, how then can we not expand our inclusion to the beings all around us?

Epilogue

Creativity Has Its Reasons

Creativity is a powerful force throughout the biosphere, at both micro and macro levels. Individual animals creatively solve problems they face in areas such as communication, building, play, tool use, sex, parenting, group living, foraging, or hunting, and sometimes pass those solutions on to others in their group. These solutions may be novel and useful to others of their species and diffused through cultural avenues over time, affecting their evolution. Humans, too, solve problems creatively, sometimes passing those solutions on to other humans, and this may have over time affected their evolution. The first creative behavior by an individual animal has not been recorded, nor have those millions of everyday creative behaviors by individuals of many species. These everyday instances of creativity, what comparative psychologists call "little-c," are valuable, perhaps only to the individual who has solved their problem, but they are still novel and useful to that individual. In the diffusion of these behaviors to large populations, we also find what could be considered Big-C creativity.[1]

Creativity is often invisible. As humans, we recognize it in the composition of a piece of music that uplifts us when the world seems unbearably dismal. We recognize it in the empathic abilities of an author to allow us to immerse ourselves in the world of another. We occasionally consider the creative jolt that a physicist may experience when one of his experiments works. But more often, it is the natural world that surprises us, excites us, astonishes us, or leaves us in awe of the immensity of what is not us. We are swimming in an ocean of creativity. It is happening all around us all the time, in all the creatures surrounding us, even in those that we do not see.

In the introduction, I suggested that asking whether animals are creative would bring up all kinds of questions. I have tried to answer those questions throughout the book, but I also want to revisit those questions here at the end of our journey together to see if answering them might spark more options. The first question was, Does describing types of animal behavior as creative mean that animals are creative in the same ways as humans? The examples of creativity in the book come from an array of species found in the animal kingdom. While a great deal of research on mammals has been done, a recent scan of the twenty-five most cited articles in the journal *Animal Behavior* between 2015 and 2019 reveals nine studies on mammals, but five on birds, six on fish, and five on insects. Seventeen concern general animal behavior methodologies concerned with emotion, social network analysis, personality traits, social cognition, exploratory behavior, cultural evolution, associative learning, social complexity, and motivational traits, indicating that these methods are useful in studying many species.[2] We have seen these methods used throughout this book to help us understand creativity in animals. According to Samuel D. Gosling writing about personality, for instance,

> Past research has established that personality (a) exists and can be measured in animals; (b) can be identified in a broad array of species, ranging from squid, crickets, and lizards, to trout, geese, and orangutans; and (c) shows considerable cross-species generality for some dimensions.[3]

But does that mean that species personalities are fixed, and therefore their ways of being creative are identical? Simply, no. If researchers are finding commonalities in the methods used to study animals, that does not automatically imply that the creative processes found are identical across species. No matter how hard I try, I will never sing like a songbird, even though songbirds have similar vocal learning brain circuits to those mediating human speech.[4] As we saw in the communication chapter, different species of songbirds sing discrete songs unique to their species and sometimes in unique dialects. I cannot make the surrounding water dance as I bellow infrasonically into the dusk as male alligators do to attract female alligators. And I certainly cannot make honey no matter how much nectar I try to collect. While researchers are trying to understand what commonalities species might share, the uniqueness of each species combined with the individual creative process ensures diversity. We are like other species *and* we are different. We need to absorb the meaning of that conclusion.

If we are serious about resisting global warming, then we need to see how vital biodiversity is to the health of the planet. Restoring and protecting biodiversity is the main aim of conservation biology. Differences between species and their unique interactions with the world drive biodiversity. Previous conservation "efforts had been framed predominantly in terms of preserving 'biodiversity' conceptualized in genetic terms."[5] With the discovery of widespread animal cultures—once thought to be only found in human animals—it is now evident that individual diversity within these diverse animal cultures has a crucial impact on the survival of species. Disregarding individual animals' creativity and its influence on the distinct cultures of animals across and within species has limited previous research on social learning, a necessary path for accumulating cultural knowledge. Philippa Brakes and 24 internationally based colleagues insist that specific conservation programs succeed due to considering the differing social structures of animal groups and their individual members.[6]

Science has recognized elephant matriarchs as essential leaders of their family units since at least 1975, although people who have lived alongside elephants in the wild have known this for much longer. The matriarch is respected as the leader of a family because she uses her knowledge gained from years of experience to guide younger elephants. She knows the best places to find food, the safest migration routes, the areas where water can be found, what predators are a real threat, and other knowledge that will allow her family to flourish.[7] Older family members of other species provide expertise learned over time, such as cod elders who provide the migratory routes to younger family members.[8] Meerkats are another species whose older members provide babysitting and mentorship in both foraging and recognizing danger.[9]

Brakes and her collaborators recognize how important traits in individuals, such as flexibility, encourage creative responses to human impacts affecting their group or family. If we are to contribute positively to "future proofing" vulnerable populations, cultural variation and the creativity it relies on need to be conserved. In many cases, this is a tall order when so much of the planet has been changed by human intrusion. But, researchers such as Brakes and her colleagues are offering paths towards that goal.[10]

This leads us to the next question: How do these findings affect how we think of our own creativity? For me, they have encouraged my understanding of how ethical arguments concerning animals are bolstered by science-based comprehension of why we need to acknowledge the limits of human creativity. Much of human creativity has been directed towards the benefit of our species, often to the detriment of other species. Within the development of new technologies, such as biotechnologies and geoengineering, to name only two, humans have created processes whose risks are as high as their assumed benefits.[11] Biotechnology changes living organisms for medicinal, agricultural, or industrial uses. Geoengineering tackles climate change by removing CO_2 from the air or limiting the sunlight reaching the planet. Both technologies interfere with natural processes, something we have been doing for centuries, but without such widespread irreversible consequences. Both have major negative consequences for the natural world. Briefly, geoengineering entails enormous risks for biodiversity, nutrient and water cycles, and land use.[12] Genetic technologies, an example of biotechnology,

> disrupt the sequence of the genetic code of the host, disturbing the functioning of neighboring genes. . . . The practical outcomes of this are unanticipated side-effects for the recipient organism and special risks that come with the use of viral genes and vectors in genetic engineering.[13]

The largest study done so far on the risks of genetically modified organisms (GMOs) revealed environmental impacts of GMO crops: the adoption of GMO soybeans correlated with a negative impact on the environment as increased herbicide use also increased contamination of local ecosystems.[14] Recent studies have discussed the increasing number of new viruses and chemicals affecting pollinators, such as bees.[15] A great deal of creative energy is invested in the development of these technologies, and humans benefit in some ways from their implementation, for a time. But repercussions of these technologies will affect humans detrimentally as well. Without consideration for the creativity that exists in the natural world, we are at risk of losing its vast diversity of species. Only one species will remain: us. The links between morality and creativity are applicable here, not only for animals as moral subjects but for us as moral agents. Because the choices we make about how we use our creativity have had and will continue to have an overwhelming impact on the common good. How is it that the goals and products of our creative behavior have led us into the environmental miasma we are experiencing today? Human activities are the major cause of the sixth great extinction of plants and animals. Species loss is equal to or worse than the loss of the dinosaurs 65 million years ago. While species extinction happens naturally, it happens at what is called a "background" rate of one to five species per year. We are losing dozens of species every day. By midcentury 30 to 50 percent of all species will head towards extinction, unless we change our thinking, our behaviors, and our industries in multiple ways.[16]

Scientists in many disciplines have begun to creatively address these issues by working together across disciplines and across global habitat. While wildlife corridors—on the land, in the sea, and in the air—have existed as long as animals have, humanly designed wildlife corridors are a relatively new addition to conservation. In a paper discussing human resistance in planning wildlife corridors, authors from a wide variety of natural and social sciences discuss three case studies: wolves in Washington State, United States; leopards in Goleston Province in Iran; and large carnivores in Central India.[17] They argue that analyzing only the physical habitat animals travel through is not enough to secure their safe passage. Human attitudes, both negative and positive, shape animals' ability to move across the landscape to find resources, locate mates, or respond to climatic change. This "anthropogenic resistance" to both the animals and the corridors often functionally dooms the animals using them or intensifies the human-animal conflict. The authors of this paper argue for combining the expertise of the natural and social sciences to more helpfully address the needs of both the humans and the animals involved in these endeavors.[18] After all, the most creative thinking exists between the disciplines, that area where past assumptions are put aside and previously hidden connections are made.

This leads to my next question: Might asking these questions change the way we define creativity? If we continue to define creativity only in human terms, we will squander the opportunity to question the limits of our current definition of creativity, which encourages a human creativity that obliterates the creativity of the rest of the world. Until we see our creativity as only a small part of that larger universal creativity of biodiversity, we will lose the very core and abundance of its gift. I am again referring to the idea of creativity as a gift, as does Lewis Hyde in the first quotation in the book. Hyde was writing about the commercialization of art and creativity and its impact on the essence of creativity as a gift that is given. This idea applies to the gifts that animals bring into the world, not merely as witnesses or guardians of the biodiversity of this planet but as its creators. We are in danger, more than ever, of stopping the circular nature of creativity, of killing off its creators and finding ourselves without a means for those gifts to return.

That is the worst-case scenario, and it is one to consider, but solutions are available and staring us in the face. We just refuse to see them. Many of these solutions require changing old thinking and established behaviors. We know this is difficult, some say impossible. I do not think this is true. Humans are also creative, as we are so fond of telling ourselves. We know that species extinction and climate change will have enormous effects on life for much of the world population of species, if not all. How do we tackle that when so much about how we have chosen to live obstructs change? We must overcome our fear that if we give up anything that we now have there will be nothing to take its place. If we can shut that proverbial door of fear, the door to recognizing the gift of a universal creativity will open for us. Only then will we gain an endowment more creatively healthy, more creatively conducive to helping others, all kinds of others, to flourish creatively as well.

I hope that the hundreds of examples in this book of the creative lives of a wide variety of animals—and I have not even mentioned the creative lives of plants—combined with the definition framed in the introduction will entice the reader to think differently about creativity. This would entail not continuing to see creativity as a mono-species process but recognizing it as one that dynamically flows through multiple species on the *individual, cultural, species, and evolutionary levels.*

Will this redefinition of creativity affect the way we perceive and act towards animals? I certainly hope so. If my initial goal in writing this book was to investigate how I could add productively to a shift in thinking and acting ethically towards animals, the result of researching and writing it was to open up a whole new comprehension of just how creative animals are. My lack of knowledge about animals' lives humbled me when I started this project, and I was overwhelmed with respect and gratitude towards the researchers who have amassed vast bodies of knowledge about the lives of animals. They have documented for us animal's intelligence, their creativity, their emotions, their agency in their own lives, and their contributions to what makes this planet as unique and deeply beautiful as it is.

Might it contribute to changing the way we view our place in the world? Discounting the profuse ways the creative process works is a major stumbling block to understanding its power. We need a redefined sense of a universal multispecies creativity. Individuals and cultures of all the beings on this planet are indispensable contributors to this creativity. We are only one species among millions of others who have been gifted with intelligence, abilities to communicate, the joy of play, the capability to build and use tools, the biodiverse exuberance of sex, the wide range of emotions that make meaning in our lives, and the ability to create cultural traditions and morals to contribute positively to the common good not just for us but for all the species with which we share this gorgeous and ineffable planet. Recognizing ourselves as one species of many is a sure road to fostering our imagination and securing our bond with how imagination and creativity flow.

ACKNOWLEDGMENTS

I wish to acknowledge the traditional homelands of the Kalapuya peoples of the Willamette Valley of Eugene, where I wrote the bulk of the book.

Great thanks go to Ilene Kalish, the editor from heaven, who acquired the book for NYU Press, and to Colin Jerolmack, the guest editor of the Animals in Context series. The process has been exquisitely supportive and anxiety free, with just the right advice from both Ilene and Sonia Tsuruoka at exactly the right moment. Great thanks are due to my copyeditor, Emily Wright, for her meticulous work and thanks for her patience to Senior Production Editor, Alexia Traganas. Everyone at NYU Press, it is truly a pleasure to work with you.

The scientists and others who accepted my interview invitations were all extremely generous with their time, experience, and knowledge. Françoise Wemelsfelder, Annie Potts, Robert Fagen, Con Slobodchikoff, Donald Kroodsma, Richard O. Prum, Hollis Taylor, Robert Crabtree, Camilla Fox, Julie Andreyev, and Mary Lee Jensvold have changed the way we think about animals, and how we study them.

Thanks to Annie Potts for sharing her thoughtful and lovingly perceptive anecdotes about the chickens who make their homes with her. Thanks and admiration are due to Gloria Grow for her warm welcome to the Fauna Foundation, and for allowing me to see firsthand the incredible care given to all the animals there. It is such a pleasure to be able to include Julie Andreyev's thoughts and writing about her creativity and how it was influenced by collaborating with animals in her immediate world. To Julie, Maria Lantin, and everyone involved in the "Interactive Futures' 11: Animal Influence" conference, your insight is visible here.

I was lucky to have astute and imaginative readers early on in the proposal process who gave inordinately helpful comments, suggestions, and support: Calder G. Lorenz, Paula Levine, Sharon Romero, Mercedes Lawry. All four were also willing to listen to what I was researching for hours on end, and without their encouragement the whole process would have been much more daunting. Particular thanks go to Jill Rothenberg and Jeff Kleinman for their generous support and edification early on. My thanks also to the anonymous reviewers who offered both encouragement and critique. The book was much better because of your feedback. To my friends and colleagues in human-animal studies and critical animal studies in many fields, I am lucky to be included among you. No matter the position, together we are making change. You know who you are! Your work is inspirational and always meaningful for this struggle.

Great thanks are also due to Marc Bekoff, Jessica Pierce, Yvette Watt, Phillip Armstrong, Deb Merskin, Lori Marino, Rod Bennison, Jessica Ulrich, Susanne Karr, John Sanbonmatsu, Carol Freeman, Jodey Castricano, Karen Davis, Char Davies, Tanya Das Neves, Ramona Lyons, Karolle Wall, Stephanie Ellis, M. Simon Levin, Sadira Rodrigues, Terra Long, Marilyn McKinley, Megan Burroughs, Lisa Zisa, Pamela Byars, and Leslie Bishko. Thank you to my sister and biggest supporter, Joanne Gigliotti, and to the rest of our family, Jennifer Valli and John Boughter and Rob and Dobrinka Valli, for your friendship and loving support through difficult times.

My very special love and thanks go to my son, Calder Lorenz, and his wife, Kendra, who have been phenomenal supporters and helpmates throughout. You are the lights of my life. And to Nancy and Tom Regan, who are always in my thoughts.

NOTES

INTRODUCTION

1 Edgar et al., "Avian Maternal Response to Chick Distress."

2 Bonetto et al., "The Paradox of Creativity."

3 Van Leeuwen, Cronin, and Haun, "A Group-Specific Arbitrary Tradition in Chimpanzees (Pan Troglodytes)."

4 Jung et al., "The Structure of Creative Cognition in the Human Brain."

5 Gordon Burghardt, "Creativity, Play, and the Pace of Evolution," in *Animal Creativity and Innovation*, ed. Allison B. Kaufman and James B. Kaufman (London: Academic Press, 2015), 200.

6 Lewis Hyde, *The Gift: Creativity and the Artist in the Modern World* (New York: Vintage, 1979), 68.

7 Stan A. Kuczaj, "Animal Creativity and Innovation," in *APA Handbook of Comparative Psychology*, ed. Josept Call et al. (Washington, DC: American Psychological Association, 2017), 630.

8 Kuczaj, "Animal Creativity and Innovation," 636.

9 Jung et al., "The Structure of Creative Cognition in the Human Brain," 1.

10 Jung et al., "The Structure of Creative Cognition in the Human Brain," 1.

11 Csikszentmiyalyi, *Creativity*.

12 David Bohm, *On Creativity* (London: Routledge, 1998).

13 Bohm, *On Creativity*, 75.

14 Simon M. Reader and Kevin N. Laland, eds., *Animal Innovation* (New York: Oxford University Press, 2003).

15 Kevin N. Laland, *Darwin's Unfinished Symphony: How Culture Made the Human Mind* (Princeton, NJ: Princeton University Press, 2017).

16 Kaufman and Kaufman, "Applying a Creativity Framework to Animal Cognition."

17 Kaufman and Kaufman, eds., *Animal Creativity and Innovation*.

18 Mora et al., "How Many Species Are There on Earth and in the Ocean?"

19 Donald R. Griffin, *The Question of Animal Awareness: Evolutionary Continuity of Mental Experience* (New York: Rockefeller University Press, 1976).

20 Gordon M. Burghardt, "Amending Tinbergen: A Fifth Aim for Ethology," in *Anthropomorphism, Anecdotes, and Animals*, ed. R. W. Mitchell, N. S. Thompson, and H. L. Miles (Albany: State University of New York Press, 1997), 268.

21 Urquiza-Haas and Kotrschal, "The Mind behind Anthropomorphic Thinking."

CHAPTER 1. ANIMAL INTELLIGENCE

1 Inoue and Matsuzawa, "Working Memory of Numerals in Chimpanzees," R1004.
2 Inoue and Matsuzawa, "Working Memory of Numerals in Chimpanzees," R1005.
3 Macrae, "I'm the Chimpion!"
4 Merriam-Webster Dictionary, 2017, s.v., "intelligence."
5 "Visible Smell," in *Animal Life*, ed. Charlotte Uhleenbroek (New York: DK Publishing, 2008), 446.
6 Payne, Langbauer, and Thomas, "Infrasonic Calls of the Asian Elephant (Elephas maximus)."
7 Knight, "Seeing and Communicating through Weak Electric Fields"; Markham et al., "Circadian and Social Cues Regulate Ion Channel Trafficking."
8 Mateos-Rodríguez and Liechti, "How Do Diurnal Long-Distance Migrants Select Flight Altitude in Relation to Wind?"
9 Fagot, Young, and Wasserman, "Discriminating the Relation between Relations."
10 Bruck, "Decades-Long Social Memory in Bottlenose Dolphins."
11 McGrane, "Moscow's Metro Dogs."
12 "Stray Dogs Master Complex Moscow Subway System."
13 Clayton and Dickinson, "Episodic-Like Memory during Cache Recovery by Scrub Jays."
14 Grainger et al., "Orthographic Processing in Baboons (Papio papio)."
15 Grainger et al., "Orthographic Processing in Baboons (Papio papio)," 248.
16 King and Janik, "Bottlenose Dolphins Can Use Learned Vocal Labels to Address Each Other."
17 Connor, "Dolphin Social Intelligence."
18 Hal Whitehead and Luke Rendell, *The Cultural Lives of Whales and Dolphins* (Chicago: University of Chicago Press, 2015).
19 Herzing, "SETI Meets a Social Intelligence."
20 Kuczaj, Yeater, and Highfill, "How Selective Is Social Learning in Dolphins?"
21 Brett H., "Dolphins Waiting to Steal Fish from a Stingray." YouTube video, 5:04, www.youtube.com/watch?v=YgwdL4xeXJw.
22 Lipkind et al., "Stepwise Acquisition of Vocal Combinatorial Capacity in Songbirds and Human Infants."
23 Iacoboni, "Imitation, Empathy, and Mirror Neurons."
24 Schilbach et al., "Toward a Second-Person Neuroscience."
25 Keysers and Gazzola, "Social Neuroscience."
26 Hickok, "Eight Problems for the Mirror Neuron Theory of Action Understanding in Monkeys and Humans."
27 Moffet, *Adventures among Ants*, 221.
28 Moffet, *Adventures among Ants*, 222.
29 Moffet, *Adventures among Ants*, 165.

30 Moffett, "Why Don't Ants Play?"

31 Wystrach, "We've Been Looking at Ant Intelligence the Wrong Way."

32 Wystrach et al., "Backtracking Behaviour in Lost Ants."

33 Marino and Colvin, "Thinking Pigs."

34 Gonzalez-Crussi, *A Short History of Medicine*.

35 Mendl, Held, and Byrne, "Pig Cognition."

36 Hatkoff, *The Inner World of Farm Animals*, 80.

37 Mendl, Held, and Byrne, "Pig Cognition."

38 Franks and Richardson, "Teaching in Tandem-Running Ants."

39 Thornton and McAuliffe, "Teaching Can Teach Us a Lot."

40 Françoise Wemelsfelder, email interview with author, December 12, 2014.

41 Wemelsfelder interview.

42 Low, "The Cambridge Declaration on Consciousness in Non-Human Animals."

43 Wemelsfelder interview.

44 Wemelsfelder interview.

45 Wemelsfelder interview.

46 Wemelsfelder interview.

47 I ran the words "sentient" and "behaviorism" on Google Ngram Viewer to find this information in graph form.

48 Bartlett, "A New Twist in the Sad Saga of Little Albert."

49 United Press, "Ecstasy Causes Depression in Pigs."

50 Rutherford et al., "Qualitative Behavioural Assessment of Emotionality in Pigs"; Wemelsfelder, "A Science of Friendly Pigs."

51 Wemelsfelder. "A Science of Friendly Pigs," 224.

52 Wemelsfelder. "A Science of Friendly Pigs," 228.

53 Wemelsfelder interview.

54 Polsby, "The Contributions of President Richard F. Fenno, Jr."

55 Wemelsfelder, "How Animals Communicate Quality of Life."

56 Wemelsfelder interview.

57 Willette, "The Enduring Symbolism of Doves."

58 Wasserman et al., "Pigeons Learn Virtual Patterned-String Problems in a Computerized Touch Screen Environment."

59 University Communication and Marketing, "Pigeons Peck for Computerized Treat."

60 Scarf, Hayne, and Colombo, "Pigeons on Par with Primates in Numerical Competence."

61 Fagot, Young, and Wasserman, "Discriminating the Relation between Relations."

62 Franks and Richardson, "Teaching in Tandem-Running Ants."

63 "Animal Cognition."

64 Gardner, *Frames of Mind*.

65 Gardner, "Frequently Asked Questions."

66 Castro and Wasserman, "Crows Understand Analogies."

CHAPTER 2. COMMUNICATION UNLIMITED

1 Lewis and Clark, *The Journals of Lewis and Clark.*
2 Lee, "Accounting for Conquest."
3 Woodger and Toropov, *Encyclopedia of Lewis and Clark Expedition,* 287.
4 "Black-Tailed Prairie Dog."
5 Slobodchikoff, *Chasing Doctor Dolittle,* 59.
6 Slobodchikoff, *Chasing Doctor Dolittle,* 59.
7 Slobodchikoff, *Chasing Doctor Dolittle,* 55.
8 Slobodchikoff, *Prairie Dogs: America's Meerkats.*
9 Slobodchikoff, *Chasing Doctor Dolittle,* 62.
10 Slobodchikoff, *Chasing Doctor Dolittle,* 61.
11 Con Slobodchikoff, Skype interview with author, March 10, 2017.
12   Slobodchikoff interview.
13 Robert Crabtree, phone interview with author, March 9, 2016.
14 Crabtree interview.
15 Slobodchikoff interview.
16 Kellogg and Kellogg, *The Ape and the Child.*
17 Slobodchikoff interview. For brain, gut, and heart connections, see Hadhazy, "Think Twice."
18 Daemen, "The Heart and the Brain."
19 Ferris Jabr, "Can Prairie Dogs Talk?"
20 Munz, *The Dancing Bees,* 220.
21 British Museum, "Everything You Ever Wanted to Know about the Rosetta Stone."
22 "Visible Smell," in *Animal Life,* ed. Charlotte Uhleenbroek (New York: DK Publishing, 2008), 446.
23 Brown, Garwood, and Williamson, "It Pays to Cheat."
24 Hanlon, Conroy, and Forsythe, "Mimicry and Foraging Behaviour of Two Tropical Sand-Flat Octopus Species off North Sulawesi, Indonesia."
25 Brown, "It Pays to Cheat," 730.
26 Randall, "Vibrational Communication," 126.
27 Caldwell et al., "Vibrational Signaling in the Agonistic Interactions of Red-Eyed Treefrogs."
28 Caldwell et al., "Vibrational Signaling in the Agonistic Interactions of Red-Eyed Treefrogs," 1016.
29 "Social Issues Update."
30 King, *How Animals Grieve,* 9.
31 Katy Payne, William Langbauer, and Elizabeth Thomas, "Infrasonic Calls of the Asian Elephant," *Behavioral Ecology and Sociobiology* 18, no. 4 (1986): 297–301.
32 Payne, ed., *Songs of the Humpback Whale.*
33 Brody, "Scientist at Work."
34 Brody, "Scientist at Work," 2.
35 Guinee and Payne, "Rhyme-Like Repetitions in Songs of Humpback Whales."

36 Guinee and Payne, "Rhyme-Like Repetitions in Songs of Humpback Whales," 305.

37 Payne, *Silent Thunder*.

38 Payne, "Infrasonic Calls of the Asian Elephant," 297–301.

39 O'Connell, *The Elephant's Secret Sense*; O'Connell-Rodwell, "Keeping an 'Ear' to the Ground."

40 O'Connell, *The Elephant's Secret Sense*.

41 Nickerson, "Elephants' Toes Get the Message, Study Finds."

42 Garstang, *Elephant Sense and Sensibility*, 44–45.

43 Kroodsma, *The Singing Life of Birds*, 373.

44 Gray et al., "The Music of Nature and the Nature of Music," 52.

45 Kroodsma, *The Singing Life of Birds*, 268.

46 Kroodsma, *The Singing Life of Birds*, 199.

47 Kroodsma, *The Singing Life of Birds*, 201.

48 Kroodsma, *The Singing Life of Birds*, 272.

49 Kroodsma, *The Singing Life of Birds*.

50 Kroodsma, phone interview with author, April 5, 2017.

51 Kroodsma interview.

52 Kroodsma interview.

53 Kroodsma interview.

54 Kroodsma interview.

55 Kroodsma interview.

CHAPTER 3. PLAY AS A CREATIVE SOURCE

1 Behncke, "Waterplay in Wild Bonobos."

2 Behncke, "Play in the Peter Pan Ape."

3 Behncke, "Play in the Peter Pan Ape," R25.

4 Csikszentmiyalyi, *Creativity*, 79.

5 Csikszentmiyalyi, *Creativity*, 79.

6 Eibes-Eibesfeldt, "On the Ontogeny of Behavior of a Male Badger (Meles Meles L.) with Particular Reference to Play Behavior."

7 Brown, "Animals at Play."

8 Burghardt, *The Genesis of Animal Play*.

9 Burghardt, *The Genesis of Animal Play*, 70.

10 O'Brien and Kellan. "Peaceful Bonobos May Have Something to Teach Humans."

11 Davila-Ross, Owren, and Zimmermann, "Reconstructing the Evolution of Laughter in Great Apes and Humans."

12 Balcombe, *What a Fish Knows*, loc. 1289 of 4678, Kindle.

13 Bateson and Martin, *Play, Playfulness, Creativity, and Innovation*, 75.

14 Bateson and Martin, *Play, Playfulness, Creativity, and Innovation*, 75.

15 Bird and Emery, "Rooks Use Stones to Raise the Water Level to Reach a Floating Worm."

16 Sharpe, "Social Foraging of the Southeast Alaskan Humpback Whale, Meguptera Novaeangliae."

17 Bateson and Martin, *Play, Playfulness, Creativity, and Innovation*, 74.

18 Hal Whitehead and Luke Rendell, *The Cultural Lives of Whales and Dolphins* (Chicago: University of Chicago Press, 2015), loc. 2064 of 11398, Kindle.

19 Huizinga, *Homo Ludens*, 1.

20 Darwin, *The Descent of Man and Selection in Relation to Sex*, 140.

21 Montaigne, "Apology for Raimond Sebond."

22 Groos, *The Play of Animals*, 75.

23 Fagen, "Selective and Evolutionary Aspects of Animal Play," 852.

24 Fagen, "Play, Five Evolutionary Gates, Paths to Art."

25 Fagen, "Animal Play and Phylogenetic Diversity of Creative Minds," 79.

26 Pleasance, "Not So Bird-Brained."

27 Diamond and Bond, *Kea, Bird of Paradox*, 93.

28 Fagen, "Animal Play and Phylogenetic Diversity of Creative Minds," 79.

29 Geoffrey North. "The Biology of Fun and the Fun of Biology," *Current Biology* 25, no. 1 (2015): 2.

30 Jonathan Pruitt, Gordon Burghardt, and Susan E. Riechert. "Non-Conceptive Sexual Behavior in Spiders: A Form of Play Associated with Body Condition, Personality Type, and Male Intrasexual Selection," *Ethology* 118, no. 1 (2011): 39.

31 Leonardo Dapporto, Stefano Turillazzi, and Elisabetta Palagi, "Dominance Interactions in Young Adult Paper Wasp (Polistes Dominulus) Foundresses: A Playlike Behavior?" *Journal of Comparative Psychology* 120, no. 3 (2006): 394–400.

32 Gordon M. Burghardt, Brian Ward, and Roger Rosscoe, "Problem of Reptile Play: Environmental Enrichment and Play Behavior in a Captive Nile Soft-Shelled Turtle, Trionyx Triunguis," *Zoobiology* 15, no. 3 (1996): 223–38.

33 Vladimir Dinets, "Play Behavior in Crocodilians," *Animal Behavior and Cognition* 2, no. 1 (2015): 49.

34 Dinets, "Play Behavior in Crocodilians," 50.

35 Dinets, "Play Behavior in Crocodilians," 53.

36 Vladimir Dinets, "Crocodylus Rhombifer (Cuban Crocodile) Mating Behavior," *Herpetological Review* 42 (2011): 232.

37 Mitchell, ed., *Pretending and Imagination in Animals and Children*.

38 Kellogg and Kellogg, *The Ape and the Child*.

39 Hayes, *The Ape in Our House*, 87.

40 Hayes, *The Ape in Our House*, 80–84.

41 Mitchell, ed., *Pretending and Imagination in Animals and Children*, 37.

42 Slobodchikoff, *Chasing Doctor Dolittle*, 237.

43 Bradshaw et al., "Building an Inner Sanctuary"; G. A. Bradshaw, Theodora Capaldo, Lorin Lindner, and Gloria Grow, "Developmental Context Effects on Bicultural Posttrauma Self Repair in Chimpanzees," *Developmental Psychology* 45, no. 5 (2009): 1376–88.

44 Gloria Grow and Mary Lee Jensvold, interview with author at Fauna Foundation, June 16, 2016.

45 Jensvold and Fouts, "Imaginary Play in Chimpanzees (Pan Troglodytes)."

46 Egan and Jensvold, "Pretend Play in Signing Chimpanzees (Pan Troglodytes)."

47 Jensvold, "Pretend Play in Chimpanzees."

48 Jensvold, "Signs of Art and Pretend Play in Chimpanzees."

49 Goodall, *The Chimpanzees of Gombe*, 591.

50 C. K. Tayler and G. S. Saayman, "Imitative Behaviour by Indian Ocean Bottlenose Dolphins (Tursiops Aduncus) in Captivity," *Behaviour* 44, nos. 3–4 (1973): 286–98, www.jstor.org/stable/4533493.

51 Hauptman, *Crow Planet*.

52 Balcombe, *Pleasurable Kingdom*, 9.

53 Balcombe, *Pleasurable Kingdom*, 11.

54 Romanes, *Mental Evolution in Animals*, 108.

55 Bekoff and Pierce, *Wild Justice*.

56 Bekoff, *The Emotional Lives of Animals*, 94.

57 Geirland, "Go with the Flow."

58 Bekoff, *The Emotional Lives of Animals*, 94.

59 Bekoff, *The Emotional Lives of Animals*, 94.

60 Marek Spinka, Ruth C. Newberry, and Marc Bekoff, "Mammalian Play: Training for the Unexpected," *Quarterly Review of Biology* 76, no. 2 (2001): 144, www.jstor.org/stable/2664002.

61 Watson and Croft, "Age-Related Differences in Playfighting Strategies of Captive Male Red-Necked Wallabies (Macropus Rufogriseus Banksianus)," 343.

62 Waal, *Good Natured*.

63 Walker et al., "Sneeze to Leave," 1.

64 Adam Grant and James Berry, "The Necessity of Others Is the Mother of Invention: Intrinsic and Prosocial Motivations, Perspective Taking, and Creativity," *Academy of Management Journal* 54, no. 1 (2011): 73–96, 93.

65 Grant and Berry, "The Necessity of Others Is the Mother of Invention," 77.

66 Grant and Berry, "The Necessity of Others Is the Mother of Invention," 74.

67 Bekoff and Pierce, *Wild Justice*, 132.

68 Gall and Gjerris, "Role of Joy in Farm Animal Welfare Legislation."

69 Gall and Gjerris, "Role of Joy in Farm Animal Welfare Legislation," 163.

70 Byrne, "Animal Curiosity."

71 Byrne, "Animal Curiosity," R470.

72 Byrne, "Animal Curiosity," R470.

CHAPTER 4. CREATING BUILT ENVIRONMENTS

1 Griffin, *Animal Minds*, 99.

2 Wolf, *Europe and the People without History*, 158.

3 Muller-Schwarze, *The Beaver*.

4 Morgan, *The American Beaver and His Works*.

5 Morgan, *The American Beaver and His Works*, 263.

6 Morgan, *The American Beaver and His Works*, 264.

7 Morgan, *The American Beaver and His Works*, 257–84.

8 Weber et al., "Alteration of Stream Temperature by Natural and Artificial Beaver Dams."

9 Muller and Watling, "The Engineering in Beaver Dams."

10 Gould and Gould, *Animal Architects*.

11 Gould and Gould, *Animal Architects*, 90.

12 Gould and Gould, *Animal Architects*, 253.

13 Morgan, *The American Beaver and His Works*, 264.

14 Griffin, *Animal Minds*, 91.

15 Gould and Gould, *Animal Architects*.

16 Collman, "These Beavers Have Been Busy!"

17 Collman, "These Beavers Have Been Busy!" 270.

18 Frisch, *Animal Architecture*, 253.

19 Frisch, *Animal Architecture*, 74.

20 Hansell, *Built by Animals*.

21 Frisch, *Animal Architecture*, 42–45.

22 Griffin, *Animal Minds*, 72.

23 Bekoff and Pierce, *Wild Justice*, 50–51.

24 Bekoff and Pierce, *Wild Justice*, 49.

25 Gooding, "Modern Research into Bees and Bee-Keeping."

26 Intergovernmental Science-Policy Platform on Biodiversity and Ecosystem Services (IPBES), "Summary for Policymakers," 11.

27 MacDonald, *The Pantheon*, 33.

28 Nazzi, "The Hexagonal Shape of the Honeycomb Cells Depends on the Construction Behavior of Bees."

29 Karihaloo, Zhang, and Wang, "Honeybee Combs," 4.

30 Frisch, *The Dancing Bees*.

31 Seeley, Visscher, and Passino, "Group Decision Making in Honey Bee Swarms."

32 Seeley, Visscher, and Passino, "Group Decision Making in Honey Bee Swarms," 222.

33 Seeley, Visscher, and Passino, "Group Decision Making in Honey Bee Swarms," 226.

34 Seeley, Visscher, and Passino, "Group Decision Making in Honey Bee Swarms," 228.

35 Seeley, Visscher, and Passino, "Group Decision Making in Honey Bee Swarms," 229.

36 Hansell, *Built by Animals*.

37 Darwin, *The Descent of Man and Selection in Relation to Sex*, vol. 1, chapter 2.

38 Prum, "Aesthetic Evolution by Mate Choice."

39 Griffin, *Animal Minds*, 87.

40 Gould and Gould, *Animal Architects*, 250.

41 Wallace, "A Theory of Birds' Nests," 74.

42 Arndt and Tautz, *Animal Architecture*.

43 Goodfellow, *Avian Architecture*, 126.

44 Arndt and Tautz, *Animal Architecture*, 41.

45 Goodfellow, *Avian Architecture*, 134–35.

46 OzBirdZ, "Male Satin Bowerbird Building Bower."

47 Borgia, Kaatz, and Condit, "Flower Choice and Bower Decoration in the Satin Bowerbird Ptilonorhynchus Violaceus."

48 Bravery, Nicholls, and Goldizen, "Patterns of Painting in Satin Bowerbirds Ptilonorhynchus Violaceus and Males' Responses to Changes in Their Paint."

49 Cornell Ornithology Lab, "He Delivers Flowers."

50 Goodfellow, *Avian Architecture*, 142.

51 Kelley and Endler, "How Do Great Bowerbirds Construct Perspective Illusions?"

52 Madden et al., "Male Spotted Bowerbirds Propagate Fruit for Use in Their Sexual Display."

53 Gould and Gould, *Animal Architects*, 221.

54 Borgia and Keagy, "Cognitively Driven Co-Option and the Evolution of Complex Sexual Displays in Bowerbirds."

55 Prum, "Aesthetic Evolution by Mate Choice," 2254.

56 Mercader et al., "4,300-Year-Old Chimpanzee Sites and the Origins of Percussive Stone Technology."

57 Pruetz et al., "New Evidence on the Tool-Assisted Hunting Exhibited by Chimpanzees (Pan Troglodytes Verus) in a Savannah Habitat at Fongoli, Sénégal."

58 Sugasawa et al., "Causes and Consequences of Tool Shape Variation in New Caledonian Crows."

59 Poole, *Coming of Age with Elephants: A Memoir*, 155–57.

60 Kruzen et al., "Cultural Transmission of Tool Use by Indo-Pacific Bottlenose Dolphins (Tursiops Sp.) Provides Access to a Novel Foraging Niche."

61 Costa et al., "Seven-Stone Spiders on the Gravel Plains of Namibia"; Henschel, "Tool Use by Spiders."

62 Dinets, Brueggen, and Brueggen, "Crocodilians Use Tools for Hunting."

63 Shumacker, Walkup, and Beck, *Animal Tool Behavior*, 36.

64 Gadow, *Amphibians and Reptiles*, 8: 217.

65 Finn, Tregenza, and Norman. "Defensive Tool Use in a Coconut-Carrying Octopus."

66 Osvath, "Spontaneous Planning for Future Stone Throwing by a Male Chimpanzee," R190.

67 Osvath, "Spontaneous Planning for Future Stone Throwing by a Male Chimpanzee," R191.

68 Osvath and Martin-Ordas, "The Future of Future-Oriented Cognition in Non-Humans."

69 Osvath and Martin-Ordas, "The Future of Future-Oriented Cognition in Non-Humans," 7.

70 Julie Andreyev, email interview with author, July 23, 2017.

71 Sewall, "The Girl Who Gets Gifts from Birds."

72 Andreyev interview.

73 Andreyev "Chapter 2," 18.

74 Andreyev interview.

CHAPTER 5. SEXUAL EXUBERANCE

1 Nordsieck, "The Leopard Slug (Limax Maximus)."

2 Bagemihl, *Biological Exuberance*.

3 Borgia and Keagy, "Cognitively Driven Co-Option and the Sexual Evolution of Complex Sexual Displays in Bowerbirds."

4 Dreger et al., "Changing the Nomenclature/Taxonomy for Intersex," 729.

5 Atwood, *Maddaddam Trilogy*.

6 Stanton and Unkrich, dirs., *Finding Nemo*.

7 Bagemihl, *Biological Exuberance*, 37.

8 Burke, Crean, and Bonduriansky, "The Role of Sexual Conflict in the Evolution of Facultative Parthenogenesis," 117.

9 Fields et al., "Facultative Parthenogenesis in a Critically Endangered Wild Vertebrate."

10 Bagemihl, *Biological Exuberance*, 106.

11 Balcombe, *Pleasurable Kingdom*, 109–10.

12 Monk et al., "An Alternative Hypothesis for the Evolution of Same-Sex Sexual Behaviour in Animals."

13 Schamel et al., "Mate Guarding, Copulation Strategies, and Paternity in the Sex-Role Reversed, Socially Polyandrous Red-Necked Phalarope (Phalaropus Lobatus)."

14 Hardt, *Sex in the Sea*, 154–55.

15 Bagemihl, *Biological Exuberance*, 370–73.

16 Bailey and Zuk, "Same-Sex Sexual Behavior and Evolution."

17 Bagemihl, *Biological Exuberance*, 51.

18 Idani, "Social Relationships between Immigrant and Resident Bonobos (Pan Paniscus) Females at Wamba."

19 Bagemihl, *Biological Exuberance*, 52–53.

20 Moscovice et al., "Stable and Fluctuating Social Preferences and Implications for Cooperation among Female Bonobos at Luikotale, Salonga National Park, DRC."

21 Monk et al., "An Alternative Hypothesis for the Evolution of Same-Sex Sexual Behaviour in Animals," 631.

22 Hardt, *Sex in the Sea*, 154–55.

23 Judson, *Dr. Tatiana's Sex Advice for All Creation*, 95.

24 Judson, *Dr. Tatiana's Sex Advice for All Creation*, 85–86.

25 Bagemihl, *Biological Exuberance*, 73–74.

26 Walker et al., "Chimpanzees Breed with Genetically Dissimilar Mates," 11.

27 Bagemihl, *Biological Exuberance*, 21.

28 Judson, *Dr. Tatiana's Sex Advice for All Creation*, 144.

29 Bagemihl, *Biological Exuberance*, 343.

30 Bagemihl, *Biological Exuberance*, 47.

31 Hennessy, Dubach, and Gehrt, "Long-Term Pair Bonding and Genetic Evidence for Monogamy among Urban Coyotes (Canis Latrans)."

32 Kessler, "Cuddling, Teasing, and Playing."

33 Vliet, "Social Displays of the American Alligator (Alligator mississippiensis)," 1021.

34 Reber et al., "Formants Provide Honest Acoustic Cues to Body Size in American Alligators."

35 Nuechterlein and Storer, "The Pair-Formation Displays of the Western Grebe."

36 Cornell Ornithology Lab, "Shape-Shifting."

37 Arnold and Houck, "Can the Fisher-Lande Process Account for Birds of Paradise and Other Sexual Radiations?"

38 Girard and Endler, "Peacock Spiders," R590.

39 Prum, *The Evolution of Beauty*, 26.

40 Darwin, *The Descent of Man, and Selection in Relation to Sex*.

41 Mivart, "Review of *The Descent of Man*, by Charles Darwin."

42 Prum, *The Evolution of Beauty*, 30–32.

43 Browne, "Wallace and Darwin."

44 Gayon, "Sexual Selection," R1072.

45 Prum, *The Evolution of Beauty*, 26.

46 Patricelli, Herberts, and Mendelson, "Book Review of Prum, R.O.," 122.

47 Mark Kirkpatrick, "Sexual Selection and the Evolution of Female Choice," *Evolution* 36, no. 1 (1982): 10.

48 Borgia and Ball, "Book Review"; Futuyma, "Evolution."

49 Prum, "Aesthetic Evolution by Mate Choice," 2254.

50 Prum, *The Evolution of Beauty*, 26.

51 Prum, *The Evolution of Beauty*, 16.

52 Prum, *The Evolution of Beauty*, 17.

53 Prum, *The Evolution of Beauty*, 13.

54 Richard O. Prum, Skype interview with author, September 14, 2017.

55 Prum interview.

56 Prum, "Coevolutionary Aesthetics in Human and Biotic Artworlds."

57 Prum interview.

58 Prum interview.

59 Prum interview.

60 Prum, *The Evolution of Beauty*, 171.

61 Prum, *The Evolution of Beauty*, 299.

CHAPTER 6. EMOTIONAL AGENCY

1 Cartmill and Byrne, "Orangutans Modify Their Gestural Signaling according to Their Audience's Comprehension."

2 Gaesser, "Constructing Memory, Imagination, and Empathy."

3 Darwin, *The Expression of the Emotions in Man and Animals*, 2nd ed.

4 Masson and McCarthy, *When Elephants Weep.*

5 Bekoff, "Animal Emotions," 867.

6 Bekoff, "Animal Emotions," 861.

7 Ligon and McGraw, "Chameleons Communicate with Complex Colour Changes during Contests."

8 Barron and Klein, "What Insects Can Tell Us about the Origins of Consciousness."

9 Waal, *Good Natured.*

10 Bekoff, *The Emotional Lives of Animals.*

11 Virginia Morell, *Animal Wise: How We Know Animals Think and Feel* (New York: Broadway Books, 2013).

12 Balcombe, *What a Fish Knows.*

13 Safina, *Beyond Words.*

14 Burghardt, *The Genesis of Animal Play.*

15 Olkowicza et al., "Birds Have Primate-Like Numbers of Neurons in the Forebrain."

16 Gleich and Langemann, "Auditory Capabilities of Birds in Relation to the Structural Diversity of the Basilar Papilla"; Marino, "Thinking Chickens."

17 Potts, *Chicken*, 46.

18 Marino, "Thinking Chickens," 127–47.

19 Perry, Barron, and Chittka, "The Frontiers of Insect Cognition."

20 Marino, "Thinking Chickens," 141.

21 Potts, *Chicken*, 46.

22 Rothschild, "Ode to Spent Hens."

23 Rothschild, "Ode to Spent Hens."

24 Potts, *Chicken*, 48.

25 Annie Potts, email interview with author, November 24, 2017.

26 Potts interview.

27 Potts interview.

28 Potts interview.

29 Davis, "Chicken Wisdom," 146.

30 Russ, *Affect and Creativity*, 105.

31 Greenberg, "The Role of Neophophilia and Neophobia in the Development of Innovative Behavior of Birds," 179.

32 Davis, "The Social Life of Chickens."

33 Edgar et al., "Avian Maternal Response to Chick Distress."

34 Pierce, "Mice in the Sink."

35 Lanzoni, "A Short History of Empathy."

36 Pierce, "Mice in the Sink," 76.
37 Waal and Preston, "Mammalian Empathy," 498.
38 Waal and Preston, "Mammalian Empathy," 505.
39 Waal and Preston, "Mammalian Empathy," 505.
40 Waal, "Putting the Altruism Back into Altruism."
41 Bates et al., "Do Elephants Show Empathy?"
42 Dvash and Shamay-Tsoory, "Theory of Mind and Empathy as Multidimensional Constructs."
43 Waal and Preston, "Mammalian Empathy," 500.
44 Church, "Emotional Reactions of Rats to the Pain of Others."
45 Waal and Preston, "Mammalian Empathy," 502.
46 Lee and Moura, "Necessity, Unpredictability, and Opportunity," 323.
47 Kummer and Goodall, "Conditions of Innovative Behaviors in Primates."
48 Kummer and Goodall, "Conditions of Innovative Behaviors in Primates," 208.
49 Waal, "What Is an Animal Emotion?"
50 Waal, "What Is an Animal Emotion?" 192.
51 Waal, "What Is an Animal Emotion?" 192.
52 Bekoff and Pierce, *Wild Justice*, 126.
53 Mech, "Alpha Status, Dominance, and Division of Labor in Wolf Packs."
54 Palagi and Cordoni, "Postconflict Third-Party Affiliation in Canis Lupus."
55 Waal, "What Is an Animal Emotion?" 192.
56 Kruuk, *The Spotted Hyena*, 274.
57 Watts and Holekamp, "Hyena Societies."
58 Watts and Holekamp, "Hyena Societies," R658.
59 Benson-Amram and Holekamp, "Innovative Problem Solving by Wild Spotted Hyenas."
60 Benson-Amram and Holekamp, "Innovative Problem Solving by Wild Spotted Hyenas," 4087.
61 Sol, "The Evolution of Innovativeness."
62 Carrere and Maestripieri, eds., *Animal Personalities*.
63 Weiss et al., "Personality in the Chimpanzees of Gombe National Park."
64 McKie, "Chimps with Everything."
65 Weiss, "Personality Traits," 7.
66 Weintraub, "Wild and Captive Chimpanzees Share Personality Traits with Humans."
67 Kummer and Goodall, "Conditions of Innovative Behaviors in Primates."
68 Kaufman and Gregoire, *Wired to Create*, xxvi.
69 Weiss, "Personality Traits," 7–8; Polderman, "Meta-Analysis of the Heritability of Human Traits Based on Fifty Years of Twin Studies."
70 Castanheira et al., "Are Personality Traits Consistent in Fish?"
71 Vila Pouca and Brown, "Contemporary Topics in Fish Cognition and Behaviour."
72 Brown, Laland, and Krause, *Fish Cognition and Behavior*.

73 Balcombe, *What a Fish Knows*, loc. 4727 of 4768, Kindle.

74 FishBase Information and Research Group, Inc., "Fishbase."

75 Balcombe, *What a Fish Knows*, loc. 104 of 4768, Kindle.

76 Abbott, "Animal Behaviour."

77 Pinto et al., "Cleaner Wrasses *Labroides Dimiadiatus* Are More Cooperative in the Presence of an Audience."

78 Myerson, *Game Theory*.

79 Pinto et al., "Cleaner Wrasses *Labroides Dimiadiatus* Are More Cooperative in the Presence of an Audience," 1140–44.

80 Salwiczek et al., "Adult Cleaner Wrasse Outperform Capuchin Monkeys, Chimpanzees, and Orang-Utans in a Complex Foraging Task Derived from Cleaner–Client Reef Fish Cooperation."

81 Abbott, "Animal Behaviour," 413.

82 Abbott, "Animal Behaviour," 414.

83 Laland, Atton, and Webster, "From Fish to Fashion," 959.

84 Balcombe, *What a Fish Knows*, loc. 2093 of 4768, Kindle.

85 Balcombe, *What a Fish Knows*, loc. 2118 of 4768, Kindle.

86 Pascal Fossat et al., "Anxiety-Like Behavior in Crayfish Is Controlled by Serotonin," *Science* 344, no. 6189 (2014): 1293–97.

87 Bateson et al., "Agitated Honeybees Exhibit Pessimistic Cognitive Biases."

CHAPTER 7. CULTURE ACROSS SPECIES

1 Akrigg and Akrigg, *1001 British Columbia Place Names*.

2 First Nations Health Authority, "Our History, Our Health."

3 Griffin and West, "Kin Discrimination and the Benefit of Helping in Cooperatively Breeding Vertebrates."

4 Kuczaj et al., "Are Animals Capable of Deception or Empathy?"

5 Allen, "Community through Culture."

6 Schuppli and Van Schaik, "Animal Cultures."

7 Whitehead and Rendell, *The Cultural Lives of Whales and Dolphins*, loc. 270 of 11399, Kindle.

8 Laland and Galef, *The Question of Animal Culture*.

9 Whiten et al., "The Extension of Biology through Culture," 7776.

10 Fisher and Hinde, "The Opening of Milk Bottles by Birds"; Goodall, "Behaviour of the Free-Ranging Chimpanzee"; Goodall, "Tool-Using and Aimed Throwing in a Community of Free-Living Chimpanzees"; Kawai, "Newly Acquired Precultural Behavior of the Natural Troop of Japanese Monkeys on Koshima Islet."

11 Marler and Tamura, "Culturally Transmitted Patterns of Vocal Behavior in Sparrows."

12 Whitehead and Rendell, *The Cultural Lives of Whales and Dolphins*, loc. 235 of 11399, Kindle.

13 Hain et al., "Feeding Behavior of the Humpback Whale, Megaptera Novaeangliae, in the Western North Atlantic."

14 Ramsey, "What Is Animal Culture?" 348.

15 Ramsey, "What Is Animal Culture?" 348.

16 Ramsey, "What Is Animal Culture?" 350.

17 Whiten, Caldwell, and Mesoudi, "Cultural Diffusion in Humans and Other Animals."

18 Ingold, "The Use and Abuse of Ethnography"; Tomicello, "The Question of Chimpanzee Culture, Plus Postscript."

19 Marino and Frohoff, "Towards a New Paradigm of Non-Captive Research on Cetacean Cognition."

20 Whitehead and Rendell, *The Cultural Lives of Whales and Dolphins*, loc. 677 of 11399, Kindle.

21 Galef and Whiten, "The Comparative Psychology of Social Learning."

22 Galef, "Culture in Animals?"

23 Kis, Huber, and Wilkinson, "Social Learning by Imitation in a Reptile (Pogona Vitticeps)."

24 Fawcett, "The Case of the Mimic Octopus."

25 Josef et al., "Camouflaging in a Complex Environment."

26 Scheel et al., "A Second Site Occupied by Octopus Tetricus at High Densities, with Notes on Their Ecology and Behavior."

27 Godfrey-Smith, *Other Minds*.

28 Frantzis and Alexiadou, "Male Sperm Whale (Physeter Macrocephalus) Coda Production and Coda-Type Usage Depend on the Presence of Conspecifics and the Behavioural Context."

29 Whitehead and Rendell, *The Cultural Lives of Whales and Dolphins*, loc. 3468 of 11399, Kindle.

30 Whitehead, "Gene-Culture Coevolution in Whales and Dolphins."

31 Whitehead and Rendell, *The Cultural Lives of Whales and Dolphins*, loc. 5216 of 11399, Kindle.

32 Whitehead and Rendell, *The Cultural Lives of Whales and Dolphins*, loc. 5233 of 11399, Kindle.

33 Patrerson and Mann, "Cetacean Tool Use."

34 Patrerson and Mann, "Cetacean Tool Use," 154.

35 Wild et al., "Multi-Network-Based Diffusion Analysis Reveals Vertical Cultural Transmission of Sponge Tool Use within Dolphin Matrilines."

36 Kopps et al., "Cultural Transmission of Tool Use Combined with Habitat Specializations Leads to Fine-Scale Genetic Structure in Bottlenose Dolphins."

37 Patrerson and Mann, "Cetacean Tool Use."

38 Whitehead, "Gene-Culture Coevolution in Whales and Dolphins," 7814–21.

39 Payne, ed., *Songs of the Humpback Whale*.

40 Magnúsdóttir and Lim, "Subarctic Singers."

41 Garland et al., "Song Hybridization Events during Revolutionary Song Change Provide Insights into Cultural Transmission in Humpback Whales."

42 Garland et al., "Song Hybridization Events during Revolutionary Song Change Provide Insights into Cultural Transmission in Humpback Whales," 7822–29.

43 Taylor, *Is Bird Song Music?*

44 "Birdsong Has Inspired Humans for Centuries: Is It Music?" *Conversation*, July 25, 2017.

45 Taylor, *Is Bird Song Music?* 134.

46 Janney et al., "Temporal Regularity Increases with Repertoire Complexity in the Australian Pied Butcherbird's Song."

47 Curry, Mullins, and Whitehouse, "Is It Good to Cooperate?"

48 Whitehead and Rendell, *The Cultural Lives of Whales and Dolphins*, loc. 6334 of 11399, Kindle.

49 For those interested in further discussion of the role rationality does or does not play in moral behavior, I point to a little light reading by the philosopher Hume in *A Treatise of Human Nature* (any edition).

50 Whitehead and Rendell, *The Cultural Lives of Whales and Dolphins*, loc. 6397 of 11399, Kindle.

51 Whitehead and Rendell, *The Cultural Lives of Whales and Dolphins*, loc. 6358–91 of 11399, Kindle.

52 Whitehead and Rendell, *The Cultural Lives of Whales and Dolphins*, loc. 6414 of 11399, Kindle.

53 Whitehead and Rendell, *The Cultural Lives of Whales and Dolphins*, loc. 6339 of 11399, Kindle.

54 Parsons, "Impacts of Navy Sonar on Whales and Dolphins."

55 Rowlands, *Can Animals Be Moral?*

56 Waal, *Good Natured*.

57 Bekoff and Pierce, *Wild Justice*.

58 Peterson, *The Moral Lives of Animals*.

59 Rowlands, *Can Animals Be Moral?*

60 Crane, ed., *Beastly Morality*.

61 Monsó, Benz-Schwarzburg, and Bremhorst, "Animal Morality."

62 Gigliotti, "Aesethics of a Virtual World."

63 Bekoff and Pierce, *Wild Justice*, x.

64 Dutcher and Dutcher, "The Social Wolf."

65 Dutcher and Dutcher, "Our Observations."

66 Bekoff and Pierce, *Wild Justice*, 142.

67 Bekoff and Pierce, *Wild Justice*, 144–45.

68 Packard, "Deferred Reproduction in Wolves (Canis Lupis)."

69 Packard, "Wolf Behavior."

70 Packard, "Wolf Social Intelligence," 1.

71 Packard, "Wolf Social Intelligence," 29.
72 Packard, "Wolf Social Intelligence," 29.

EPILOGUE

1 Dean Keith Simonton, "Commentary on Chapter 13: Defining Animal Creativity; Little-C, Often; Big-C, Sometimes." In *Animal Creativity and Innovation: An Integrated Look at the Field*, ed. Allison B. Kaufman and James C. Kaufman (Cambridge, MA: Academic Press, 2015), 390–97.

2 "The Most Cited Articles from *Animal Behaviour* Published since 2018, Extracted from Scopus."

3 Samuel D. Gosling, "Personality in Non-Human Animals," *Social and Personality Psychology Compass* 2, no. 2 (March 2008): 985.

4 Coen P. H. Elemans et al., "Universal Mechanisms of Sound Production and Control in Birds and Mammals," *Nature Communications* 6, no. 8978 (2015). https://doi.org/10.1038/ncomms9978.

5 United Nations Environment Programs, "Report on 1st CMSE Workshop on Conservation Implications of Animal Culture and Social Complexity, Parma, Italy."

6 Brakes et al., "Animal Cultures Matter for Conservation," 1032.

7 McComb et al., "Leadership in Elephants."

8 Brakes et al., "Animal Cultures Matter for Conservation," 1034.

9 Brakes et al., "A Deepening Understanding of Animal Culture Suggests Lessons for Conservation," 4.

10 Brakes et al., "A Deepening Understanding of Animal Culture Suggests Lessons for Conservation," 8.

11 Alex Gray, "What New Technologies Carry the Biggest Risk?" World Economic Forum, January 11, 2017, www.weforum.org/.

12 Vera Heck et al., "Biomass-Based Negative Emissions Difficult to Reconcile with Planetary Boundaries," *Nature Climate Change* 8 (2018): 151–55.

13 Carol Gigliotti, "Introduction," in *Leonardo's Choice: Genetic Technologies and Animals*, ed. Carol Gigliotti, xi–xxviii. Dorchedt, Netherlands: Springer, 2009, xvi.

14 Edward D. Perry et al., "Genetically Engineered Crops and Pesticide Use in U.S. Maize and Soybeans," *Science Advances* 2, no. 8 (2016:): e1600850.

15 "Pollinators Vital to Our Food Supply under Threat" (Rome, Italy: Food and Agricultural Organization of the United Nations, 2016).

16 Gerardo Ceballos et al., "Accelerated Modern Human-Induced Species Losses: Entering the Sixth Mass Extinction," *Science Advances* 1, no. 5 (June 19, 2015): e140025. https://doi.org/10.1126/sciadv.1400253.

17 Ghoddousi et al., "Anthropogenic Resistance," 43–44.

18 Ghoddousi et al., "Anthropogenic Resistance," 45–46.

BIBLIOGRAPHY

Abbott, Alison. "Animal Behaviour: Inside the Cunning, Caring, and Greedy Minds of Fish." *Nature*, May 26, 2015, 412–14.

Akrigg, Helen B., and George Phillip Vernon Akrigg. *1001 British Columbia Place Names*. Vancouver: Discovery Press, 1973.

Allen, Jenny A. "Community through Culture: From Insects to Whales." *BioEssays* 41, no. 11 (2019): 1900060.

Andreyev, Julie. "Chapter 2: Crows and Stones." In *Biophilic Ethics and Creativity with More-Than-Human Beings. Doctoral dissertation*, Simon Fraser University, 2017.

"Animal Cognition: An Interview with Ed Wasserman." *Talk of Iowa*, edited by Charity Nebbe, Iowa Public Radio, August 22, 2012.

Arndt, Ingo, and Jurgen Tautz. *Animal Architecture*. New York: Abrams, 2014.

Arnold, Stevan J., and Lynne D. Houck. "Can the Fisher-Lande Process Account for Birds of Paradise and Other Sexual Radiations?" *American Naturalist* 187, no. 6 (June 2016): 717–35.

Atwood, Margaret. *MaddAddam Trilogy*. Book 1, *Oryx and Crake*, Book 2, *The Year of the Flood*, Book 3, *MaddAddam*. New York: Anchor, 2014.

Bachelard, Gaston. *The Poetics of Reverie*. Boston: Beacon Press, 1969.

———. *The Poetics of Space*. Trans. Maria Jolas. Boston: Beacon Press, 1969.

Bagemihl, Bruce. *Biological Exuberance: Animal Sexuality and Natural Diversity*. New York: St. Martin's Press, 1999.

Bailey, Nathan, and Marlene Zuk. "Same-Sex Sexual Behavior and Evolution." *Trends in Ecology & Evolution* 24 (2009): 439–46.

Balcombe, Jonathan. *Pleasurable Kingdom: Animals and the Nature of Feeling Good*. New York: Macmillan, 2006.

———. *What a Fish Knows*. New York: Farrar, Straus, and Giroux, 2016.

Barron, Andrew B., and Colin Klein. "What Insects Can Tell Us about the Origins of Consciousness." *Proceedings of the National Academy of Sciences (USA)* 113, no. 18 (2016): 4900–08.

Bartlett, Tom. "A New Twist in the Sad Saga of Little Albert." *Chronicle of Higher Education*, January 25, 2012.

Bass, Andrew H., Edwin H. Gilland, and Robert Baker. "Evolutionary Origins for Social Vocalization in a Vertebrate Hindbrain–Spinal Compartment." *Science* 321, no. 5887 (2008): 417–21.

Bates, Lucy A., Phyllis C. Lee, Norah Njiraini, Joyce H. Poole, Katito Sayialel, Soila Sayialel, Cynthia J. Moss, and Richard W. Byrne. "Do Elephants Show Empathy?" *Journal of Consciousness Studies* 15, nos. 10–11 (2008): 204–25.

Bateson, Melissa, Suzanne Desire, Sarah E. Gartside, and Geraldine A. Wright. "Agitated Honeybees Exhibit Pessimistic Cognitive Biases." *Current Biology* 21, no. 12 (2011): P1070–73. https://doi.org/10.1016/j.cub.2011.05.017.

Bateson, Patrick, and Paul Martin. *Play, Playfulness, Creativity, and Innovation*. Cambridge: Cambridge University Press, 2013.

Bear, KB. "A Skunk Chases a Bobcat—& the Bobcat's Two Kittens Appear!" YouTube video, September 9, 2016, www.youtube.com/watch?v=I7fvhzaajew.

Behncke, Isabel. "Play in the Peter Pan Ape." *Current Biology* 25, no. 2 (January 5, 2015): PR25–27. https://doi.org/10.1016/j.cub.2014.11.020.

———. "Waterplay in Wild Bonobos." YouTube vidoeo, November 3, 2014, www.youtube.com/watch?v=geWv5__IOjk.

Bekoff, Marc. "Animal Emotions: Exploring Passionate Natures." *BioScience* 50, no. 10 (October 2000): 861–70.

———. *Animal Passions and Beastly Virtues: Reflections on Redecorating Nature*. Philadelphia: Temple University Press, 2005.

———. "Do Animals Know Who They Are? (Op-Ed)." *LiveScience: Expert Voices*, September 19, 2013.

———. *The Emotional Lives of Animals: A Leading Scientist Explores Animal Joy, Sorrow, and Empathy and Why They Matter*. Navato, CA: New World Library, 2008.

———. "How and Why Dogs Play, Revisited: Who's Confused?" *Psychology Today* (blog), November 29, 2015, www.psychologytoday.com/us/blog/animal-emotions/201511/how-and-why-dogs-play-revisited-who-s-confused.

Bekoff, Marc, and Jessica Pierce. *Wild Justice: The Moral Lives of Animals*. Chicago: University of Chicago Press, 2009.

Benson-Amram, Sarah, and Kay E. Holekamp. "Innovative Problem Solving by Wild Spotted Hyenas." *Proceedings of the Royal Society B* 278 (2012): 4087–95. https://doi.org/10.1098/rspb.2012.1450.

Bird, Christopher David, and Nathan John Emery. "Rooks Use Stones to Raise the Water Level to Reach a Floating Worm." *Current Biology* 19 (2009): 1410–14. https://doi.org/10.1016/j.cub.2009.07.033.

"Black-Tailed Prairie Dog." Center for Biological Diversity, accessed January 3, 2022, www.biologicaldiversity.org.

Bonetto, Eric, Nicolas Pichott, Jean-Baptiste Pavani, and Jaïs Adam-Troïan. "The Paradox of Creativity." *New Ideas in Psychology* 60 (January 2021): 100820.

Borgia, Gerald, and Gregory F. Ball. Review of *The Evolution of Beauty: How Darwin's Forgotten Theory of Mate Choice Shapes the Animal World—and Us*, by Richard O. Prum. *Animal Behaviour* 137 (2018): 187–88.

Borgia, Gerald, Ingrid M. Kaatz, and Richard Condit. "Flower Choice and Bower Decoration in the Satin Bowerbird Ptilonorhynchus Violaceus: A Test of

Hypotheses for the Evolution of Male Display." *Animal Behavior* 35 (1987): 1129–39.

Borgia, Gerald, and Jason Keagy. "Cognitively Driven Co-Option and the Evolution of Complex Sexual Displays in Bowerbirds." In *Animal Signaling and Function: An Integrative Approach*, edited by Duncan J. Irschick, Mark Briffa, and Jeffrey Podos, 75–109. Hoboken, NJ: Wiley, 2015.

Bradshaw, G. A., Theodora Capaldo, Lorin Lindner, and Gloria Grow. "Building an Inner Sanctuary: Complex PTSD in Chimpanzees." *Journal of Trauma & Dissociation* 9, no. 1 (2008): 9–34.

Brakes, Philippa, Emma L. Carroll, Sasha R. X. Dall, Sally A. Keith, Peter K. McGregor, Sarah L. Mesnick, Michael J. Noad, et al. "A Deepening Understanding of Animal Culture Suggests Lessons for Conservation." *Proceedings of the Royal Society B: Biological Sciences* 288, no. 1949 (2021): 1–10.

Brakes, Phillipa, Sasha R. X. Dall, Lucy M. Aplin, Stuart Bearhop, Emma L. Carroll, Paolo Ciucci, Vicki Fishlock, et al. "Animal Cultures Matter for Conservation." *Science* 363, no. 6431 (2019): 1032–34.

Bravery, Benjamin, James A. Nicholls, and Anne W. Goldizen. "Patterns of Painting in Satin Bowerbirds Ptilonorhynchus Violaceus and Males' Responses to Changes in Their Paint." *Journal of Avian Biology* 37, no. 1 (2006): 75–85.

British Museum. "Everything You Ever Wanted to Know about the Rosetta Stone." In *Objects in Focus*. London: British Museum, 2016.

Brody, Jane E. "Scientist at Work: Katy Payne; Picking up Mammals' Deep Notes." *New York Times*, November 9, 1993, 2.

Brothers, Leslie. "The Neural Basis of Primate Social Communication." *Motivation and Emotion* 14, no. 2 (1990): 81–91.

Brown, Culum, Martin P. Garwood, and Jane E. Williamson. "It Pays to Cheat: Tactical Deception in a Cephalopod Social Signalling System." *Biology Letters* 8, no. 5 (2012): 729–32. https://doi.org/10.1098/rsbl.2012.0435.

Brown, Culim, Kevin Laland, and Jens Krause. *Fish Cognition and Behavior*, 1st ed. London: Wiley-Blackwell, 2005.

Brown, Stuart L. "Animals at Play." *National Geographic Magazine* 186, no. 6 (December 1994).

———. *Play: How It Changes the Brain, Opens the Imagination, and Invigorates the Soul.* 1st ed. New York: Avery, 2009.

Browne, Janet. "Wallace and Darwin." *Current Biology* 23, no. 24 (2013): R1071–72.

Bruck, Jason N. "Decades-Long Social Memory in Bottlenose Dolphins." *Proceedings of the Royal Society B* 280, no. 1768 (2013).

Burghardt, Gordon M. *The Genesis of Animal Play: Testing the Limits.* Cambridge, MA: MIT Press, 2006.

Burghardt, Gordon M., and Kerrie Lewis Graham. "Current Perspectives on the Biological Study of Play: Signs of Progress." *Quarterly Review of Biology* 85, no. 4 (December 2010): 394.

Burke, Nathan, Angela Crean, and Russell Bonduriansky. "The Role of Sexual Conflict in the Evolution of Facultative Parthenogenesis: A Study on the Spiny Leaf Stick Insect." *Animal Behaviour* 101 (2015): 117–27.

Byrne, Richard W. "Animal Curiosity." *Current Biology* 23, no. 11 (June 3, 2013): R469–70. https://doi.org/10.1016/j.cub.2013.02.058.

———. "The What as Well as the Why of Animal Fun." *Current Biology* 25, no. 1 (2015): R2–4.

Caldwell, Michael S., Gregory R. Johnston, J. Gregory McDaniel, and Karen M. Warkentin. "Vibrational Signaling in the Agonistic Interactions of Red-Eyed Treefrogs." *Current Biology* 20, no. 11 (2010): 1012–17. https://doi.org/10.1016/j.cub.2010.03.069.

Carrere, Claudio, and Dario Maestripieri, eds. *Animal Personalities: Behavior, Psychology, and Evolution*. Chicago: University of Chicago Press, 2013.

Cartmill, Erika, and Richard Byrne. "Orangutans Modify Their Gestural Signaling according to Their Audience's Comprehension." *Current Biology* 17, no. 15 (2007): 1345–48. https://doi.org/10.1016/j.cub.2007.06.069.

Castanheira, Maria Filipa, Marco Cerqueira, Sandie Millot, Rui A. Gonçalves, Catarina C. V. Oliveira, Luís E. C. Conceição, and Catarina I. M. Martins. "Are Personality Traits Consistent in Fish? The Influence of Social Context." *Applied Animal Behaviour Science* 178 (May 2016): 96–101. https://doi.org/10.1038/ng.3285.

Castro, Leyre, and Ed Wasserman. "Crows Understand Analogies." *Scientific American*, February 10, 2015.

Church, Russell. "Emotional Reactions of Rats to the Pain of Others." *Journal of Comparative Physiology and Psychology* 52 (1959): 132–34. https://doi.org/10.1037/h0043531.

Clayton, Nicola S., and Anthony Dickinson. "Episodic-Like Memory during Cache Recovery by Scrub Jays." *Nature*, September 17, 1998, 272–74.

Collman, Ashley. "These Beavers Have Been Busy! Explorer Crosses 200 Miles of Wilderness to Become First Person to Visit the World's Largest Beaver Dam." *MailOnline*, December 24, 2014.

Connor, Richard C. "Dolphin Social Intelligence: Complex Alliance Relationships in Bottlenose Dolphins and a Consideration of Selective Environments for Extreme Brain Size Evolution in Mammals." *Philosophical Transactions of the Royal Society B* 362, no. 1480 (2007): 587–602.

Cornell Ornithology Lab. "He Delivers Flowers: Vogelkop Bowerbird." YouTube video, May 18, 2015, 00.52, www.youtube.com/watch?v=_Dq437HuhOo.

———. "Shape-Shifting." In *The Birds-of-Paradise Project*, edited by Tim Lahman and Ed Scholes. Video, May 2, 2017, https:birdsofparadiseproject.org.

Costa, G., A. Petralia, E. Conti, C. Hanel, and M. K. Seely. "Seven-Stone Spiders on the Gravel Plains of Namibia." *Bollettino della Accademia Gioenia di Scienze Naturali* 26, no. 345 (1993): 77–83.

Crane, Jonathan K., ed. *Beastly Morality: Animals as Ethical Agents*. New York: Columbia University Press, 2015.

———. "Introduction: Beastly Morality; A Twisting Tale." In *Beastly Morality*, edited by Jonathan K. Crane. New York: Columbia University Press, 2015.

Csikszentmihalyi, Mihaly. *Creativity: Flow and the Psychology of Discovery and Invention*. New York: HarperCollins, 1996.

Curry, Oliver Scott, Daniel Austin Mullins, and Harvey Whitehouse. "Is It Good to Cooperate? Testing the Theory of Morality-as-Cooperation in 60 Societies." *Current Anthropology* 60, no. 1 (2019): 47–69. https://doi.org/10.1086/701478.

Daemen, Mat. "The Heart and the Brain: An Intimate and Underestimated Relation." *Netherlands Heart Journal* 21 (2013). https://doi.org/10.1007/s12471-012-0371-x.

Darwin, Charles. *The Descent of Man, and Selection in Relation to Sex*. 2 vols. London: John Murray, 1871.

———. *The Descent of Man, and Selection in Relation to Sex*. 2nd ed. New York: Appleton, 1889.

———. *The Expression of the Emotions in Man and Animals*. New York: Appleton, 1899.

Davila-Ross, Marina, Michael J. Owren, and Elke Zimmermann. "Reconstructing the Evolution of Laughter in Great Apes and Humans." *Current Biology*, July 14, 2009, 1106–11. https://doi.org/10.1016/j.cub.2009.05.028.

Davis, Karen. "Chicken Wisdom." Review of *Chicken*, by Annie Potts. *Humanimalia: A Journal of Human/Animal Interface Studies* 4, no. 1 (2012): 144–48.

———. "The Social Life of Chickens." In *Experiencing Animal Minds: An Anthology of Animal-Human Encounters*, edited by Julie A. Smith and Robert W. Mitchell. New York: Columbia University Press, 2012.

Diamond, Judy, and Alan B. Bond. *Kea, Bird of Paradox: The Evolution and Behavior of a New Zealand Parrot*. Oakland: University of California Press, 1999.

Dinets, Vladimir, Jen C. Brueggen, and John D. Brueggen. "Crocodilians Use Tools for Hunting." *Ethology, Ecology & Evolution* 27, no. 1 (2015): 74–78.

Dreger, Alice D., Cheryl Chase, Aron Sousa, and Joel Frader. "Changing the Nomenclature/Taxonomy for Intersex: A Scientific and Clinical Rationale." *Journal of Pediatric Endocrinology and Metabolism* 18, no. 8 (2005): 729–33.

Dutcher, Jim, and Jamie Dutcher. "Our Observations." Living with Wolves. Accessed January 3, 2022. www.livingwithwolves.org/.

———. "The Social Wolf." Living with Wolves. Accessed January 3, 2022. www.livingwithwolves.org/.

Dvash, Jonathan, and Simone G. Shamay-Tsoory. "Theory of Mind and Empathy as Multidimensional Constructs: Neurological Foundations." *Topics in Language Disorders* 34, no. 4 (2104): 282–95.

Edgar, Joanne, J. C. Lowe, E. S. Paul, and Christine Nicol. "Avian Maternal Response to Chick Distress." *Proceedings of the Royal Society B: Biological Sciences* 278 (2011): 3129–34. https://doi.org/10.1098/rspb.2010.2701.

Egan, Tennyson E., and Mary Lee A. Jensvold. "Pretend Play in Signing Chimpanzees (Pan Troglodytes)." In *Animal Communication and Cognition: Principles, Evolution, and Development*, edited by T. Wagner. New York: Nova, 2015.

Eibes-Eibesfeldt, Irenäus. "On the Ontogeny of Behavior of a Male Badger (Meles Meles L.) with Particular Reference to Play Behavior." In *Evolution of Play Behavior*, edited by Dietland Müller-Schwarze, 142–48. Stroudsburg, PA: Dowden, Hutchinson, and Ross, 1978.

Emery, Christopher D., and Nathan J. Bird. "Insightful Problem Solving and Creative Tool Modification by Captive Nontool-Using Rooks." *Proceedings of the National Academy of Sciences* 106, no. 25 (2009): 103070–75.

Emes, Richard D., Andrew J. Pocklington, Christopher N. G. Anderson, Alex Bayes, Mark O. Collins, Catherine A. Vickers, Mike D. R. Croning, et al. "Evolutionary Expansion and Anatomical Specialization of Synapse Proteome Complexity." *Nature Neuroscience* 11, no. 7 (2008): 799–806.

Estes, James A., M. Tim Tinker, Tom M. Williams, and David F. Doak. "Killer Whale Predation on Sea Otters Linking Oceanic and Nearshore Ecosystems." *Science* 282, no. 5388 (October 16, 1998): 473–76. https://doi.org/10.1126/science.282.5388.473.

Fagen, Robert. "Animal Play and Phylogenetic Diversity of Creative Minds." *Journal of Social and Biological Structures* 11, no. 1 (January 1988): 79–82.

———. "Play, Five Evolutionary Gates, Paths to Art." In *Play: An Interdisciplinary Synthesis*, edited by Donald E. Lytle, Felicia Faye McMahon, and Brian Sutton-Smith, 9–42. Lanham, MD: United Press of America, 2005.

———. "Selective and Evolutionary Aspects of Animal Play." *American Naturalist* 108, no. 964 (1974): 850–58.

Fagot, Joel, Michael E. Young, and Edward A. Wasserman. "Discriminating the Relation between Relations." *Journal of Experimental Psychology: Animal Behavior Processes* 27, no. 4 (2001): 318–28.

Fawcett, Leesa. "The Case of the Mimic Octopus: Agency and Worldmaking." *Antennae: The Journal of Nature in Visual Culture*, no. 21 (Summer 2012): 58–66.

Fields, Andrew T., Kevin A. Feldheim, Gregg R. Poulakis, and Demian D. Chapman. "Facultative Parthenogenesis in a Critically Endangered Wild Vertebrate." *Current Biology* 25, no. 11 (2015): R446–47.

Finn, Julian K., Tom Tregenza, and Mark D. Norman. "Defensive Tool Use in a Coconut-Carrying Octopus." *Current Biology* 19, no. 23 (2009): R1069–70. https://doi.org/10.1016/j.cub.2009.10.052.

First Nations Health Authority. "Our History, Our Health." FNHA, accessed December 2, 2021, www.fnha.ca/.

FishBase Information and Research Group, Inc. "Fishbase." Catalogue of Life, accessed December 2, 2021, www.catalogueoflife.org/.

Fisher, J., and R. A. Hinde. "The Opening of Milk Bottles by Birds." *British Birds* 42 (1949): 347–57.

Fitzgerald, F. Scott. "The Crack-Up." *Esquire*, February 1, 1936.

Franks, Nigel, and Tom Richardson. "Teaching in Tandem-Running Ants." *Nature,* January 11, 2006.

Frantzis, Alexandros, and Paraskevi Alexiadou. "Male Sperm Whale (Physeter Macrocephalus) Coda Production and Coda-Type Usage Depend on the Presence of Conspecifics and the Behavioural Context." *Canadian Journal of Zoology* 86, no. 1 (2008): 62–75. https://doi.org/10.1139/Z07–114.

Frisch, Karl von. *Animal Architecture.* New York: Harcourt Brace Jovanovich, 1974.

———. *The Dancing Bees: An Account of the Life and Senses of the Honey Bee.* 1st ed. Vienna, Austria: Springer-Verlag Wien, 1954. A translation of *Aus dem Leben der Bienen.* https://doi.org/10.1007/978-3-7091-4697-2.

Futuyma, Donald J. "Evolution." Review of *The Evolution of Beauty: How Darwin's Forgotten Theory of Mate Choice Shapes the Animal World—and Us*, by Richard O. Prum. *Quarterly Review of Biology* 93 (2018): 150–51.

Gadow, Hans. *Amphibians and Reptiles.* Cambridge Natural History vol. 8. London: Macmillan, 1901.

Gaesser, Brendan. "Constructing Memory, Imagination, and Empathy: A Cognitive Neuroscience Perspective." *Frontiers in Psychology* 3, no. 576 (January 9, 2013). https://doi.org/10.3389/fpsyg.2012.00576.

Galef, Bennett G. "Culture in Animals?" In *The Question of Animal Culture*, edited by Kevin N. Laland and Bennett G. Galef, 222–46. Cambridge, MA: Harvard University Press, 2009.

———. "The Question of Animal Culture." *Human Nature* 3 (1992): 157–78.

———. "Where's the Beef? Evidence of Culture, Imitation, and Teaching, in Cetaceans?" *Behavioral and Brain Sciences* 24 (2001): 335.

Galef, Bennett G., and Andrew Whiten. "The Comparative Psychology of Social Learning." In *APA Handbook of Comparative Psychology.* Vol. 2, *Perception, Learning, and Cognition*, edited by Josep Call, 441–60. Washington, DC: American Psychological Association, 2017.

Gall, Philipp von, and Mickey Gjerris. "Role of Joy in Farm Animal Welfare Legislation." *Society and Animals* 25, no. 2 (2017): 163–79. https://doi.org/10.1163/15685306-12341444.

Gardner, Howard. *Frames of Mind: The Theory of Multiple Intelligences.* 3rd ed. New York: Basic Books, 2011.

———. "Frequently Asked Questions: Multiple Intelligences and Related Educational Topics." *Howard Gardner* (blog), March 20, 2013, https://howardgardner01.files.wordpress.com/2012/06/faq_march2013.pdf.

Garland, Ellen C., Luke Rendell, Luca Lamoni, M. Michael Poole, and Michael J. Noad. "Song Hybridization Events during Revolutionary Song Change Provide Insights into Cultural Transmission in Humpback Whales." *Proceedings of the National Academy of Sciences* 114, no. 30 (July 25, 2017): 7822–29. https://doi.org/10.1371/journal.pone.0210057.

Garstang, Michael. *Elephant Sense and Sensibility.* London: Academic Press, 2015.

Gayon, Jean. "Sexual Selection: Another Darwinian Process." *Comptes Rendus Biologies* 333, no. 2 (2010): 134–44.

Geirland, John. "Go with the Flow: An Interview with Mihaly Csikszentmihalyi." *Wired*, September 1, 1996.

Ghoddousi, Arash, Erin K. Buchholtz, Alia M. Dietsch, Matthew A. Williamson, Sandeep Sharma, Niko Balkenhol, Tobias Kuemmerle, and Trishna Dutta. "Anthropogenic Resistance: Accounting for Human Behavior in Wildlife Connectivity Planning." *One Earth* 4, no. 1 (January 22, 2021): 39–48.

Gieling, Elise Titia, Rebecca Elizabeth Nordquist, and Franz Josef van der Staay. "Assessing Learning and Memory in Pigs." *Animal Cognition* 14, no. 2 (2011): 151–73.

Gigliotti, Carol. "Aesthetics of a Virtual World." *Leonardo: Journal of Arts, Sciences, and Technology* 28, no. 4 (1995): 289–95.

Girard, Madeline B., and John A. Endler. "Peacock Spiders." *Current Biology* 24, no. 13 (July 7, 2014): R588–90.

Gleich, Otto, and Ulrike Langemann. "Auditory Capabilities of Birds in Relation to the Structural Diversity of the Basilar Papilla." *Hearing Research* 273, nos. 1–2 (January 29, 2010): 80–88. https://doi.org/10.1016/j.heares.2010.01.009.

Godfrey-Smith, Peter. *Other Minds: The Octopus, the Sea, and the Deep Origins of Consciousness*. New York: Farrar, Straus, and Giroux, 2016.

Gonzalez-Crussi, Frank. *A Short History of Medicine*. New York: Modern Library, 2009.

Goodall, Jane. "Behaviour of the Free-Ranging Chimpanzee." Doctoral thesis, Cambridge University, 1966.

———. *The Chimpanzees of Gombe*. Cambridge, MA: Harvard University Press, 1986.

———. "Tool-Using and Aimed Throwing in a Community of Free-Living Chimpanzees." *Nature*, March 28, 1964, 1264–66. https://doi.org/10.1038/2011264a0.

Goodfellow, Peter. *Avian Architecture: How Birds Design, Engineer, and Build*. Princeton, NJ: Princeton University Press, 2011.

Gooding, Stanley. "Modern Research into Bees and Bee-Keeping." *Journal of the Royal Society of Arts* 106, no. 5021 (1958): 303–21.

Gould, James L., and Carol Grant Gould. *Animal Architects: Building and the Evolution of Intelligence*. New York: Basic Books, 2012.

Grainger, Jonathan, Stéphane Dufau, Marie Montant, Johannes C. Ziegler, and Joël Fagot. "Orthographic Processing in Baboons (Papio Papio)." *Science* 13 (April 2012): 245–48.

Gray, Patricia M., Bernie Krause, Jelle Atema, Roger Payne, Carol Krumhansl, and Luis Baptista. "The Music of Nature and the Nature of Music." *Science* 291, no. 5 (January 2001): 52–54.

Greenberg, Russell. "The Role of Neophophilia and Neophobia in the Development of Innovative Behavior of Birds." In *Animal Innovation*, edited by Simon M. Reader and Kevin N. Laland. New York: Oxford University Press, 2003.

Griffin, Ashleigh S., and Stuart A. West. "Kin Discrimination and the Benefit of Helping in Cooperatively Breeding Vertebrates." *Science* 302 (October 24, 2003): 634–36.

Griffin, Donald R. *Animal Minds*. Chicago: University of Chicago Press, 1994.

Groos, Karl. *The Play of Animals*. Translated by E. L. Baldwin. New York: Appleton, 1898.

Guinee, Linda N., and Katherine B. Payne. "Rhyme-Like Repetitions in Songs of Humpback Whales." *Ethology* 79 (1988): 295–306.

Hadhazy, Adam. "Think Twice: How the Gut's 'Second Brain' Influences Mood and Well-Being." *Scientific American*, February 12, 2010.

Hain, James, Gary R. Carter, Scott Kraus, Charles A. Mayo, and Howard E. Winni. "Feeding Behavior of the Humpback Whale, Megaptera Novaeangliae, in the Western North Atlantic." *Fishery Bulletin* 80 (1981).

Hanlon, Roger T., Lou-Anne Conroy, and John W. Forsythe. "Mimicry and Foraging Behaviour of Two Tropical Sand-Flat Octopus Species off North Sulawesi, Indonesia." *Biological Journal of the Linnean Society* 93 (2008): 23–38. https://doi.org/10.1111/j.1095–8312.2007.00948.x.

Hansell, Mike. *Animal Architecture*. Oxford Animal Biology Series. 1st ed. Oxford: Oxford University Press, 2005.

———. *Built by Animals: The Natural History of Animal Architecture*. Oxford: Oxford University Press, 2007.

Hardt, Marah J. *Sex in the Sea*. New York: St. Martin's Press, 2016.

Hatkoff, Amy. *The Inner World of Farm Animals*. New York: Stewart, Tabori & Chang, 2009.

Hauptman, Lyanda Lynn. *Crow Planet: Essential Wisdom from the Urban Wilderness*. New York: Back Bay Books, 2011.

Hayes, Catherine. *The Ape in Our House*. New York: Harper, 1951.

Heidborn, Tina. "Dancing with Bees." *Max Planck Research* 2 (2010): 74–80.

Hennessy, Cecilia A., Jean Dubach, and Stanley D. Gehrt. "Long-Term Pair Bonding and Genetic Evidence for Monogamy among Urban Coyotes (Canis Latrans)." *Journal of Mammalogy* 93, no. 3 (2012): 732–42.

Henschel, Joh R. "Tool Use by Spiders: Stone Selection and Placement by Corolla Spiders Ariadna (Segestriidae) of the Namib Desert." *Ethology* 101, no. 3 (1995): 187–99.

Herzing, Denise L. "Seti Meets a Social Intelligence: Dolphins as a Model for Real-Time Interaction and Communication with a Sentient Species." *Acta Astronautica* 67 (2010): 1451–54.

Heyes, Cecilia. "Where Do Mirror Neurons Come From?" *Neuroscience & Biobehavioral Review* 34, no. 4 (March 2010): 575–83.

Hickok, Gregory. "Eight Problems for the Mirror Neuron Theory of Action Understanding in Monkeys and Humans." *Journal of Cognitive Neuroscience* 21, no. 7 (2008): 1229–43.

Huizinga, Johan. *Homo Ludens: A Study of the Play Element in Culture*. Translated by R. F. C. Hull. 1st ed. Boston: Beacon Press, 1955 (first published 1938).

Hyde, Lewis. *The Gift: Creativity and the Artist in the Modern World*. New York: Vintage, 1979.

Iacoboni, Marco. "Imitation, Empathy, and Mirror Neurons." *Annual Review of Psychology* 60 (2009): 653–70.

Idani, Giorgio. "Social Relationships between Immigrant and Resident Bonobos (Pan Paniscus) Females at Wamba." *Folio Primatologica* 57 (1991): 83–95.

"The Impact of Smallpox on First Nations on the West Coast." *Working Effectively with Indigenous People* (blog), April 17 2017. www.ictinc.ca/.

Ingold, Timothy. "The Use and Abuse of Ethnography." *Behavioral and Brain Sciences* 24 (2001): 337.

Inoue, Sana, and Tetsuro Matsuzawa. "Working Memory of Numerals in Chimpanzees." *Current Biology* 17, no. 23 (2007): R1004–5.

Intergovernmental Science-Policy Platform on Biodiversity and Ecosystem Services (IPBES). "Summary for Policymakers of the Assessment Report of the Intergovernmental Science-Policy Platform on Biodiversity and Ecosystem Services on Pollinators, Pollination, and Food Production." Bonn, Germany: Secretariat of the IPBES, 2016.

Isabel Behncke, "Evolution's Gift of Play, from Bonobo Apes to Humans." TED2011 video, 7:01, March 22, 2011, www.youtube.com/watch?v=WjBwhwe5-cc.

———. "Play in the Peter Pan Ape." *Current Biology* 25, no. 1 (January 5, 2015): R24–27.

Jabr, Ferris. "Can Prairie Dogs Talk?" *New York Times Magazine*, March 12, 2017.

Janmaat, Karline R. L., Leo Polansky, Simone Dagui Ban, and Christophe Boesch. "Wild Chimpanzees Plan Their Breakfast Time, Type, and Location." *Proceedings of the National Academy of Sciences of the United States of America* 111, no. 46 (2014): 6343–48.

Janney, Eathan, Hollis Taylor, Constance Scharff, David Rothenberg, Lucas C. Parra, and Ofer Tchernichovski. "Temporal Regularity Increases with Repertoire Complexity in the Australian Pied Butcherbird's Song." *Royal Society Open Science* 3 (2016): 160357.

Jensvold, Mary Lee. "Pretend Play in Chimpanzees." Fauna, May 25, 2016, www.faunafoundation.org.

———. "Signs of Art and Pretend Play in Chimpanzees." Paper presented at the Workshop on the Origins of Awe and Wonder, University of Indiana–Bloomington, April 3, 2016.

Jensvold, Mary Lee Abshire, and Roger Fouts. "Imaginary Play in Chimpanzees (Pan Troglodytes)." *Human Evolution* 8, no. 3 (July 1993): 217–27.

Josef, Noam, Piero Amodio, Graziano Fiorito, and Nadav Shashar. "Camouflaging in a Complex Environment: Octopuses Use Specific Features of Their Surroundings for Background Matching." *PLoS ONE* 7, no. 5 (2012): e37579. https://doi.org/10.1371/journal.pone.0037579.

Judson, Olivia. *Dr. Tatiana's Sex Advice for All Creation*. New York: Henry Holt, 2002.

Julian K. Finn, Tom Tregenza, and Mark D. Norman. "Defensive Tool Use in a Coconut-Carrying Octopus." *Current Biology* 19, no. 23 (2009): R1069–70.

Jung, Rex E., Brittany S. Mead, Jessica Carrasco, and Ranee A. Flores. "The Structure of Creative Cognition in the Human Brain." *Frontiers in Human Neuroscience* 7, no. 330 (2013): 9.

Kaplan, Gisela. "Animal Communication." *Wiley Interdisciplinary Reviews: Cognitive Science* 5, no. 6 (2014): 661–77.

Karihaloo, Bhushan, Kai Zhang, and Jianping Wang. "Honeybee Combs: How the Circular Cells Transform into Rounded Hexagons." *Journal of the Royal Society Interface* 10, no. 20130299 (2013). https://doi.org/10.1098/rsif.2013.0299.

Kaufman, Allison B., and James C. Kaufman, eds. *Animal Creativity and Innovation.* Cambridge, MA: Academic Press, 2015.

Kaufman, James C., and Allison B. Kaufman, "Applying a Creativity Framework to Animal Cognition." *New Ideas in Psychology* 22 (2004): 143–55. https://doi.org/10.1016/j.newideapsych.2004.09.006.

Kaufman, Scott Barry, and Carolyn Gregoire. *Wired to Create: Unraveling the Mysteries of the Creative Mind.* New York: Tarcher Perigee/Penguin, 2015.

Kawai, M. "Newly Acquired Precultural Behavior of the Natural Troop of Japanese Monkeys on Koshima Islet." *Primates* 6 (1965): 1–30.

Kelley, Laura A., and John A. Endler. "How Do Great Bowerbirds Construct Perspective Illusions?" *Royal Society Open Science* 4, no. 160661 (2017).

Kellogg, Winthrop Niles, and Luella Agger Kellogg. *The Ape and the Child: A Study of Environmental Influence upon Early Behavior.* New York: Hafner, 1967.

Kessler, Janet. "Cuddling, Teasing, and Playing." Coyote Yipps, January 11, 2019, https://coyoteyipps.com/.

Keysers, Christine, and Valeria Gazzola. "Social Neuroscience: Mirror Neurons Recorded in Humans." *Current Biology* 20, no. 8 (2010): R353–54.

King, Barbara J. *How Animals Grieve.* Chicago: University of Chicago Press, 2013.

King, Stephanie L., and Vincent Janik. "Bottlenose Dolphins Can Use Learned Vocal Labels to Address Each Other." *Proceedings of the Royal Society B* 110, no. 32 (2013): 13216–21.

Kis, Anna, Ludwig Huber, and Anna Wilkinson. "Social Learning by Imitation in a Reptile (Pogona Vitticeps)." *Animal Cognition* 18, no. 1 (January 15, 2015): 325–31. https://doi.org/10.1371/journal.pone.0024121.

Knight, Kathryn. "Seeing and Communicating through Weak Electric Fields." *Journal of Experiential Biology* 216, nos. i–iv (2013).

Kopps, Anna M., Corinne Y. Ackermann, William B. Sherwin, Simon J. Allen, Lars Bejder, and Michael Krützen. "Cultural Transmission of Tool Use Combined with Habitat Specializations Leads to Fine-Scale Genetic Structure in Bottlenose Dolphins." *Proceedings of the Royal Society B* 281, no. 1782 (March 19, 2014): 20133245. https://doi.org/10.1098/rspb.2013.3245.

Kottler, Malcolm Jay. "Darwin, Wallace, and the Origin of Sexual Dimorphism." *Proceedings of the American Philosophical Society* 124, no. 3 (1980): 203–26.

Kroodsma, Donald. *The Singing Life of Birds*. New York: Houghton Mifflin, 2005.

Kruuk, Hans. *The Spotted Hyena: A Study of Predation and Social Behaviour*. Berkeley: University of California Press, 1972.

Kruzen, Michael, Sina Kreicker, Colin D. MacLeod, Jennifer Learmonth, Anna M. Kopps, Pamela Walsham, and Simon J. Allen. "Cultural Transmission of Tool Use by Indo-Pacific Bottlenose Dolphins (Tursiops Sp.) Provides Access to a Novel Foraging Niche." *Proceedings of the Royal Society B: Biological Sciences* 281 (2014). https://doi.org/10.1098/rspb.2014.0374.

Kuczaj, Stan, Kevin Tranel, Marie Trone, and Heather Hill. "Are Animals Capable of Deception or Empathy? Implications for Animal Consciousness and Animal Welfare." *Animal Welfare* 10, no. S (2001): 161–73.

Kuczaj, Stan A., II, Deirdre Yeater, and Lauren Highfill. "How Selective Is Social Learning in Dolphins?" *International Journal of Comparative Psychology* 25 (2012): 221–36.

Kummer, Hans, and Jane Goodall. "Conditions of Innovative Behaviors in Primates." In *Animal Innovation*, edited by Simon M. Reader and Kevin N. Laland. New York: Oxford University Press, 2003.

LaBelle, Brandon. *Lexicon of the Mouth: Poetics and Politics of Voice and the Oral Imaginary*. New York: Bloomsbury Academic, 2014.

Laland, Kevin N., Nicholas Atton, and Mike M. Webster. "From Fish to Fashion: Experimental and Theoretical Insights into the Evolution of Culture." *Philosophical Transactions of the Royal Society B* 366 (2011): 958–68. https://doi.org/10.1098/rstb.2010.0328.

Laland, Kevin, and Bennet G. Galef. *The Question of Animal Culture*. New York: Oxford University Press, 2009. https://doi.org/10.1073/pnas.1707630114.

Langlois, Krista. "First Nations Fight to Protect the Rare Spirit Bear from Hunters." *National Geographic*, October 26, 2017. www.nationalgeographic.com/.

Lanzoni, Susan. "A Short History of Empathy." *Atlantic*, October 2015.

Laws, Richard M., I. S. C. Parker, and Ronald C. B. Johnstone. *Elephants and Their Habitats; The Ecology of Elephants in North Bunyoro, Uganda*. Oxford: Clarendon Press, 1975.

Lee, Phyllis C., and Antonio C. de A. Moura. "Necessity, Unpredictability, and Opportunity: An Exploration of Ecological and Social Drivers of Behavioral Innovation." In *Animal Creativity and Innovation*, edited by Allison B. Kaufman and James C. Kaufman. New York: Academic Press, 2016.

Lee, Robert. "Accounting for Conquest: The Price of the Louisiana Purchase of Indian Country." *Journal of American History* 103, no. 4 (2017): 921–42.

Leeuwen, Edwin J. C. van, Katherine A. Cronin, and Daniel B. M. Haun. "A Group-Specific Arbitrary Tradition in Chimpanzees (Pan Troglodytes)." *Animal Cognition* 17, no. 6 (2014): 1421–25.

Levenson, Richard M., Elizabeth A. Krupinski, Victor M. Navarro, and Edward A. Wasserman. "Pigeons (Columba Livia) as Trainable Observers of Pathology and Radiology Breast Cancer Images." *PLOS ONE* 10, no. 11 (2015): e0141357.

Lewis, Meriwether, and William Clark. *The Journals of Lewis and Clark, 1804–1806.* Project Gutenberg, 2005, www.gutenberg.org/.

Ligon, Russell A., and Kevin J. McGraw. "Chameleons Communicate with Complex Colour Changes during Contests: Different Body Regions Convey Different Information." *Biology Letters* 9, no. 6 (2013): 20130892.

Lipkind, Dina, Gary F. Marcus, Douglas K. Bemis, Kazutoshi Sasahara, Nori Jacoby, Miki Takahashi, Kenta Suzuki, Olga Feher, Primoz Ravbar, Kazuo Okanoya, and Ofer Tchernichovski. "Stepwise Acquisition of Vocal Combinatorial Capacity in Songbirds and Human Infants." *Nature*, June 6, 2013, 104–9.

Lovgren, Stefan. "Animals Laughed Long before Humans, Study Says." *National Geographic News*, March 31, 2005.

Low, Philip. "The Cambridge Declaration on Consciousness in Non-Human Animals." Paper presented at the Francis Crick Memorial Conference on Consciousness in Human and Non-Human Animals, Cambridge, UK, June 7, 2012.

Lusseau, D. 2007. "Evidence for Social Role in a Dolphin Social Network." *Evolutionary Ecology* 21: 357–66.

Lusseau, D., and M. E. J. Newman. "Identifying the Role That Animals Play in Social Networks." *Proceedings of the Royal Society of London B* 271 (2004): S477–81.

MacDonald, William L. *The Pantheon: Design, Meaning, and Progeny.* Cambridge, MA: Harvard University Press, 1976.

Macrae, Fiona. "I'm the Chimpion! Ape Trounces the Best of the Human World in Memory Competition." *Daily Mail UK,* January 26, 2008, www.dailymail.co.uk/.

Madden, Joah R., Caroline Dingle, Jess Isden, Janka Sparfeld, Anne W. Goldizen, and John A. Endler. "Male Spotted Bowerbirds Propagate Fruit for Use in Their Sexual Display." *Current Biology* 22, no. 8 (2012): R264–65. https://doi.org/10.1016/j.cub.2012.02.057.

Magnúsdóttir, Edda E., and Rangyn Lim. "Subarctic Singers: Humpback Whale (Megaptera Novaeangliae) Song Structure and Progression from an Icelandic Feeding Ground during Winter." *PLoS ONE* 14, no. 1 (January 2019): e0210057. https://doi.org/10.1371/journal.pone.0210057.

Marek, Spinka, Ruth C. Newberry, and Marc Bekoff. "Mammalian Play: Training for the Unexpected." *Quarterly Review of Biology* 76, no. 2 (June 2001): 144.

Marino, Lori. "Thinking Chickens: A Review of Cognition, Emotion, and Behavior in the Domestic Chicken." *Animal Cognition* 20 (2017): 127–47.

Marino, Lori, and Christina M. Colvin. "Thinking Pigs: A Comparative Review of Cognition, Emotion, and Personality in Sus Domesticus." *International Journal of Comparative Psychology* 28 (2015).

Marino, Lori, Richard C. Connor, R. Ewan Fordyce, Louis M. Herman, Patrick R. Hof, Louis Lefebvre, Brenda McCowan, David Lusseau, Esther A. Nimchinsky, Adam A. Pack, Luke Rendell, Joy S. Reidenberg, Diana Reiss, Mark D. Uhen, Estel Van der Gucht, and Hal Whitehead. "Cetaceans Have Complex Brains for Complex Cognition." *PlosBiol* 5 (2007): 0966–72.

Marino, Lori, and Toni Frohoff. "Towards a New Paradigm of Non-Captive Research on Cetacean Cognition." *PLoS One* 6, no. 9 (2011): e24121. https://doi.org/10.1371/journal.pone.0024121.

Markham, Michael R., M. Lynne McAnelly, Philip K. Stoddard, and Harold H. Zakon. "Circadian and Social Cues Regulate Ion Channel Trafficking." *PLoS Biology* 7, no. 9 (2009): e1000203.

Marler, Peter, and M. Tamura. "Culturally Transmitted Patterns of Vocal Behavior in Sparrows." *Science* 146 (1964): 1483–86.

Masson, Jeffrey Moussaieff, and Susan McCarthy. *When Elephants Weep: The Emotional Lives of Animals.* New York: Delta, 1996.

Mateos-Rodríguez, María, and Felix Liechti. "How Do Diurnal Long-Distance Migrants Select Flight Altitude in Relation to Wind?" *Behavioral Ecology* 23 (2012): 403–9.

Matisse, Henri, and J. D. Flam. *Matisse on Art.* Revised edition. Documents of Twentieth-Century Art. Berkeley: University of California Press, 1995.

McComb, Karen, Graeme Shannon, Sarah M. Durant, Katito Sayialel, Rob Slotow, Joyce Poole, and Cynthia Moss. "Leadership in Elephants: The Adaptive Value of Age." *Proceedings of the Royal Society B: Biological Sciences* 278, no. 1772 (2011): 3270–76.

McGrane, Sally. "Moscow's Metro Dogs." *New Yorker*, July 8, 2013.

McKie, Robin. "Chimps with Everything: Jane Goodall's 50 Years in the Jungle." *Guardian*, June 26, 2010.

McLendon, Aidan K. "Classics Revisited: 'The Evolution of Nests and Nest-Building in Birds,' by Dr Nicholas E Collias (1964) *American Zoologist* 4(2): 175–190." *Progress in Physical Geography: Earth and Environment* 43, no. 3 (2019): 462–67.

Mech, David L. "Alpha Status, Dominance, and Division of Labor in Wolf Packs." *Canadian Journal of Zoology* 77 (1999): 1196–1203.

Mendl, Michael, Suzanne Held, and Richard W. Byrne. "Pig Cognition." *Current Biology* 20, no. 18 (2010): R796–98.

Mercader, Julio, Huw Barton, Jason Gillespie, Jack Harris, Steven Kuhn, Robert Tyler, and Christophe Boesch. "4,300-Year-Old Chimpanzee Sites and the Origins of Percussive Stone Technology." *Proceedings of the National Academy of Sciences* 104, no. 9 (2007): 3043–48.

Metcalfe, John. "Pigeons Might Be Way Smarter Than We Give Them Credit For." *Bloomberg CityLab*, June 3, 2013, www.bloomberg.com/.

Mitchell, Robert W. "A History of Pretense in Animals and Children." In *Pretending and Imagination in Animals and Children*, edited by Robert W. Mitchell, chapter 2. Cambridge: Cambridge University Press, 2002.

———, ed. *Pretending and Imagination in Animals and Children.* Cambridge: Cambridge University Press, 2002.

Mivart, St. George. "Review of *The Descent of Man*, by Charles Darwin." *Quarterly Review*, July 1871, 47–90.

Moffet, Mark W. *Adventures among Ants: A Global Safari with a Cast of Trillions.* Berkeley: University of California Press, 2010.

———. "Why Don't Ants Play? An Interview with Mark Moffett." *American Journal of Play* 7, no. 1 (2014): 20–26.

Monk, Julian D., Erin Giglio, Ambika Kamath, Max R. Lambert, and Caitlin E. McDonough. "An Alternative Hypothesis for the Evolution of Same-Sex Sexual Behaviour in Animals." *Nature Ecology and Evolution* 3 (2019): 1622–31.

Monsó, Susana, Judith Benz-Schwarzburg, and Annika Bremhorst. "Animal Morality: What It Means and Why It Matters." *Journal of Ethics* 22 (2018): 283–310.

Montaigne, Michel de. "Apology for Raimond Sebond." In *The Essays of Michel de Montaigne*, edited by William Carew Hazlett. London: Reeves and Turner, 1877. www.project.gutenberg.org.

Mora, Camilo, et al. "How Many Species Are There on Earth and in the Ocean?" *PLoS Biology* 9, no. 8 (2011): e1001127. https://doi.org/10.1371/journal.pbio.1001127.

Morgan, Lewis Henry. *The American Beaver and His Works.* Philadelphia: Lippincott, 1868.

Moscovice, Liza R., Pamela Heidi Douglas, Laura Martinez-Iñigo, Martin Surbeck, Linda Vigilant, and Gottfried Hohmann. "Stable and Fluctuating Social Preferences and Implications for Cooperation among Female Bonobos at Luikotale, Salonga National Park, DRC." *Journal of Physical Anthropology* 163, no. 1 (2017): 158–72.

"The Most Cited Articles from *Animal Behaviour* Published since 2018, Extracted from Scopus." Elsevier, accessed December 2, 2012, www.journals.elsevier.com.

Muller, Gerald, and James Watling. "The Engineering in Beaver Dams." Paper presented at the River Flow 2016: Eighth International Conference on Fluvial Hydraulics, St. Louis, Missouri, July 16, 2016. https://doi.org/10.1201/9781315644479-326.

Muller-Schwarze, Dietland. *The Beaver: Its Life and Impact.* 2nd ed. Ithaca, NY: Comstock, 2011.

Munz, Tania. *The Dancing Bees: Karl von Frish and the Discovery of the Honey Bee Language.* Chicago: University of Chicago Press, 2016.

Myerson, Roger. *Game Theory: Analysis of Conflict.* Cambridge, MA: Harvard University Press, 1991.

Nazzi, Francesco. "The Hexagonal Shape of the Honeycomb Cells Depends on the Construction Behavior of Bees." *Scientific Reports* 6, no. 28341 (2016). https://doi.org/10.1038/srep28341.

Nichols, Henry. "The Truth about Spotted Hyenas." *BBC Earth*, October 28, 2014, www.bbc.com/.

Nickerson, Colin. "Elephants' Toes Get the Message, Study Finds." *Boston Globe*, June 28, 2007.

Nordsieck, Robert. "The Leopard Slug (Limax Maximus)." The Living World of Molluscs, accessed December 2, 2012, www.molluscs.at/.

Nuechterlein, Gary, and Robert Storer. "The Pair-Formation Displays of the Western Grebe." *Condor: Journal of the Cooper Ornithological Society* 84, no. 4 (1982): 350–69.

O'Brien, Miles, and Ann Kellan. "Peaceful Bonobos May Have Something to Teach Humans." Report, *phys.org*, March 8, 2011, https://phys.org/news/.

O'Connell, Caitlin. *The Elephant's Secret Sense: The Hidden Life of the Wild Herds of Africa*. New York: Free Press, 2007.

O'Connell-Rodwell, Caitlin E. "Keeping an 'Ear' to the Ground: Seismic Communication in Elephants." *Physiology* 22 (2007): 287–94. https://doi.org/10.1152/physiol.00008.2007.

O'Connell-Rodwell, Caitlin E., Jason D. Wood, Colleen Kinsley, Timothy C. Rodwell, Joyce H. Poole, and Sunil Puria. "Wild African Elephants (Loxodonta Africana) Discriminate between Familiar and Unfamiliar Conspecific Seismic Alarm Calls." *Journal of the Acoustical Society of America* 122, no. 2 (September 2007): 823–30.

Olkowicza, Seweryn, Martin Kocoureka, Radek K. Lučana, Michal Porteša, W. Tecumseh Fitchb, Suzana Herculano-Houzelc, and Pavel Nemeca. "Birds Have Primate-Like Numbers of Neurons in the Forebrain." *Proceedings of the National Academy of Sciences* 113, no. 26 (2016): 7255–60. https://doi.org/10.1073/pnas.1517131113.

Osvath, Mathias. "Spontaneous Planning for Future Stone Throwing by a Male Chimpanzee." *Current Biology* 19, no. 5 (2009): R190. https://doi.org/10.1016/j.cub.2009.10.052.

Osvath, Mathias, and Gemma Martin-Ordas. "The Future of Future-Oriented Cognition in Non-Humans: Theory and the Empirical Case of the Great Apes." *Philosophical Transactions of the Royal Society B* 369, no. 20130486 (2014). https://doi.org/10.1098/rstb.2013.0486.

OzBirdZ. "Male Satin Bowerbird Building Bower." YouTube video, July 21, 2014, www.youtube.com/watch?v=HINXP7kBm_g.

Packard, Jane M. "Deferred Reproduction in Wolves (Canis Lupis)." Dissertation, University of Minnesota, 1980.

———. "Wolf Behavior: Reproductive, Social, and Intelligent." In *Wolves: Behavior, Ecology, and Conservation*, edited by L. David Mech and Luigi Boitani, chapter 2. Chicago: University of Chicago Press, 2003.

———. "Wolf Social Intelligence." In *Wolves: Biology, Behavior, and Conservation*, edited by Ana Paula Maia and Henrique F. Crussi, chapter 1. Hauppauge, NY: Nova Science Publishers, 2012.

Palagi, Elisabetta, and Giada Cordoni. "Postconflict Third-Party Affiliation in Canis Lupus: Do Wolves Share Similarities with the Great Apes?" *Animal Behaviour* 78 (2009): 979–86.

Parsons, E. Christien Michael. "Impacts of Navy Sonar on Whales and Dolphins: Now Beyond a Smoking Gun?" *Frontiers in Marine Science* 4, no. 295 (September 13, 2017). https://doi.org/10.3389/fmars.2017.00295.

Patrerson, Eric, and Janet Mann. "Cetacean Tool Use." In *Deep Thinkers*, edited by Janet Mann, chapter 7. Chicago: University of Chicago Press, 2017.

Patricelli, Gail L., Eileen A. Herberts, and Tamra C. Mendelson. "Book Review of Prum, R. O. 2018. *The Evolution of Beauty: How Darwin's Forgotten Theory of Mate*

Choice Shapes the Animal World—and Us, by R. O. Prum." *Evolution* 73, no. 1 (2018): 115–24.

Payne, Katy. *Silent Thunder: In the Presence of Elephants*. New York: Penguin, 1999.

Payne, Katy, William H. Langbauer Jr., and Elizabeth Thomas. "Elephant Calling Patterns as Indicators of Group Size and Composition: The Basis for an Acoustic Monitoring System." *African Journal of Ecology* 41 (2003): 99–107.

———. "Infrasonic Calls of the Asian Elephant." *Behavioral Ecology and Sociobiology* 18, no. 4 (1986): 297–301.

Payne, Robert B., and Laura L. Payne. "Song Copying and Cultural Transmission in Indigo Buntings." *Animal Behaviour* 46, no. 6 (1993): 1045–65. https://doi.org/10.1006/anbe.1993.1296.

Payne, Roger, ed. *Songs of the Humpback Whale*. CRM Records, 1970.

Perlman, David. "Toadfish's Steamy Love Life Is Revealed: Singing Fish Sometimes Let Meek Males Join a Menage à Trois." *SF Gate*, December 18, 2003. www.sfgate.com.

Perry, Clint J., Andrew B. Barron, and Lars Chittka. "The Frontiers of Insect Cognition." *Behavioral Sciences* 16 (2017): 111–18. https://doi.org/10.1016/j.cobeha.2017.05.011.

Peterson, Dale. *The Moral Lives of Animals*. New York: Bloomsbury Press, 2011.

Pierce, Jessica. "Mice in the Sink: On the Expression of Empathy in Animals." *Environmental Philosophy* 5, no. 1 (Spring 2008): 75–96. https://doi.org10.1098/rspb.2010.2701.

Pinto, Ana, Jennifer Oates, Alexandra Grutter, and Redouan Bshary. "Cleaner Wrasses *Labroides Dimiadiatus* Are More Cooperative in the Presence of an Audience." *Current Biology* 21 (2011): 1140–44.

Pleasance, Chris. "Not So Bird-Brained: Cheeky Keas Caught Dragging Cones into the Road So People in Cars Will Stop to Feed Them." *Daily Mail*, December 1, 2016, www.dailymail.com.

Polderman, Tinca J. C. "Meta-Analysis of the Heritability of Human Traits Based on Fifty Years of Twin Studies." *Nature Genetics* 47 (2015): 702–9. https://doi.org/10.1038/ng.3285.

Polsby, Nelson W. "The Contributions of President Richard F. Fenno, Jr." *Political Science* 17, no. 4 (1984): 778–81.

Poole, Joyce. *Coming of Age with Elephants: A Memoir*. 1st ed. Chicago: Trafalgar Square, 1996.

Potts, Annie. *Chicken*. London: Reaktion Books, 2012.

Pruetz, Jill D., Paco Bertolani, Kelly M. Boyer Ontl, Stacy Lindshield, Mark C. Shelley, and Erin G. Wessling. "New Evidence on the Tool-Assisted Hunting Exhibited by Chimpanzees (Pan Troglodytes Verus) in a Savannah Habitat at Fongoli, Sénégal." *Royal Society Open Science* 2, no. 4 (April 15, 2015): 140507. https://doi.org/10.1098/rsos.140507.

Prum, Richard O. "Aesthetic Evolution by Mate Choice: Darwin's *Really* Dangerous Idea." *Philosophical Transactions of the Royal Society B* 367 (2012): 2253–65. https://doi.org/:10.1098/rstb.2011.0285.

———. "Coevolutionary Aesthetics in Human and Biotic Artworlds." *Biological Philosophy* 28 (2013): 811–32.

———. *The Evolution of Beauty: How Darwin's Forgotten Theory of Mate Choice Shapes the Animal World—and Us.* New York: Knopf Doubleday, 2017.

Ramsey, Grant. "What Is Animal Culture?" In *Routledge Handbook of Philosophy of Animal Minds*, edited by Kristan Andrews and Jacob Beck, 345–53. London: Routledge, 2017.

Randall, Jan A. "Vibrational Communication: Spiders to Kangaroo Rats." In *Biocommunication of Animals*, 103–33. Dordecht: Springer Science + Business Media, 2014.

Reber, Stephan A., Judith Janisch, Kevin Torregrosa, Jim Darlington, Kent A. Vliet, and W. Tecumseh Fitch. "Formants Provide Honest Acoustic Cues to Body Size in American Alligators." *Scientific Reports* 7, no. 1816 (2017).

Rendall, Drew, Michael J. Owren, and Michael. J. Ryan. "What Do Animal Signals Mean?" *Animal Behaviour* 78 (2009): 233–40. https://doi.org/10.1016/j.anbehav.2009.06.007.

Rizzolatti, Guisseppi, and Laila Craighero. "The Mirror-Neuron System." *Annual Review of Neuroscience* 27 (2004): 169–92.

Romanes, George John. *Mental Evolution in Animals.* E-book ed. Cambridge: Cambridge University Press, 2011. First published in 1883.

———. *Mental Evolution in Man.* E-book ed. Cambridge: Cambridge University Press, 2012. First published in 1888.

Rothschild, Pat. "Ode to Spent Hens." Listen to Your Horse, January 21, 2017, https://listentoyourhorse.com.

Rowlands, Mark. *Can Animals Be Moral?* Oxford: Oxford University Press, 2012.

Russ, Sandra Walker. *Affect and Creativity: The Role of Affect and Play in the Creative Process.* London: Psychology Press, 1993.

Rutherford, Kenneth, Ramona D. Donald, Alistair B. Lawrence, and Francoise Wemelsfelder. "Qualitative Behavioural Assessment of Emotionality in Pigs." *Applied Animal Behaviour Science* 139 (2012): 218–24.

Saayman, G. S., and C. K. Tayler. "Imitative Behaviour by Indian Ocean Bottlenose Dolphins (Tursiops Aduncus) in Captivity." *Behaviour* 44, nos. 3–4 (1973): 286–98.

Safina, Carl. *Beyond Words: What Animals Think and Feel.* New York: Henry Holt, 2016.

Salwiczek, Lucie H., Laurent Prétôt, Lanila Demarta, Darby Proctor, Jennifer Essler, Ana I. Pinto, Sharon Wismer, et al. "Adult Cleaner Wrasse Outperform Capuchin Monkeys, Chimpanzees, and Orang-Utans in a Complex Foraging Task Derived from Cleaner–Client Reef Fish Cooperation." *PLoS ONE* 7, no. 11 (2012): e49068. https://doi.org/10.1371/journal.pone.0049068.

Scarf, Damian, Harlene Hayne, and Michael Colombo. "Pigeons on Par with Primates in Numerical Competence." *Science* 334, no. 23 (December 2011).

Schamel, Douglas, Diane M. Tracy, David B. Lank, and David F. Westneat. "Mate Guarding, Copulation Strategies, and Paternity in the Sex-Role Reversed, Socially

Polyandrous Red-Necked Phalarope (Phalaropus Lobatus)." *Behavioral Ecology and Sociobiology* 57 (2004): 110–18.

Scheel, David, Stephanie Chancellor, Martin Hing, Matthew Lawrence, Stefan Linquist, and Peter Godfrey-Smith. "A Second Site Occupied by Octopus Tetricus at High Densities, with Notes on Their Ecology and Behavior." *Marine and Freshwater Behaviour and Physiology* 50, no. 4 (2107): 285–91. https://doi.org/10.1080/10236244.2017.1369851.

Schilbach, Leonhard, Bert Timmermans, Vasudevi Reddy, Alan Costall, Gary Bente, Tobias Schlicht, and Kai Vogeley. "Toward a Second-Person Neuroscience." *Behavioral and Brain Sciences* 36 (2013): 393–414.

Schimtz, James H. "Second Night of Summer." *Galaxy Science Fiction*, 1950, 4–31.

Schroepfer-Walker, Kara, Victoria Wobber, and Brian Hare "Experimental Evidence That Grooming and Play Are Social Currency in Bonobos and Chimpanzees." *Behaviour* 152, nos. 3–4 (2015): 545–62.

Schultz, Ted R., Ulrich G. Mueller, Cameron R. Currie, and Stephen A. Rehner. "Reciprocal Illumination: A Comparison of Agriculture in Humans and in Fungus-Growing Ants." In *Insect-Fungal Associations: Ecology and Evolution*, edited by Fernando E. Vega and Meredith Blackwell Boyd, 149–90. New York: Oxford University Press, 2005.

Schuppli, Caroline, and Carel P. Van Schaik. "Animal Cultures: How We've Only Seen the Tip of the Iceberg." *Evolutionary Human Sciences* 1, no. E2 (2019).

Scott-Philips, Thomas C. "Animal Communication: Insights from Linguistic Pragmatics." *Animal Behavior* 79, no. 2010 (2009): e1–4.

Seeley, Thomas D., P. Kirk Visscher, and Kevin M. Passino. "Group Decision Making in Honey Bee Swarms." *American Scientist* 94, no. 4 (May–June 2006): 220–29.

Sewall, Katy. "The Girl Who Gets Gifts from Birds." *BBC Magazine*, February 25, 2015.

Sharpe, Frederick A. "Social Foraging of the Southeast Alaskan Humpback Whale, Meguptera Novaeangliae." PhD dissertation, Simon Fraser University, 2001.

Shumacker, Robert W., Kristina R. Walkup, and Benjamin Beck. *Animal Tool Behavior: The Use and Manufacture of Tools by Animals.* Revised and updated ed. Baltimore, MD: Johns Hopkins University Press, 2011.

Slobodchikoff, Con. *Chasing Doctor Dolittle: Learning the Language of Animals.* New York: St. Martins, 2012.

––––––. *Prairie Dogs: America's Meerkats—Language. Prairiedogchatter.* YouTube video, 2011. www.youtube.com/watch?v=y1kXCh496U0.

Smolker, Rachel, Andrew Richards, Richard Connor, Janet Mann, and Per Berggren. "Sponge Carrying by Dolphins (Delphinidae, Tursiops Sp.): A Foraging Specialization Involving Tool Use?" *Ethology* 103, no. 6 (1997): 454–65.

"Social Issues Update: Elephants Who Appeared to Mourn Their Human Friend Remain Protected." *George Stroumboulopoulos Tonight.* CBC/Radio Canada, July 26, 2012. www.cbc.ca.

Sol, Daniel. "The Evolution of Innovativeness: Exaptation or Specialized Adaptation?" In *Animal Creativity and Innovation*, edited by Allison B. Kaufman and James B. Kaufman, 163–78. Cambridge, MA: Academic Press, 2016.

Stanton, Andrew, and Lee Unkrich, dirs. *Finding Nemo*. Emeryville, CA: Disney Productions, 2003.

"Stray Dogs Master Complex Moscow Subway System." *ABC News*, March 19, 2010.

Sugasawa, Shoko, Barbara C. Klump, James J. H. St. Clair, and Christian Rutz. "Causes and Consequences of Tool Shape Variation in New Caledonian Crows." *Current Biology* 27, no. 24 (2017): 3885–90. https://doi.org/10.1016/j.cub.2017.11.028.

Taylor, Hollis. "Birdsong Has Inspired Humans for Centuries: Is It Music?" *Conversation*, July 25, 2017.

———. *Is Bird Song Music? Outback Encounters with an Australian Songbird*. Bloomington: Indiana University Press, 2017.

Thomas, Chris D., Alison Cameron, Rhys E. Green, Michel Bakkenes, Linda J. Beaumont, Yvonne C. Collingham, Barend F. N. Erasmus, et al. "Extinction Risk from Climate Change." *Nature*, January 8, 2004, 145–48.

Thornton, Alex, and Katherine McAuliffe. "Teaching Can Teach Us a Lot." *Animal Behaviour* 83, no. 4 (2012): e6–9.

Tomicello, Michael. "The Question of Chimpanzee Culture, Plus Postscript." In *The Question of Animal Culture*, edited by Kevin N. Laland and Bennett G. Galef, 198–221. Cambridge, MA: Harvard University Press, 2009.

United Nations Environment Programs. "Report on 1st CMS Workshop on Conservation Implications of Animal Culture and Social Complexity, Parma, Italy." April 12–14, 2018. www.cms.int.

United Press. "Ecstasy Causes Depression in Pigs." News release, *phys.org*, March 10, 2006, https://phys.org/.

University Communication and Marketing. "Pigeons Peck for Computerized Treat." IowaNow, May 29, 2013, https://now.uiowa.edu/.

Urquiza-Haas, Esmeralda, and Kurt Kotrschal, "The Mind behind Anthropomorphic Thinking: Attribution of Mental States to Other Species." *Animal Behaviour* 109 (2015): 167–76. https://doi.org/10.1016/j.anbehav.2015.08.01.

Vieira, Sofia, Manuel Biscoito, Helena Encarnação, João Delgado, and Theodore W. Pietsch. "Sexual Parasitism in the Deep-Sea Ceratioid Anglerfish *Centrophryne spinulosa* Regan and Trewavas (Lophiiformes: Centrophrynidae)." *Copeia* 2013, no. 4 (December 30, 2013): 666–69. https://doi.org10.1643/CI-13-035.

Vila Pouca, Catarina, and Culum Brown. "Contemporary Topics in Fish Cognition and Behaviour." *Current Opinion in Behavioral Sciences* 16 (2017): 46–52. https://doi.org/10.1016/j.cobeha.2017.03.002.

Vliet, Kent A. "Social Displays of the American Alligator (Alligator Mississippiensis)." *American Zoology*, no. 29 (1989): 1019–31.

Waal, Frans B. M. de. *Are We Smart Enough to Know How Smart Animals Are?* New York: Norton, 2017.

———. *Good Natured: The Origins of Right and Wrong in Humans and Other Animals.* Cambridge, MA: Harvard University Press, 1996.

———. "Putting the Altruism Back into Altruism: The Evolution of Empathy." *Annual Review of Psychology* 59 (2008): 279–300.

———. "What Is an Animal Emotion?" *Annals of the New York Academy of Sciences* 1224 (2011): 191–206. https://doi.org/10.1111/j.1749-6632.2010.05912.x.

Waal, Frans B. M. de, and Stephanie D. Preston. "Mammalian Empathy: Behavioural Manifestations and Neural Basis." *Nature Reviews/Neuroscience* 18, no. 8 (August 2017): 498–509.

Walker, Kara, Rebecca Rudicell, Yingying Li, Beatrice Hahn, Emily Wroblewski, and Anne Pusey. "Chimpanzees Breed with Genetically Dissimilar Mates." *Royal Society Open Science* 4, no. 160422 (2017).

Walker, Reena H., Andrew J. King, J. Weldon McNutt, and Neil R. Jordan. "Sneeze to Leave: African Wild Dogs (Lycaon Pictus) Use Variable Quorum Thresholds Facilitated by Sneezes in Collective Decisions." *Proceedings of the Royal Society B: Biological Sciences* 284, no. 1862 (2017). https://doi.org/10.1098/rspb.2017.0347.

Wallace, Alfred Russel. "A Theory of Birds' Nests: Shewing the Relation of Certain Sexual Differences of Colour in Birds to Their Mode of Nidification (S139: 1868)." *Journal of Travel and Natural History* S, no. 139 (1868): 74.

Wasserman, Edward A., Yasuo Nagasaka, Leyre Castro, and Stephen J. Brzykcy. "Pigeons Learn Virtual Patterned-String Problems in a Computerized Touch Screen Environment." *Animal Cognition* 16 (2013): 737–53.

Watson, Duncan M., and David B. Croft. "Age-Related Differences in Playfighting Strategies of Captive Male Red-Necked Wallabies (Macropus Rufogriseus Banksianus)." *Ethology* 102 (1996): 226–346.

Watts, Heather E., and Kay E. Holekamp. "Hyena Societies." *Current Biology* 17, no. 16 (2007): R657–60. https://doi.org/10.1016/j.cub.2007.06.002.

Weber, Nicholas, Nicolaas Bouwes, Michael M. Pollock, Carol Volk, Joseph M. Wheaton, Gus Wathen, Jacob Wirtz, and Chris E. Jordan. "Alteration of Stream Temperature by Natural and Artificial Beaver Dams." *PLoS ONE* 12, no. 5 (2017): e0176313.

Weintraub, Karen. "Wild and Captive Chimpanzees Share Personality Traits with Humans." *New York Times*, October 24, 2017.

Weiss, Alexander. "Personality Traits: A View from the Animal Kingdom." *Journal of Personality* 86, no. 1 (February 2018): 12–22. htps://doi.org/10.1111/jopy.1231.

Weiss, Alexander, Michael L. Wilson, D. Anthony Collins, Deus Mjungu, Shadrack Kamenya, Steffen Foerster, and Anne E. Pusey. "Personality in the Chimpanzees of Gombe National Park." *Scientific Data* 4, no. 170146 (2017).

Wemelsfelder, Françoise. "How Animals Communicate Quality of Life: The Qualitative Assessment of Behaviour." *Animal Welfare* 16, no. S (2007): 25–31.

———. "A Science of Friendly Pigs: Carving out a Conceptual Space for Addressing Animals as Sentient Beings." In *Crossing Boundaries: Investigating Human-Animal Relationships*, edited by L. I. A. Birke and J. Hockenhull, 225–51. The Hague: Brill, 2012.

Wemelsfelder, Françoise, and Siobhan Mullan. "Applying Ethological and Health Indicators to Practical Animal Welfare Assessment." *Review of Science and Technology OIE* 33, no. 1 (2014): 111–20.

Whitehead, Hal. "Gene-Culture Coevolution in Whales and Dolphins." *Proceedings of the National Academy of Sciences* 114, no. 30 (July 25, 2017): 7814–21. https://doi.org/10.1073/pnas.1620736114.

Whitehead, Hal, and Luke Rendell, eds. *The Cultural Lives of Whales and Dolphins.* Chicago: University of Chicago Press, 2015.

Whiten, Andrew, Francisco J. Ayalab, Marcus W. Feldmanc, and Kevin N. Laland. "The Extension of Biology through Culture." *Proceedings of the National Academy of Sciences* 114, no. 30 (2017): 7775–81.

Whiten, Andrew, Christine A. Caldwell, and Alex Mesoudi. "Cultural Diffusion in Humans and Other Animals." *Current Opinion in Psychology* 8 (2016): 15–21.

Wiggins, Geraint A., Peter Tyack, Constance Scharff, and Martin Rohrmeier. "The Evolutionary Roots of Creativity: Mechanisms and Motivations." *Philosophical Transactions of the Royal Society B* 370, no. 20140099 (2015).

Wild, Sonja, Simon J. Allen, Michael Krützen, Stephanie King, Livia Gerber, and J. E. William Hoppitt. "Multi-Network-Based Diffusion Analysis Reveals Vertical Cultural Transmission of Sponge Tool Use within Dolphin Matrilines." *Biology Letters* 15 (2019).

Willette, Dorothy. "The Enduring Symbolism of Doves: From Ancient Icon to Biblical Mainstay." *Bible History Daily,* September 1, 2014, www.biblicalarchaeology.org/.

Wojcieszek, Janine M., James A. Nicholls, N. Justin Marshall, and Anne W. Goldizen. "Theft of Bower Decorations among Male Satin Bowerbirds (Ptilonorhynchus Violaceus): Why Are Some Decorations More Popular Than Others?" *Emu* 106, no. 3 (2006): 175–80.

Wolf, Erik R. *Europe and the People without History.* Berkeley: University of California Press, 1982.

Woodger, Elin, and Brandon Toropov. *Encyclopedia of Lewis and Clark Expedition.* Facts on File Library of American History. 2nd ed. New York: Infobase Publishing, 2009.

Woolf, Virginia. *Orlando: A Biography.* Boston: Mariner, 1973.

Wystrach, Antonie. "We've Been Looking at Ant Intelligence the Wrong Way." *Conversation,* August 30, 2013.

Wystrach, Antoine, Sebastian Schwarz, Alice Baniel, and Ken Cheng. "Backtracking Behaviour in Lost Ants: An Additional Strategy in Their Navigational Toolkit." *Proceedings of the Royal Society B* 280, no.1769 (2013): 1677.

INDEX

abstract thinking, 21–22, 40–41, 42–43, 113
adaptive behavior, 87, 99. *See also* flexibility
Advertising Calls, 150
aesthetics: animal-centered understanding and, 128, 161; architecture and, 122–123, 125–126, 127–128, 129; choice and, 159; vs. creativity, 123; sexual selection and, 155–159
African Mormyridae, 161
African wild dogs, 102–103
agency: captivity vs. natural environments and, 95–96; sexual selection and, 156–159, 161, 163
aggression: animal-human similarities and, 80; communication and, 63–64
alarm calls, 50–52, 59, 68
alligators: courtship, 149–150; play, 90, 91
alloparenting, 198
altruism, 103, 178
Amazon Molly, 140
American Beaver and His Works, The (Morgan), 108
amphibians: communication, 62; tool use, 132
analogical thinking, 43, 44
Andreyev, Julie, 135–136
angler fish, 143–144
Animal Architecture: Building and the Evolution of Intelligence (Gould and Gould), 109, 113
animal-centered understanding: aesthetics and, 128, 161; architecture and, 110; communication and, 21, 59–60, 65, 66, 68–69, 74, 75; complexity and, 74–75;

culture and, 201; diversity and, 226–227; dogs as catalyst for, 187; emotions and, 167, 169–170; intelligence and, 20–22, 38–39, 44–45, 74; meaning and, 137; methodology and, 14; play and, 79, 85
Animal Creativity and Innovation (Kaufman and Kaufman), 12
"Animal Creativity and Innovation" (Kuczaj), 7
animal-human similarities: aggression and, 80; animal research and, 33; anthropomorphism and, 14–15, 166–167; birdsong and, 70–71; emotions and, 84, 166, 182; intelligence and, 30, 44; language and, 57–58; laughter and, 80–81; learning and, 2, 27; personality and, 187; play and, 84, 102; QBA approach and, 38; sexual selection and, 155. *See also* bonobos; chimpanzees
Animal Innovation (Reader and Laland), 10–11
Animal Minds (Griffin), 107, 108–110
animal research, 33, 38, 95
animal sanctuaries, 94–96
animal subjectivity, 159–161
Animal Tool Behavior (Burghardt), 130
Animalwise: How We Know Animals Think and Feel (Morell), 167
Anthony, Lawrence, 64–65, 68
anthropomorphism, 14–15, 166–167
ants: cultural transmission, 44; intelligence, 30–32
Apology for Raymond Sebold (Montaigne), 85

Applying a Creative Framework to Animal Cognition (Kaufman and Kaufman), 11, 12
appropriateness, 6
archerfish, 131–132
architecture, 106–121; aesthetics and, 122–123, 125–126, 127–128, 129; courtship and, 2, 106, 122–129; decision-making and, 118–121; ecological benefits of, 108, 116–117; flexibility and, 109–111, 113, 115; insects and, 114–115, 116–117; intelligence and, 108; interspecies interactions and, 111; physical processes of, 109, 111, 112, 115, 117–118; social groups and, 109, 111, 115–116
ASL (American Sign Language), 96–97
Atwood, Margaret, 140
autonomy, 162
Ayumu (chimpanzee), 19–21

babbling, 28
baboons: intelligence, 25; play, 105
Bachelard, Gaston, 76, 106
badgers, 78
Bagemihl, Bruce, 138–139, 140, 142, 143, 144–145, 146–147, 148
Balcombe, Jonathan, 81, 99, 142, 143, 167, 189, 190, 192–193
Baptista, Luis, 71
Bateson, Patrick, 5, 81–82, 83, 201
Baya Weaver bird, 124
bearded dragons, 203–204
Beastly Virtues: Animals as Ethical Agents (Crane), 216
beavers, 106–112; canals, 112–113; dams, 111–112, 113–114; hunting of, 107–108; intelligence, 108
bees: architecture, 116–117; decision-making, 118–121; emotions, 193; language, 58–59, 118–120
behavioral diversity: empathy and, 179–180; innovation and, 185

behaviorism, 37–38, 59
Behncke, Isabel, 76–77
Bekoff, Marc, 39, 99–100, 101, 102, 116, 164, 166–167, 181, 216, 217, 220
Benson-Amram, Sarah, 183–185
Berry, Adam, 103
Beyond Words: What Animals Think and Feel (Safina), 167
bill tip organ, 169
biodiversity: human impacts on, 229–231; individuality and, 227; sexual selection and, 129, 143, 158, 159; social groups and, 227–228
biotechnology, 228–229
birds: architecture, 2, 106, 122–129; courtship, 2, 106, 122–129, 150–154; deception, 24–25, 27–28, 179; emotions, 169–175; intelligence, 24–25, 27–28; interspecies creativity, 135–136; memory, 24; migration, 21; play, 82, 86–87, 98, 99; sexuality, 141, 143, 148, 162; tool use, 130–131
birds of paradise, 152–154
birdsong, 69–75; anatomy and, 69–70; animal-human similarities and, 70–71; complexity and, 71; cultural transmission and, 43, 70, 200; human exceptionalism and, 72–74; language and, 75; learning and, 2, 28, 162; as music, 70, 212
bobcats, 86
Bohm, David, 10
Bond, Alan, 87
bonobos: play, 76–78, 79–80; sexuality, 144–145
Booth, Warren, 141
boredom, 39
Borgia, Gerald, 123, 128–129
bowerbirds, 2, 106, 122–129
Brakes, Philippa, 227, 228
Brennan, Patricia, 162
Bronson, Sarah, 191–192

Brothers, Lesley, 115
Brown, Culum, 61, 189
Brown thrasher, 71–72
Bruck, Jason, 24
Bshary, Redouan, 190, 191–192
built environments. *See* architecture
Buiski, Peter, 186
Burghardt, Gordon, 6, 15, 78–79, 87, 89, 90, 130, 167
Burke, Nathan, 141
Byrne, Richard, 104

caddisflies, 114–115
Caldwell, Michael S., 62–64
Cambridge Declaration of Consciousness, 36, 57
camouflage, 61, 204
Can Animals Be Moral (Rowland), 216
canines: animal-centered understanding and, 187; flexibility, 221–222; learning, 24; morality, 217–219, 220; personality, 220–221; play, 100–101; reconciliation, 181–182
cannibalism, 146
captivity vs. natural environments: agency and, 95–96; boredom and, 39; culture and, 202–203; Free Choice Profiling and, 39–40; intelligence and, 20, 21, 36; language and, 27, 56; neophilia and, 4–5; tool use and, 133–134
capuchins, 209
"Case of the Mimic Octopus, The: Agency and World-Making" (Fawcett), 204
Castanheira, Maria Filipa, 188
Castro, Leyre, 46
catbirds, 73
cetaceans, 30. *See also* dolphins; whales
chameleons, 167
Chasing Dr. Dolittle: Learning the Language of Animals (Slobodchikoff), 50
chemical communication, 60
Chica (chicken), 171–172

chickens, 168–175; communication, 3, 169; emotions, 173, 174–175; empathy, 3, 174–175; friendship, 170–172; sensory abilities, 169; social diplomacy, 2–3
Chimpanzee and Human Communication Institute, 96
chimpanzees: empathy, 179; human adoption of, 56, 92–94; individuality, 4; intelligence, 19–21; language and, 93; personality, 186, 187; play, 82; sanctuaries for, 94–96; sexuality, 147; similarity to humans, 30, 80; tool use, 130, 209; Washoe Project, 96
choice. *See* agency; judgment
Church, Russell, 178
Clark's Grebe, 150–151
cleaner fish, 191–193
clownfish, 140
Coastal Guardian Watchmen, 197
"Coevolutionary Aesthetics in Human and Biotic Artworlds" (Prum), 161
cognition. *See* intelligence
Coming of Age with Elephants (Poole), 131
communal spiders, 88–89
communication, 50–75; aesthetics and, 136; animal-centered understanding and, 21, 59–60, 65, 66, 68–69, 74, 75; chemical, 60; courtship and, 60–61; creative process and, 212–213; cultural transmission and, 43, 70, 200; culture and, 210–211, 212–213; deception and, 60–61; emotions and, 167; gestures and, 190; individuality and, 52; infrasound, 65, 66–68; innovation and, 53–55; intelligence and, 27, 46, 165; interspecies interactions and, 52–53; vs. language, 55–56; learning and, 2, 70, 162, 211; music and, 65–66, 70, 211–212; naming and, 26; perspective taking and, 169; social groups and, 3, 50–51, 68; ubiquity of, 69; vibrational, 61–65, 66–68; visual, 60–61. *See also* language

community. *See* social groups

complexity: animal-centered understanding and, 74–75; communication and, 71

conflict resolution: empathy and, 179; play and, 79–80

cooperation: interspecies interactions and, 190–193; morality as, 213

Cordoni, Giada, 181–182

Corolla spiders, 131

courtship: aesthetics and, 129, 155–159; architecture and, 2, 106, 122–129; communication and, 60–61; dance and, 149–154; intelligence and, 128; play and, 81, 88–89, 91; sexual selection and, 123, 129, 155–159, 161, 163. *See also* sexuality

coyotes: communication, 54–55; pair bonding, 148–149

Crabtree, Robert, 54–55

Crane, Jonathan K., 216

crayfish, 193

Creativity: Flow and the Psychology of Discovery and Invention (Csikszentmihalyi), 77

creativity: vs. aesthetics, 123; author's definition, 4; continuum of, 6–7, 225; decision-making and, 120–121; deep source of, 3, 10, 22; definitions of, 3–4, 5, 6, 7–8, 230, 231–232; diversity of, 4–5, 226–227, 230; emotions and, 3, 165–166, 173–174; empathy and, 3, 166, 178; evolution and, 162; flow and, 9, 100; fluid nature of, 8, 123; human exceptionalism and, 72–74; individuality and, 4, 18; vs. innovation, 5–6, 11, 81–82; innovation and, 54, 55; vs. intelligence, 22, 23; interspecies interactions and, 135–136; morality and, 217–220; motivations for, 4–5; music and, 70; obsessiveness and, 105; personality and, 187–188; play and, 78, 86; process of, 4, 5–6, 7–8, 9,

77–78, 212–213; sexuality and, 139, 143; ubiquity of, 139, 225

critical anthropomorphism, 15, 167–168

crocodiles: play, 89–91; tool use, 131

Croft, David, 101

cross-fostering, 56, 92–94

Crow Planet (Haupt), 98

crows: interspecies creativity, 135–136; play, 98; tool use, 130–131

Croze, Harvey, 177

Csikszentmihalyi, Mihaly, 77–78, 99

cultural hitchhiking, 207, 209

Cultural Lives of Whales and Dolphins, The (Whitehead and Rendell), 199

cultural transmission: communication and, 43, 70, 200; definitions of culture and, 193, 201–202; ecotypes and, 206–207; intelligence and, 43–44; language and, 205; play and, 84; tool use and, 130, 131

culture: animal-centered understanding and, 201; captivity vs. natural environments and, 202–203; communication and, 210–211, 212–213; cooperation and, 192–193; definitions of, 193, 199, 201–202, 205; ecotypes and, 206–207; human exceptionalism and, 11, 13, 199–201; imitation and, 203–204; innovation and, 200, 202; intelligence and, 46, 203; language and, 205, 206; learning and, 212–213; mitochondrial DNA and, 207–208, 209; morality and, 213; play and, 84; tool use and, 130, 147, 200, 208–209. *See also* cultural transmission

curiosity: animal-centered understanding and, 74; creativity and, 7; play and, 104, 105

cuttlefish: communication, 60–61; tactical deception, 179

dance: courtship and, 149–154; as language, 58–59, 118–120, 121

Dancing Bees, The: Karl von Frisch and the Discovery of the Honeybee Language (Munz), 59

Dapporto, Leonardo, 89

Darwin, Charles: on architecture, 117, 122–123; on courtship, 127; on emotions, 84, 166; on morality, 216; on sexuality, 143; on sexual selection, 129, 155, 156, 157–158

Darwin's Unfinished Symphony: How Culture Made the Human Mind (Laland), 11

David Graybeard (chimpanzee), 130

Davis, Karen, 173, 174

deception: courtship and, 60–61; empathy and, 179; intelligence and, 24–25, 27–28, 31, 34–35, 169

decision-making: creativity and, 120–121; language and, 118–120; perspective taking and, 103–104; sexuality and, 139; social groups and, 102–104

decoration. *See* aesthetics

Deep Thinkers (Mann), 208

depression, 37, 39

Descent of Man and Selection in Relation to Sex, The (Darwin), 122–123, 156

de Waal, Frans, 19, 102, 167, 175–177, 178, 180, 181, 182, 216

dialects, 43, 70, 72, 200, 205, 206

Diamond, Jared, 123

Diamond, Judy, 87

Dinets, Vladimir, 89–91

discourse system theory, 57–58

discriminating among individuals: communication and, 52; intelligence and, 34, 169; social groups and, 3

dogs: animal-centered understanding and, 187; learning, 24; play, 100–101; reconciliation, 181

dolphins: learning, 212–213; memory, 26–27; morality, 214–215; naming, 25–26;

play, 81, 98; sexuality, 147–148; tool use, 131, 208–209

Dr. Tatiana's Sex Advice to All Creation (Judson), 146

ducks, 162

Dutcher, Jamie, 219

Dutcher, Jim, 219

ecotypes, 206–207

Edgar, Barry, 194

Edgar, Joanne, 174–175

Egan, Tennyson E., 96

Eibl-Eibesfeldt, Irenäus, 78

Einfühlung, 175

elephants: biodiversity and, 227–228; communication, 21, 64–65; empathy, 177–178; intelligence, 21; play, 105; tool use, 131

Ella (elephant), 177–178

Emery, Nathan, 82

Emotional Lives of Animals (Bekoff), 167

emotions, 164–182; altruism, 103, 178; animal-centered understanding and, 167, 169–170; animal-human similarities and, 84, 166, 182; anthropomorphism and, 166–167; communication and, 167; creativity and, 3, 165–166, 173–174; current studies, 167–168; innovation and, 185; intelligence and, 36, 39; interspecies interactions and, 165; mirror neurons and, 28–29; morality and, 216; neophilia, 4–5, 184; personality and, 193; reconciliation, 180–182; sexuality and, 143; social groups and, 220–221. *See also* empathy

empathy, 164–165, 174–178; behavioral diversity and, 179–180; creativity and, 3, 166, 178; deception and, 179; mirror neurons and, 29; morality and, 220; parenting/parental bonds and, 3, 174–175, 177–178, 198–199, 222–223; social groups and, 177–178, 179–180

Endler, John, 127
episodic memory, 25
Erasistratus of Ceos, 33
Eudora (elephant), 177–178
evolution, 187. *See also* Darwin, Charles; sexual selection
Evolution of Beauty: How Darwin's Forgotten Theory of Mate Choice Shapes the Animal World—and Us (Prum), 155
exploration: innovation and, 77, 184–185; play and, 76–77
Expression of the Emotions in Man and Animals, The (Darwin), 166

facultative parthenogenesis (FP), 141
Fagen, Joanna, 86
Fagen, Robert, 86, 87
Fauna Foundation, 94–95
Fawcett, Leesa, 204
feelings. *See* emotions
Field, Andrew, 141–142
Finding Nemo, 140
Finn, Julian, 132
First Nations people, 196–198
Fish Cognition and Behavior (Brown, Laland, and Krause), 189
Fisher, Ronald, 157
fishes: aesthetics and, 161; communication, 21, 60–61, 161; cooperation, 190–193; culture, 192–193; hermaphroditism, 140, 145–146; intelligence, 21, 191–192; parthenogenesis, 141; personality, 188, 189; play, 81, 86; sexuality, 143–144; tool use, 131–132
fission-fusion societies, 26
Fitch, Tecumseh, 150
flexibility: architecture and, 109–111, 113, 115; social groups and, 221–222. *See also* adaptive behavior
flow, 9, 99–100
forced perspective, 127
forgiveness. *See* reconciliation

Fouts, Roger and Debbie, 96
FOXP2 gene, 57
Franks, Nigel, 35
Free Choice Profiling (FCP), 39–40
friendship, 170–172, 219
Frohoff, Tony, 203
future planning: human exceptionalism and, 134–135; mirror neurons and, 29; tactical deception and, 179; tool use and, 132, 133–134

Galef, Bennet G., 199–200
game theory, 191
Gardner, Beatrix and Allen, 96
Gardner, Howard, 45–46
Garstang, Michael, 68
garter snakes, 60
Genesis of Animal Play, The: Testing the Limits (Burghardt), 78–79
genetics: biotechnology and, 228–229; culture and, 207; language and, 57–58; mitochondrial DNA, 207–208, 209; sexuality and, 147; sexual selection and, 157
geniuses, 7, 8
geoengineering, 228
gestures, 190
Gjerris, Mickey, 104
Goodall, Jane, 98, 130, 166, 179, 186
Good Natured: The Origins of Right and Wrong in Humans and Other Animals (de Waal), 167, 216
Gosling, Samuel D., 226
Gould, Carol, 109, 110, 111, 112, 113, 115, 123, 127, 128
Gould, James L., 109, 110, 111, 112, 113, 115, 123, 127, 128
Grainger, Jonathan, 25
grammar, 51
Grant, Adam, 103
Gray, Patricia, 71
Grayback (wolf), 222

Great Animal Orchestra, The (Krause), 71
Great Bear Rainforest, 194–198
Great Bowerbirds, 127
Greenberg, Russell, 174, 184
Gregoire, Carolyn, 187
Greylag Goose, 148
grieving, 64–65, 172–173
Griffin, Donald, 14, 107, 108–110, 111, 115, 123, 127
grizzly bears, 194–195, 197–198
Groos, Karl, 85
Grow, Gloria, 94–96
Gua (chimpanzee), 56, 92
Guinee, Linda, 66

Hansell, Mike, 114, 122, 127
Hardt, Marah J., 146
Hare, Brian, 80
Haupt, Lyanda Lynn, 98
Hawking, Stephen, 36
Hayes, Keith and Kathy, 92–93
Held, Susan, 34–35
hermaphroditism, 139–140, 145–146
Hermit thrush, 72
higher-order alliances, 26
Hinemoa (chicken), 171–172
hive mind, 4, 31–32, 115–117
Holekamp, Kay E., 183–185
honeybees: architecture, 116–117; emotions, 193
horned frogs, 132
How Animals Grieve (King), 64
Huber, P., 84
Huizinga, Johan, 84
human-animal similarities. *See* animal-human similarities
human creativity: definitions of, 3–4; negative impacts of, 13, 228–229, 230–231
human exceptionalism, 9–10; aesthetics and, 155–156; agency and, 163; altruism and, 178; architecture and, 114; behaviorism and, 37–38, 59; captivity vs. natural

environments and, 40; communication and, 46, 50, 58–59; creativity and, 72–74; culture and, 11, 13, 199–201; dangers of, 44, 159–160; future planning and, 134–135; intelligence and, 21, 44; interspecies creativity and, 136; morality and, 214; personality and, 186; play and, 89–90; reconciliation and, 180; sexual selection and, 156; tool use and, 129–130. *See also* animal-centered understanding
Humboldt Penguin, 148
Hume, David, 216
humpback whales, 82–83, 215
Humphrey, Nicholas, 115
Hyde, Lewis, 1, 7, 230
hyenas, 182–184

iguanas: communication, 60; intelligence, 21
illusions, creation of, 127
imagination, 166
imitation: communication and, 70; culture and, 203–204; learning and, 27–28, 29; pretend play and, 98. *See also* social learning
improvisation, 70, 73
incest, 146–147
incubation, 77–78
indigenous people, 46, 196–198
Indigo Bunting, 162
individuality: biodiversity and, 227; communication and, 52; creativity and, 4, 18; emotions and, 170; fishes, 189; social groups and, 227–228
infrasound, 65, 66–68
innovation: architecture and, 112, 113; communication and, 53–55; vs. creativity, 5–6, 11, 81–82; creativity and, 54, 55; culture and, 200, 202; evolution and, 162; exploration and, 77, 184–185; intelligence and, 21; personality and, 183–185; play and, 76, 77, 82–83, 87–88

insects: architecture, 114–115, 116–117; cultural transmission, 44; decision-making, 118–121; emotions, 193; hive mind, 4, 115–117; intelligence, 30–32; language, 58–59, 118–120; play, 89; sexuality, 146

intelligence, 10, 19–48; abstract thinking and, 21–22, 40–41, 42–43, 113; analogical thinking and, 43, 44; animal-centered understanding and, 20–22, 38–39, 44–45, 74; architecture and, 108; behaviorism on, 37–38; boredom and, 39; captivity vs. natural environments and, 20, 21, 36; communication and, 27, 46, 165; courtship and, 128; vs. creativity, 22, 23; cultural transmission and, 43–44; data on, 23–24; deception and, 24–25, 27–28, 31, 34–35, 169; emotions and, 36, 39; language and, 27, 46; learning and, 24, 27, 28, 33, 34; measurement of, 42; memory and, 19–21, 24, 26–27, 34; mirror neurons and, 28–30; multiple intelligences theory, 45–46; naming and, 25–26; personality and, 30–31; reading and, 25; self-awareness and, 30, 42; sentience and, 36–37; social groups and, 26, 31–32, 34, 115–116, 169; social learning and, 27–28, 29, 35, 169; teaching and, 34, 35–36, 44–45; tool use and, 129–130

interspecies interactions: aesthetics and, 135; architecture and, 111; communication and, 52–53; cooperation, 190–193; creativity and, 135–136; emotions and, 165; First Nations people and, 196–198; friendship, 170–171; intelligence and, 27; play and, 91, 105; rationality and, 214–215

Is Birdsong Music? Outback Encounters with an Australian Songbird (Taylor), 212

jays: intelligence, 24–25, 27–28; play, 82
Jensvold, Mary Lee, 94, 96, 97
Jolly, Allison, 115
joy. *See* pleasure
judgment, 102–103, 217. *See also* decision-making
Judson, Olivia, 146, 147
Julie (chimpanzee), 4
jumping spiders, 154
Jung, Rex, 5, 7–8

Karihaloo, Bhushan, 117
Kaufman, Allison B., 11, 12
Kaufman, James C., 11, 12
Kaufman, Scott Barry, 187
Kea, Bird of Paradox: The Evolution and Behavior of a New Zealand Parrot (Diamond and Bond), 87
Keagy, Jason, 128–129
keas, 86–87
Kellog, Winthrop and Luella, 56, 92
Kelly, Laura, 127
Kessler, Janet, 148–149
King, Barbara, 64
Kirkpatrick, Mark, 157
Kitasoo/Xai'xais First Nation, 196–198
Krause, Bernie, 71
Krause, Jens, 189
Kroodsma, Donald, 70, 71, 72–75, 123, 162
Kuczaj, Stanley, 7

Lakota (wolf), 219
Laland, Kevin N., 10–11, 189, 192, 199–200
Laman, Tim, 152, 153
Lande, Russell, 157
Lande-Kirkpatrick (LK) theory, 157
Langberger, William, 66, 67
Langlois, Krista, 194
language: animal-centered understanding and, 59–60; babbling, 28; birdsong and, 75; captivity vs. natural

environments and, 27, 56; vs. communication, 55–56; cross-fostering and, 56, 93; culture and, 205, 206; decision-making and, 118–120; dialects, 205, 206; discourse system theory, 57–58; genetics and, 57–58; human exceptionalism and, 46, 58–59; innovation in, 53–55; intelligence and, 27, 46; memory and, 56; play and, 97–98; reading, 25; social groups and, 51, 55–56; social learning and, 97. *See also* communication

laughter, 80–81

Lawrence, Matthew, 204

learning: communication and, 2, 70, 162, 211; courtship and, 154; culture and, 212–213; intelligence and, 24, 27, 28, 33, 34. *See also* cultural transmission

leopard slugs, 138, 139

Lindauer, Martin, 118, 119

Lion King, The, 183

Lipps, Theodor, 175

"Little Albert" experiment, 38

LK (Lande-Kirkpatrick) theory, 157

Loulis (chimpanzee), 96–97

macaque monkeys, 28, 200

Madden, Joah, 127

magpies, play, 82

Mann, Janet, 208, 209

Marino, Lori, 169, 203

Marler, Peter, 65

Marshall, Alan John, 123

Marshall, Elizabeth, 66

Martin, Paul, 5, 81–82, 83

Martin-Ordas, Gemma, 134–135

Masson, Jeffrey Moussaieff, 166

masturbation, 147

Matsi (wolf), 219

Mech, David L., 181, 220–221

meerkats: cultural transmission, 43; social groups, 228

memory: episodic, 25; intelligence and, 19–21, 24, 26–27, 34; rhyme and, 66; social groups and, 56

Mendl, Michael, 34–35

mental state attribution, 15

midges, 146

mirror neurons, 28–30

mischievousness, 86–87, 105

Mitchell, Robert W., 92

mitochondrial DNA, 207–208, 209

Mivart, St. George Jackson, 155–156

mobula rays, 81

mockingbird, 70

Moffett, Mark, 30, 31–32

monkeys: innovation, 200; intelligence, 28; reconciliation, 180; tool use, 209

Montaigne, 85

morality, 213–220; as cooperation, 213; creativity and, 217–220; empathy and, 220; judgment and, 102–103; perspective taking and, 103–104; play and, 100–102, 220; rationality and, 214–215

Moral Lives of Animals (Peterson), 216

Morell, Virginia, 167

Morgan, Lewis Henry, 108

Moss, Cynthia, 67, 177

Motaki (wolf), 219

mothering. *See* parenting/parental bonds

multiple intelligences (MI) theory, 45–46

Munz, Tania, 59

music, 65–66, 70, 211–212

naming, 25–26

natural selection, 156, 158, 159

navigation, 32

Neasloss, Doug, 194–195, 197–198

neophilia, 4–5, 184

neuroscience, 5

Nile softshell turtle, 89

Nipples (wolf), 222–223

Norris, Ken, 215

North, Geoffrey, 88

novelty: creativity vs. innovation and, 81–82; neophilia and, 4–5, 184. *See also* innovation

obsessiveness, 105
O'Connell-Rodwell, Caitlin, 67–68
octopuses: imitation, 204; tool use, 132
On Creativity (Bohm), 10
one-trial learning, 33
orangutans: empathy, 164–165; sexuality, 147
orcas, 206
Orlando (Woolf), 140
orthographic processing, 25
Osvarth, Mathias, 133–135
other minds, 52–53. *See also* interspecies interactions
otters, 91

Packard, Jane A., 220–223
pair bonding, 148–149
Palagi, Elisabetta, 89, 181–182
Panamanian red-eyed tree frogs, 62
paper wasps, 89
parenting/parental bonds: cross-fostering and, 93–94; culture and, 208–209; empathy and, 3, 174–175, 177–178, 198–199, 222–223; mitochondrial DNA and, 207–208, 209. *See also* social groups
Parotia, 152–153
parthenogenesis, 140–142
Patricelli, Gail, 157
Payne, Katy, 65–67, 210
Payne, Roger, 71, 162, 210
peacocks, 159
peacock spiders, 154
Pepperberg, Irene, 36
personality, 183–189; cooperation and, 190–191; creativity and, 187–188; emotions and, 193; innovation and, 183–185; intelligence and, 30–31; social groups and, 188–189, 191–192, 221; trait theory on, 187–188. *See also* individuality

perspective taking, 103–104, 169, 176
Peterson, Dale, 216
Piaget, Jean, 92
Pierce, Jessica, 99, 100, 102, 116, 175, 181, 216, 217, 220
pigeons, 40–43, 47–48
Pigface (turtle), 89
pigs: animal research and, 33; boredom, 39; captivity vs. natural environments and, 36, 39–40; intelligence, 33, 34–35, 36; QBA approach and, 38; sentience, 37; similarity to humans, 33, 38
pit viper snakes, 141
planning. *See* future planning
plant cultivation, 122, 127
Play, Playfulness, Creativity, and Innovation (Bateson and Martin), 81–82
play, 76–93, 97–105; adaptive behavior and, 87, 99; animal-centered understanding and, 79; animal-human similarities and, 84, 102; boredom and, 89; conflict resolution and, 79–80; courtship and, 81, 88–89, 91; creative process and, 7, 77–78; criteria for, 79; cultural transmission and, 84; exploration and, 76–77; flow and, 99–100; freedom from stress and, 78; human exceptionalism and, 89–90; innovation and, 76, 77, 82–83, 87–88; interspecies interactions and, 91, 105; language and, 97–98; mischievousness and, 86–87, 105; morality and, 100–102, 220; novelty and, 76, 77; pleasure and, 77, 84, 98–99, 104–105; as practice, 85–86; pretending and, 92–93, 96–98; problem-solving and, 80, 82; reconciliation and, 181, 182; in reptiles, 89–91; sexuality and, 88–89
"play bow", 100–101

Pleasurable Kingdom (Balcombe), 142
pleasure: emotions and, 170; play and, 77, 84, 98–99, 104–105; sexuality and, 139, 142, 143. *See also* aesthetics
Poiarkov, Andrei, 24
Poole, Joyce, 67, 131, 177
Potts, Annie, 170–172
Pouca, Catarina Vila, 189
prairie dogs, 49–54, 59
Preston, Stephanie, 175–177, 178
Pretending and Imagination in Children and Animals, 92
pretend play, 92–93, 96–98
Pridmore, Ben, 19
primates: empathy, 164–165; human adoption of, 56, 92–94; intelligence, 25; laughter in, 80–81; play, 76–78, 79–80, 92–93, 105; sexuality, 144–145, 147; tool use, 147, 200. *See also* bonobos; chimpanzees
problem-solving: emotions and, 174; play and, 80, 82
prosocial motivation, 103. *See also* morality
Pruetz, Jill, 130
Prum, Richard O., 129, 138, 143, 155, 156–163
Pyburn, William F., 63

Qualitative Behavior Assessment (QBA), 37, 38
Question of Animal Awareness, The: Evolutionary Continuity of Mental Experience (Griffin), 14
Question of Animal Culture, The (Laland and Galef), 199–200

Ramsey, Grant, 201
ratchet-pointing, 151
rationality, 214–215. *See also* intelligence
rats, 178
Reader, Simon M., 10–11

reading, 25
Reber, Stephan, 150
reconciliation, 180–182
Red-Necked Phalarope, 143
Rendell, Luke, 83–84, 199, 200–201, 202–203, 205–206, 207, 209, 213–216
reptiles: communication, 60; courtship, 149–150; intelligence, 21; parthenogenesis, 141; play, 89–91; tool use, 131
rhesus monkeys, 180
rhyme, 66
Richardson, Tom, 35
Rizzolatti, Giacomo, 28
"Role of Joy in Farm Animal Welfare Legislation" (von Gall and Gjerris), 104
role reversal, 101
Romanes, George John, 130
rooks, 82
Rosetta Stone, 59–60
Rothschild, Pat, 171
Rowlands, Mark, 216
Rushing Dance, 150
Russ, Sandra, 173
rusty angelfish, 145–146

Safina, Carl, 167
same-sex sexuality, 140, 142, 144–145, 148
Santino (chimpanzee), 133–134, 179
Satin Bowerbird, 125–126
Scheel, David, 204
Scholes, Ed, 152, 153, 154
Schuett, Gordon, 141
scrub jays: deception, 179; intelligence, 24–25, 27–28
Seeley, Tom, 118, 119, 121
self-awareness, intelligence and, 30, 42, 169
self-handicapping, 101
sentience, 36–37
serial polyandry, 143
sex differences: aesthetics and, 123; communication and, 72

Sex in the Sea (Hardt), 146
sexual antagonistic evolution, 162
sexuality, 138–149; cannibalism and, 146; female autonomy and, 162; hermaphroditism, 139–140, 145–146; incest, 146–147; pair bonding, 148–149; parthenogenesis, 140–142; play and, 88–89; same-sex, 140, 142, 144–145, 148; tool use and, 147; variety in, 143–144. *See also* courtship
sexual selection, 123, 129, 155–159, 161, 163
shape shifting, 152–154
Sharpe, Fred, 83
Silver Gull, 148
simultaneous hermaphroditism, 139
Singing Life of Birds, The (Kroodsma), 72
Skinner, B. F., 37
Slobodchikoff, Con, 49, 50–51, 53, 54, 56, 57–58, 59, 75
slugs, 138
smalltooth sawfish, 141
snakes, 60, 141
Sociable Weaver bird, 124
social brain hypothesis, 115–116
social diplomacy, 3
social groups: architecture and, 109, 111, 115–116; biodiversity and, 227–228; communication and, 3, 50–51, 68; conflict resolution and, 179; courtship and, 154; culture and, 205; decision-making and, 102–103; emotions and, 220–221; empathy and, 177–178, 179–180; flexibility and, 221–222; friendship and, 170–172, 219; game theory on, 191–192; hive mind, 4, 31–32, 115–117; individuality and, 227–228; intelligence and, 26, 31–32, 34, 115–116, 169; language and, 51, 55–56; memory and, 56; morality and, 219, 220; personality and, 188–189, 191–192, 221; play and, 79, 80, 82–83; reconciliation and, 180–182; sexuality and, 147; social

diplomacy and, 3. *See also* cultural transmission; parenting/parental bonds; social learning
social learning: culture and, 199, 206–207; fishes and, 192; intelligence and, 27–28, 29, 35, 169; language and, 97; play and, 83. *See also* cultural transmission
Songs of the Humpback Whale (Payne and Payne), 65, 210
Sonja (chicken), 174, 176, 177
South American Gymnotiformes, 161
South American knife fish, intelligence, 21
sperm whales: culture, 205–206, 207–208; morality, 215–216
spiders: courtship, 154; play, 88–89; sexuality, 146; tool use, 131
spiny leaf stick insects, 141
Spirit Bear, 197
Spotted Bowerbird, 127
spotted hyena, 182–184
state matching, 176
string test, 42–43
Sturla, Kim, 34
Superb Bird of Paradise, 152–154
superiority assumptions. *See* human exceptionalism
superorganisms, 4, 31–32, 115–117

tactical deception, 24–25, 31, 60–61, 179. *See also* deception
Tatu (chimpanzee), 96
Taylor, Hollis, 212
teaching: cultural transmission and, 43–44; intelligence and, 34, 35–36, 44–45
"Theory of Bird's Nests, A" (Wallace), 124
Thompson, Kevin, 87
Thornton, Alex, 35
thrush, 71
tick-pointing, 151
Titchener, Edward, 175
titmice, 200

toadfish, 86
tool use, 129–135; architecture and, 125; captivity vs. natural environments and, 133–134; cultural transmission and, 130, 131; culture and, 130, 147, 200, 208–209; human exceptionalism and, 129–130; sexuality and, 147
Tooth-billed Bowerbird, 124–125
traditional assumptions. *See* human exceptionalism
trait theory, 187–188
tremulation, 62–64
Turillazzi, Stefano, 89
turkeys, 141
turtles, 89

United Poultry Concerns, 173
van Schaik, Carel, 192
veiled chameleon, 167
vibrational communication, 61–65, 66–68
Viki (chimpanzee), 92–93
virgin births, 140–141
visual communication, 60–61
Vogelkop Bowerbird, 126
von Frisch, Karl, 58–59, 113, 118, 123
von Gall, Philipp, 104
Vygotsky, Lev, 92

wallabies, 101
Wallace, Alfred Russel, 124, 156
walruses, 144
Washoe Project, 96
wasps, 89

Wasserman, Ed, 42, 44, 46
Watson, Duncan, 101
Watson, John B., 37
Weiss, Andrew, 186, 187
Wemelsfelder, Françoise, 36–37, 38–39, 40, 219–220
Western Bowerbird, 125
Western Grebe, 150–151
whales: communication, 43, 65–66, 71, 210–212; culture, 203, 205–206, 207–208, 210–212; language, 205; morality, 215–216; play, 81, 82–83
What a Fish Knows (Balcombe), 81, 167, 189
Whiptail Lizard, 140
White, Thomas, 214–215
Whitehead, Hal, 83–84, 199, 200–201, 202–203, 205–207, 208, 209, 213–216
Whiten, Andrew, 200, 202
Why Elephants Weep (Masson), 166
Wild Justice (Bekoff and Pierce), 116, 216, 217
Wilkinson, Anna, 204
Winkle (chimpanzee), 179–180
Wolfinger, Raymond, 39
wolves: flexibility, 221–222; morality, 217–219, 220; personality, 220–221; reconciliation, 181–182
Woods, Vanessa, 80
Woolf, Virginia, 140
Wunda (chimpanzee), 98
Wystrach, Antonie, 32

zebra finches, 28

ABOUT THE AUTHOR

CAROL GIGLIOTTI is Professor Emerita at Emily Carr University of Art and Design in Vancouver, British Columbia. She is the editor of the book *Leonardo's Choice: Genetic Technologies and Animals* and was the recipient of the John and Betty Gray Writing Residency at the Sitka Center for the Arts and Ecology, Oregon, and a Writing Residency at Coppermoss, Tuwanek, British Columbia.

Lightning Source UK Ltd.
Milton Keynes UK
UKHW041925031222
413217UK00004B/92/J

9 781479 815449